BILLFISHING

BILLFISHING

THE QUEST FOR

MARLIN, SWORDFISH

SPEARFISH & SAILFISH

PETER GOADBY

International Marine

Camden, Maine

To the Ladies, to Lorrie Fay, Kay Mulholland and Sandra Clarry, and to the many others from a mere male fisherman.

In the past, fishing offshore for the big fish has been regarded as the province of male activity and achievement. Nowhere has this been more evident than with billfishing – the epitome of the saltwater challenge on balanced tackle.

Lady anglers, lady fishing administrators and lady scientists have met and beaten challenges from the fish and male competition.

This book acknowledges the achievements of all the lady anglers from all countries for all species – particularly billfish.

It has been and is a privilege to know and to fish with and against the ladies. It is appropriate that recognition of the ladies extends to the great ocean fish sought by the anglers, where the females of the gamefish species make up most of the record listings for the species.

First published in the United States of America by International Marine,
a division of The McGraw-Hill Companies.

Originally published in Australia in 1996
by HarperCollins*Publishers* (Australia) Pty Limited Group.

Copyright © Peter Goadby 1996

ISBN 0–07–011779–9
Cataloging-in-Publication information for this title can be obtained
from the Library of Congress.

Questions regarding the ordering of this book should be addressed to:
The McGraw-Hill Companies
Customer Service Department
P.O. Box 547
Blacklick, OH 43004
Retail customers: 1–800–262–4729
Bookstores: 1–800–722–4726

Cover: *Photo: Sean Wallace*
Title page: Master angler, Marsha Bierman, exerts maximum pressure
on her PENN stand up tackle. *Photo: Darrell Jones*

Printed in Hong Kong

CONTENTS

▲ Billfishing from shore. The latest challenge. (See page 57.).
Photo: Greg Finney.

FOREWORD

Peter Goadby's previous books on gamefishing, *Big Fish and Blue Water* (1970) and *Saltwater Gamefishing* (1991) were coffee table compendiums of all the knowledge available at the time for aspiring anglers, captains and crew. These books showed that Peter had 'been there and done that' and, most importantly, that the knowledge and experience gained was freely passed on.

Billfishing — the quest for marlin, swordfish, spearfish & sailfish will be considered as the on-board as well as the at-home reference on how to find and fish successfully for the billfish of the world.

This new book has the exciting colorful action photographs and clear drawings that accompany a clear text, the trade mark of his previous books.

Here is emphasis on conservation of the big fish and the importance of the marine food chain. Tag and release is the fishing ethic of the 90s and the future. Modern fishing practice recycles a billfish, even a grander, to fight another day. Catch and kill is fast being replaced by catch and release. Tag and release is the order of the day. As *Billfishing* says, 'Billfish are too valuable to be caught only once'.

This book sets out the problems of the indiscriminate pressure fishing method, the pelagic longliner, on the the pelagic fish population and the need for management. In this new 'how-to' book Peter Goadby gives anglers, captains and crews, in his concise style, tips on how to specialize with billfish whether by trolling, spinfishing or saltwater fly fishing within the IGFA rules, the world-wide standard for ethical fishing.

Peter has had the opportunity to fish with, and to observe and to learn from many of the world's great anglers, captains and crews. This knowledge, when combined with his own practical and successful involvement in all phases of saltwater fishing ensures that the readers of his books have a unique opportunity for knowledge and expertize as well as the excitement that is billfishing, and billfish around the world. In his writings, Peter's thirst for knowledge, for history, to know the people and the great animals of the oceans, is clearly evident. It is now more than thirty years since this Australian first fished and competed successfully in the Hawaiian islands in the Hawaiian International Billfish Tournament. Since then our Board of Governors have used his knowledge and judgement in fishing rules and ethics as have administrators in his own country, in New Zealand and internationally.

His scientific involvement has also spread widely. It has been said of Peter Goadby that 'fishing is not just a sport, it is a way of life'.

As we move towards the next century we are vividly aware of the problems created for the billfish stocks by commercial longliners.

We are lucky there is this book *Billfishing* that gives the 'how-to' and the 'where' in regard to the great fish, for all tackle disciplines.

Peter's up-to-date knowledge and involvement will greatly increase all saltwater anglers' appreciation of the blue water challenge of the billfish, the mightiest of all fish.

Many tight lines and much aloha.
Peter S Fithian

TRUSTEE, IGFA
CHAIRMAN, HIBA
CHAIRMAN, PORF, HONOLULU, HAWAII

INTRODUCTION

There is a special challenge and charisma associated with the offshore fish species known as billfish.

These are the fish that dominate the records and other memorable photographs of fish, angler, crew and tackle. Billfish are the dream fish that trigger heightened fishing excitement and numerous descriptive clichés. Their speed, power, endurance and acrobatic, aerial activity have forced tackle improvements, the evolution of special boats, and carefully thought-out techniques.

Even the names of the billfish are exciting. The heavyweights, such as the broadbill swordfish, the blue marlin and the black marlin, are the food chain peak predators in their tropical and temperate environments weighing up to and over 445 kg (1000 lb) – the magic weight in fishing, the granders. The striped marlin is the middle weight champion growing to 250 kg (550 lb). The white marlin of the Atlantic is smaller and equally acrobatic, requiring expert angler skill from hook-up to boatside. Sailfish are, and always will be, the lightweight champions that establish charter industries and light tackle feats. The spearfish are the smallest of the billfish. Here again, pound for pound, they are tough fighters on balanced tackle and active jumpers.

Billfish are the superfish, even those who do not rate the name 'giant' before their name. Their color, conformation and power are a tribute to nature's evolution of speed and power. The unsolved answers to many questions about them are sought by scientists, fishermen and fishery managers alike. Billfish have gripped the imagination and triggered our quest for knowledge as have no other fish. They are the stars of the fishing world.

At sea and in every film image of them, billfish make fishermen look and absorb the fascinating qualities of these mighty fish. Photographs, paintings and sculptures bring back vivid memories for those of us who are fortunate enough to seek and find the fish in their natural environment. In print, great writers such as Zane Grey, Ernest Hemingway and Philip Wylie, who were also keen fishermen, created written images that brought the billfish to life. Their works are recognized, even by non-fishmen, as classics today.

The object of this book is to record the 'how to' for maximum results, and to further encourage the fishing ethic of 'tag and release', the sport fishing of the present and even more of the future. Tag and release is a tribute to the fish themselves. The feeling shown by the fishermen at the culmination of a successful tag and release of any billfish, but especially giant billfish, is a very special mix of common sense and euphoria.

The book deplores the frightening effects of commercial longlining on billfish, and recognizes the damage done by thoughtless exploitation of the food chain.

Billfishing gives current and future anglers everywhere the opportunity to be aware not only of the fish but the methods that have evolved and stood the test of time through years of fishing in the world famous hot spots. The tackle methods and techniques have changed over the years and will refine even more as our understanding develops.

Photographs shot by some of the world's great fishing cameramen bring the visual impact of first-hand contact with these colorful purpose-evolved and graceful predators to the reader. Photographers who have helped beyond thanks include Darrell Jones, Gilbert Keech, Captain Paul Murray, Biff Lampton, Bill Harrison, Jacquie Acheson, James Watts, Vic Dunaway, Graham Farmer, Syd Kraul, Kim Holland, Mike Kenyon, Jim Witten, Peter Hoogs, John Jordan, Greg Finney, Tudor Collins, Lyndon Rea, G. Angus, Simon Cassetarri, Andrew Taulerman, Tim Simpson, Greg Edwards, Shaun Wallace, Bob Bury, David Rogers, Julian Pepperell, Mark Deeney, and all the others credited in the photographs in the book. I would also like to thank my designer, Louise McGeachie, who has showcased their work to such good effect.

Billfishing has become the epitome of the challenge of saltwater fishing in the 90s. As we move towards the turn of the century the sport is no longer with heavy knucklebusting tackle. Billfishing is now whatever is your tackle preference. There is the more traditional method of trolling tackle, with special brake materials and two speeds of reel and line from 1 kg to 60 kg (2 lb to 130 lb line). Saltwater fly fishing has been improved to cope with the power and action of the billfish. To this is added the thrill of raising and teasing the fish within casting range and the skill of fly presentation. The third recent tackle evolution is the powerful spinning tackle. Spinning, once the domain of fresh water, now has the benefits of casting and performance and capacity that make its use routine.

The question of the ingredients for success in saltwater gamefishing can be briefly summed up. A mix of preparation, concentration and perspiration, to which is added a little luck, will ensure success. Even though the necessary proportions may vary with the type of fish, the first three are the most necessary. The experience factor can be offset to some degree by communication and coaching from skipper, crew or another experienced anger. One of these assisting is enough. Participation by all creates possible confusion.

It is hoped *Billfishing* will give information and direction to the anglers and charter fishermen interested in billfish of all sizes and all species — the memory creators.

Billfishing is many things to many people. It is a special challenge. Tag and release will give another dimension to this sport as we move towards the year 2000.

This book, like fishing itself, is a team effort.

THE BILLFISH

Of all the world's fish, the billfish are the supercaptures. In recent times, the tag and release ethic has added a new dimension — a new feeling — to billfishing. Anglers fishing even the super hot spots such as Cairns for black marlin and Madeira for blue marlin are tagging and releasing giants weighing over 450 kg (1000 lb). Anglers who have experienced first hand the thrill of billfish alongside the boat, seeing them recover their color and become active, rate the act of release as one of fishing's top experiences.

Saltwater fly fishing originated when Webster Robinson took the world's first billfish on fly. This, and subsequent pioneer efforts, triggered incredible expansion, acceptance and tackle development for one of the fastest growing sport fishing methods.

Fly fishing devotees are now showing that even the peak pelagic species are open to those who choose the fly reel in preference to the long-established familiar overhead trolling and spinning reels. There is a whole new world of developing techniques and fishing challenges.

◀ A 300 kg (660 lb) black marlin jumps alongside Ted Naftzger in the cockpit. *Photo: Peter Goadby*

▲ World record angler, Kay Mulholland with a 230 kg (500 lb) black marlin on Captain Peter Wright's boat *Duyfken*. *Photo: Peter Goadby*

Much scientific study has been directed at the world's billfish, particularly because the pressure from commercial fisheries adversely affects stocks. The long-lining activities of many fishing nations — each boat running up to 3000 hooks on miles of long line — take billfish both as by-catch and deliberate targets.

This is a serious problem as all billfish are worth much more, in dollar value, as a recreational sport fish than as a dead, commercial fish. The tag and release of billfish increases their value to a fishing area. In fact, they are too valuable to be caught and killed; they should be caught, tagged and released for the benefit of scientific information gathering and the good of the various billfish species.

Experienced anglers, skippers and crews are often asked which is the mightiest of the billfish. From personal experience and listening to hundreds of people around the world who should know, the rating for adult fish may be: broadbill; blue marlin and black marlin; striped marlin; white marlin; Pacific sailfish (because of their size) and Atlantic sailfish; and finally, longnose and shortnose spearfish.

This is a quick way to get into an argument as all billfish are great. Each species has characteristics that mean special degrees of difficulty in hook-up, in fighting, and in just plain orneryness. Some specialize in power acrobatics close to the boat, others at a distance. Naturally there is a difference in fighting characteristics depending on the age, weight and condition of the fish. The equal rating of black marlin and blue marlin, whether Atlantic or Indo-Pacific, will no doubt trigger many cries of dissent from devotees of one particular fishing location.

One thing for certain is that all billfish are a challenge and surefire generators of adrenalin. Sport fishermen are fortunate to have the opportunity to see these great fish in their natural environment, displaying their power and savagery — an experience unknown by other fishermen and those who don't venture into the deep blue of the ocean.

BROADBILL SWORDFISH

Xiphias Gladius
LINNAEUS 1758

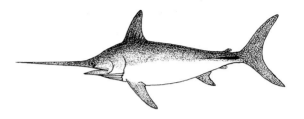

OTHER COMMON NAMES
Swordfish, broadbill.

IDENTIFYING FEATURES
Upper body dark blue, often with bronze coloration, lower body silvery white, colors merge to light brown. Maximum weight 680 kg (1500 lb). Long flat bill. High, rigid sickle dorsal, equal in height and similar in shape to upper caudal lobe. Straight lower jaw. No visible lateral line. Fixed sickle pectoral. Wide single body keel at junction of body and tail.

EXPECTED TEMPERATURE RANGE
13°C–22°C (55°F–72°F).

TYPICAL LOCATION
Open water deeper than 110 meters (60 fathoms) to 1850 meters (1000 fathoms) or more, over canyons and submarine peaks and banks, cruising to reoxygenate along current lines.

FISHING METHODS
In daylight, presenting trolled baits of squid, barracuda or chub mackerel, striped tuna or small tuna to broadbill cruising on surface with dorsal and tail clear of surface. Drifting at night with live or dead squid, spotted mackerel, small tuna, bonito or bottom fish species obtained from commercial trawlers. Eating quality is excellent.

TYPICAL FIGHTING CHARACTERISTICS
Regarded as the king of fishes, broadbill are dogged deep and mid water fighters that

occasionally jump in a spectacular fashion. At night they often run to the surface immediately after hook-up. Use of a light stick shows the position and depth of swordfish in night fighting. The soft mouth and body flesh and skin dictates that these fish be fought with maximum 10 kg (22 lb) brake. 24 kg (50 lb) and 37 kg (80 lb) tackle is balanced for most broadbill, with 60 kg (130 lb) for the superfish.

MAJOR SPORTFISHING AREAS
Chile, Peru, Panama, Ecuador, Mexico, north-east coast USA, Florida, Venezuela, Portugal, New Zealand, Australia, South Africa, Hawaii.

ATLANTIC BLUE MARLIN

Makaira Nigricans

LACEPEDE 1802

OTHER COMMON NAMES
Blue marlin.

IDENTIFYING FEATURES
Back dark blue with light blue stripes of dots and bars, belly silvery white. In life, fins and tail electric blue. Maximum weight 900 kg (2000 lb). Start of second dorsal behind start of second anal fin. Pectoral fins fold flat. Lateral line generally does not show in adults. When scales or skin are removed the lateral line shows as multiple, up to four, chain loops. Bill medium long. Lower jaw turns down slightly at tip. Dorsal fin and anal fin pointed and medium height.

EXPECTED TEMPERATURE RANGE
21°C–30°C (70°F–86°F).

TYPICAL LOCATION
Open ocean along continental shelf drop off over deeper canyons along 110 meter (60 fathom) reefs and submarine mountains and peaks and ledges, along current lines, around bait schools of tuna, mahi mahi (dolphin fish), squid, around logs, weed lines.

FISHING METHODS
Trolling lures of hard and soft plastic, trolling dead baits, tuna, mullet, Spanish mackerel, squid, trolling live baits, drifting with live or dead baits. Eating quality good.

TYPICAL FIGHTING CHARACTERISTICS
Whether in the Caribbean, the Atlantic or the Indo-Pacific, blue marlin are the heavyweights — very fast, tough fighters and spectacular jumpers that tend to fish deeper than black or striped marlin.

MAJOR SPORTFISHING AREAS
Puerto Rico, Walker's Cay, Bimini, Virgin Islands, Jamaica, Bermuda and other east Atlantic and Caribbean islands, Costa Rica, North and South Carolina, Florida, Gulf of Mexico, Mexico, Venezuela, Brazil, Azores, Canary Islands, Cape Verde Islands, Ivory Coast of Africa, Madeira.

BLACK MARLIN

Makaira Indica

CUVIER 1832

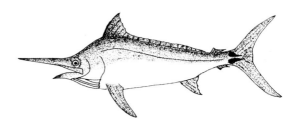

OTHER COMMON NAMES
White marlin (in Japan, possibly from color of flesh), giant black marlin, silver marlin.

IDENTIFYING FEATURES

Temperate waters: back and fins dark slatey blue or black, belly silvery white. Tropical waters: back dark blue, sometimes with light blue stripes that fade after death, belly silver, dorsal fin lavender, other fins and tails electric blue, sometimes spots on dorsal. Maximum weight 863 kg (1900 lb). Start of second dorsal forward of start of second anal fin. Fixed pectoral fins in marlin in excess of 50 kg (110 lb). In black marlin less than 50 kg (110 lb) the pectorals can often be moved despite rigor mortis, but will not fold flat against body. Short lower jaw curved down. Short, heavy, round bill.

EXPECTED TEMPERATURE RANGE

21°C–30°C (70°F–86°F).

TYPICAL LOCATION

Along current lines. Open ocean around schools of bait species and small tuna, along reefs, along continental shelf drop-off 182 meters (100 fathoms) and submarine peaks, along shore where warm currents are running, around logs. A few 'local' fish on reefs, even in cooler waters off-season. Juveniles move in schools of similar age and class along coast and islands.

FISHING METHODS

Adults: trolling tuna, Spanish mackerel, mullet. Trolling lures of hard and soft plastic. Drifting or anchor live and dead bait. Juveniles: trolling mullet, ballyhoo (garfish), chub mackerel, strips often in combination with plastic squid, feather jigs. Trolling live baits, skipjack and other small tuna, kawa kawa (mackerel tuna), trevally. Fly fishing after teasing occasionally from rocky headland with live bait. Trolling small lures, spoons, konaheads, knuckleheads, big and bibless minnows, plastic squid.

TYPICAL FIGHTING CHARACTERISTICS

A dogged deep fighter and aerial performer that usually mixes jumping, fast runs with deep fighting characteristics. Will jump at any time

▲ The crew cut the leader to complete the tag and release. *Photo: Mike Kenyon.*

during fight, and right alongside boat when leader is in hand.

MAJOR SPORTFISHING AREAS

East and west coast of Australia, Panama, Peru, Costa Rica, Mexico, Ecuador, Tahiti, Papua New Guinea, Pacific islands, southern Asia, New Zealand, Fiji, Mauritius, Mozambique, East Africa.

INDO-PACIFIC BLUE

Marlin Makaira Mazara
JORDAN & SNYDER 1901

OTHER COMMON NAMES

Pacific blue marlin, blue marlin.

IDENTIFYING FEATURES

Back dark blue with light blue stripes of dots and bars, belly silvery white. In life, fins and tail are electric blue. Maximum weight 1181 kg (2600 lb). Start of second dorsal behind start of second anal. Pectoral fins fold flat. Lateral line generally does not show in adults, but with scales or skin removed is single line of chain. Bill medium and long. Lower jaw turns down slightly at tip. Dorsal fin and anal fin pointed and medium height.

EXPECTED TEMPERATURE RANGE

21°C–30°C (70°F–86°F).

TYPICAL LOCATION

Open ocean along continental shelf drop-off. Over deeper canyons along current lines. Along 110 meter (60 fathom) reefs, submarine mountains and peaks and ledges, weed line, around bait schools of tuna, mahi mahi (dolphin fish), squid, and around logs.

FISHING METHODS

Trolling lures of hard or soft plastic, trolling dead baits of tuna, mullet, Spanish mackerel, trolling live baits, drifting and at anchor with live or dead baits.

TYPICAL FIGHTING CHARACTERISTICS

At all weights a very tough fighter and spectacular jumper that tends to fight deeper than black or striped marlin. Will spin and reverse direction when jumping and greyhounding, a tactic that often causes cut or broken lines. The first run will sometimes spool the reel.

MAJOR SPORTFISHING AREAS

Hawaii, Tahiti, Fiji, Guam, other Pacific islands (including Tonga and Vanuatu), Mexico, Panama, Ecuador, Costa Rica, east and west coast of Australia, New Zealand, Papua New Guinea, Mauritius, southern Asia, East Africa, Mozambique.

STRIPED MARLIN

Tetrapturus Audax
PHILLIPI 1887

OTHER COMMON NAMES

Striper, stripey.

IDENTIFYING FEATURES

Upper body dark with powder blue, cobalt or lavender stripes, lower body silvery white. Maximum weight 250 kg (550 lb). High dorsal fin in which three high rays are of almost equal height. Single prominent lateral line. Pectoral fins fold in against body. Start of second dorsal behind start of second anal fin. Tail veed, cuts away at tip of each lobe of tail. Anal fin high. Bill long and slender. Lower jaw straight.

EXPECTED TEMPERATURE RANGE
20°C–26°C (68°F–79°F).

TYPICAL LOCATION
Around bait schools, chub mackerel, sardines, pilchards, anchovies, small tuna, squid.

FISHING METHODS
Trolling dead baits, chub mackerel, kahawai, yellowtail, squid. Trolling strip baits, sometimes with plastic squid in combination. Trolling live bait, chub mackerel, small tuna, kahawai. Trolling lures, hard and soft plastic lures, minnows, plastic fish or squid replicas. Casting live bait, chub mackerel, yellowtail scad, sardines, anchovies. Drifting with live bait, kahawai, small tuna, yellowtail, chub mackerel. Eating quality good. Excellent for sashimi.

TYPICAL FIGHTING CHARACTERISTICS
Exciting jumper, a greyhounding and tailwalking fighter that gives long runs and sounds deep. The marlin that is a challenge on tackle of all weights up to 37 kg (80 lb). In many areas is an ideal opponent on 13.6 kg (30 lb) tackle.

MAJOR SPORTFISHING AREAS
California, Mexico, Panama, Costa Rica, Ecuador, Chile, New Zealand, east and west coast of Australia, East Africa, Kenya, Japan, Okinawa, Hawaii and other Pacific islands, Indian Ocean islands, Western Arabian sea.

WHITE MARLIN
Tetrapturus Albidus
POEY 1860

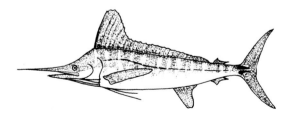

OTHER COMMON NAMES
Atlantic white marlin.

IDENTIFYING FEATURES
Back dark blue, belly silvery white, light stripes along body, dorsal fin dark blue with spots. Maximum weight 90 kg (200 lb). Dorsal, anal and pectoral fins rounded at tips. Single lateral line. Dorsal fin high and rounded. Slender bill. Slender, straight lower jaw. Second dorsal starts forward of start of second anal fin. Pelvic fins long.

EXPECTED TEMPERATURE RANGE
20°C–29°C (68°F–84°F).

TYPICAL LOCATION
Open water around bait schools (ballyhoo, mullet squid, flying fish). Over deep reefs, canyons, drop-offs and holes in the sea bed. Along current lines and weed lines.

FISHING METHODS
Trolling dead bait (ballyhoo (garfish), mullet, squid, chub mackerel, eel). Often rigged with plastic squid or feather jigs. Trolling with small hard and soft plastic lures. Trolling with live bait, ballyhoo (garfish), chub mackerel. Spin casting live bait. Eating quality good.

TYPICAL FIGHTING CHARACTERISTICS
This aggressive ocean acrobat is a most spectacular jumper, with all the surface tricks punctuated with long runs and sounding to depths. Ideal for light tackle up to 15 kg (30 lb).

MAJOR SPORTFISHING AREAS
Bahamas, Walker's Cay, Cat Cay, Bimini, Chub Key, Puerto Rico, St Thomas, Gulf of Mexico, Florida, east coast of USA north to Hudson Canyon, Bermuda, Mexico, Costa Rica, Venezuela, Brazil, Cuba.

Even though white marlin are the lightest of the marlin species, acrobatic jumps and their fighting ability make them memorable opponents on light tackle.

SPEARFISH

Longbill
Tetrapturus Pfleugeri
ROBINS & DE SYLVA 1963

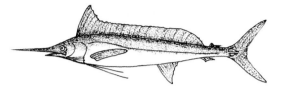

Mediterranean
Tetrapturus Belone
RAFINESQUE 1810

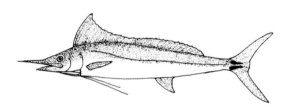

OTHER COMMON NAMES

Long-nosed spearfish, Atlantic spearfish.

IDENTIFYING FEATURES

Longbill spearfish: bill longer than head length, lower jaw straight and slender, long pelvic fin. Long, wide, rounded pectoral fins, prominent single lateral line, dorsal fin high and wide or if not, curved as it tapers to body. Distance between anus and anal fin nearly equal to depth of anal fin. Tail veed. Mediterranean spearfish: bill shorter than head length, lower jaw straight and slender. Prominent single lateral line, short, tapered pectoral fins, long pelvic fins. High dorsal rounded at front, dorsal curved as it tapers to body. Distance between anus and anal fin nearly equal to depth of anal fin. Tail veed. Maximum weight of both species 40 kg (90 lb).

EXPECTED TEMPERATURE RANGE

21°C–30°C (70°F–86°F).

TYPICAL LOCATION

Open ocean along current lines, over drop-offs and ledges, around flotsam and logs.

FISHING METHODS

Trolling hard or soft plastic lures, trolling small baits, ballyhoo (garfish), and squid sometimes in combination with small plastic squid or feather jigs. Usually taken by accident when trolling for other billfish, tuna or current-dwelling species. Eating quality excellent.

TYPICAL FIGHTING CHARACTERISTICS

Billfish lightweights with splashing jumps and long surface runs if tackle allows. Ideal on light tackle: unable to show their real fighting ability on heavier tackle on which they are usually taken.

MAJOR SPORTFISHING AREAS

Longbill spearfish: Bahamas, Venezuela, Portugal, Azores, Florida. Mediterranean spearfish: open Mediterranean. Not common anywhere.

SHORTBILL SPEARFISH

Tetrapturus Angustirostris
TANAKA 1915

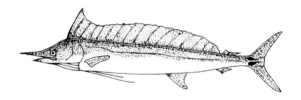

OTHER COMMON NAMES

Short-nose spearfish, Pacific spearfish.

IDENTIFYING FEATURES

Back dark blue, belly silvery. Life colors bright electric blue and silver, rarely show stripes. Maximum size up to 45 kg (100 lb). Very short bill, almost equal to length of lower jaw. Prominent single lateral line. Straight, slender lower jaw. Pectoral fins narrow and short. Long pelvic fins. Dorsal fin high in front, curves before joining body. Distance between anus and anal fin nearly equal to height of anal fin. Anal fin pointed.

EXPECTED TEMPERATURE RANGE
21°C–30°C (70°F–86°F).

TYPICAL LOCATION
Open ocean along current lines, over drop-offs and ledges, around logs and flotsam.

FISHING METHODS
Trolling hard or soft plastic lures. Trolling small baits — ballyhoo (garfish), mullet. Trolling strips sometimes squid, chub mackerel in combination with mostly squid and scad. Usually taken accidentally when trolling for other billfish, tuna or current-dwelling species. Eating quality excellent.

TYPICAL FIGHTING CHARACTERISTICS
Has characteristics of billfish and mackerels (splashing jumps and surface runs). Ideal on light tackle; unable to show their real fighting ability on the heavier tackle on which they are usually taken.

MAJOR SPORTFISHING AREAS
Hawaii (believed to be a spawning area). Sporadically in the Indian and Pacific Oceans' sportfishing areas. Apart from Hawaii, they are not commonly encountered.

ATLANTIC SAILFISH

Istiophorus Albicans
LATREILLE 1804

OTHER COMMON NAMES
Sailfish.

IDENTIFYING FEATURES
Upper body and sail dorsal spotted with dark and light blue spots, lower body silvery white, body spots in vertical rows, bright colors in life. Maximum weight 60 kg (130 lb). Very high dorsal fin highest in center, tail veed. Very long pelvic fins with membrane. Prominent single lateral line. Slender, straight lower jaw. Long, slender bill.

EXPECTED TEMPERATURE RANGE
21°C–30°C (70°F–86°F).

TYPICAL LOCATION
Open water around bait schools of small bait fish — ballyhoo (garfish), mullet, small sea toads, squid, flying fish. Along reefs where warm currents are close inshore. Over deep reefs and canyons.

FISHING METHODS
Trolling with dead bait, ballyhoo (garfish), mullet, goggle eye, chub mackerel, often rigged in combination with plastic squid or feather jigs. Fly casting after teasing. Trolling strip bait. Trolling or drifting with live baits — ballyhoo (garfish), mullet, goggle eye (yellowtail scad), chub mackerel, blue runner. Trolling small lures. Spin casting live bait. Occasionally from rocky headlands with drifting live bait. Kite fishing live baits. Deep trolling baits or lures. Eating quality poor. Improved by smoking.

TYPICAL FIGHTING CHARACTERISTICS
A spectacular jumping jack whose aerial performances and fast surface runs have established its reputation as a top sport fish, particularly on light tackle up to 10 kg (20 lb). Really big sailfish, those in excess of 70 kg (150 lb) warrant the use of 15 kg (30 lb) and 24 kg (50 lb) tests.

MAJOR SPORTFISHING AREAS
Florida, Mexico, Venezuela, Brazil, Senegal, Angola, Gulf of Mexico. Most records are held in Senegal and Angola.

A 350 kg (770 lb) black marlin jumps with the surf, with the Great Barrier Reef as a background. ▶
Photo: Peter Goadby

PACIFIC SAILFISH

Istiophorus Platypterus

SHAW & NODDER 1792

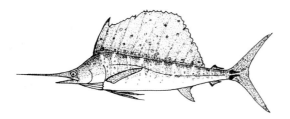

OTHER COMMON NAMES

Indo-Pacific sailfish, sailfish.

IDENTIFYING FEATURES

Body and sail dorsal spotted with dark and light blue spots, body spots in vertical rows, bright colors in life, brighter than those of the Atlantic species. Maximum weight 120 kg (265 lb). Very high dorsal fin, highest in center, tail veed, very long pelvic fins with membrane, prominent single lateral line, slender, straight lower jaw, long, slender bill.

EXPECTED TEMPERATURE RANGE

21°C–30°C (70°F–86°F).

TYPICAL LOCATION

Open water around bait schools of small bait fish, ballyhoo (garfish), mullet, small sea toads, squid, flying fish. Reefs where warm currents are close inshore.

FISHING METHODS

Trolling with dead baits, ballyhoo (garfish), mullet, goggle eye (yellowtail scad), chub mackerel, often rigged in combination with plastic squid or feather lures. Trolling strip baits. Trolling or drifting live baits, ballyhoo (garfish), mullet, yellowtail scad, chub mackerel. Trolling small lures. Fly casting after teasing. Occasionally from rocky headlands with drifting live baits. Spincasting live bait. Kite fishing live bait. Deep trolling baits or lures.

TYPICAL FIGHTING CHARACTERISTICS

Spectacular jumper whose aerial performance and fast surface runs have established its reputation as a top sport fish, particularly on light tackle. Sailfish over 45 kg (100 lb) are tough fighters.

MAJOR SPORTFISHING AREAS

Galapagos Islands, Ecuador, Costa Rica, Mexico, Panama, Fiji, Tahiti, Philippines, all Pacific and Indian Ocean islands, north-east and west coast tropical Australia, southern Asia, East African coast, Kenya. Most records are held in Mexico, Panama, Ecuador, Australia, Vanuatu and Fiji.

GENERAL IDENTIFICATION

It is a characteristic of fishermen that they have an innate desire to know what species they have caught or released. There is often confusion and debate about correct identification when fish are active in the water at boatside. It is even more difficult when the fish simply appears as a brown shape following a bait. (Billfish appear brown, sharks yellow.) It can even be hard when the billfish is brought into the boat. While broadbill and sailfish are easy to identify, the other species are more tricky. It is important to know which species occur in which oceans. Scientists are now analysing DNA to understand billfish more clearly. Dr John Graves of Virginia, USA, has found that many assumptions made before the DNA test program began need to be re-evaluated.

There has been long-standing controversy on the number of species of billfish in the world's oceans, with scientists, fishermen and taxidermists disagreeing about some species, such as blue marlin. In the 1960s scientists everywhere finally agreed that the Atlantic offers two species of marlin — blue marlin and white marlin — whereas the Indo-Pacific produces three: blue, black and striped. To these add Atlantic and Indo-Pacific sailfish, broadbill swordfish and short-nose spearfish of the Pacific and Indian Oceans, the long-nose spearfish of the Atlantic, plus the spearfish in the Mediterranean, and identification can provide a basis for continuing fiery debate.

The argument can be further spiced by discussing variations between juvenile and adult, midget and monster, plus variations in build and outline. Color is not a big help in identification and tends to add further controversy. The colors of all billfish vary between live and dead fish, wet and dry fish, the neon blue of a lit up fish and the dark bronze of the fish after a fight, and between tropical and temperate waters. All these colors are evident at various times.

It is incredible that English-speaking scientists only recognized the existence of blue marlin in the Pacific and Indian Oceans as recently as 1954. Even when scientific papers were published, some people — particularly those in areas far from where these super fish live and terrorize the bait fish, tuna and squid schools — disputed the classification and identification.

It was scientifically 'neat' to have white and blue marlin in the Atlantic, and striped and black marlin in the Indo-Pacific. However, nature is not always neat, and added one species, so there are three, not two, species in the Indo-Pacific oceans.

Additional confusion was created by experienced fishermen and the taxidermists who recognized species. These practical people had unique opportunities to work with all the giant fish in life and action, opportunities not often available to scientists. The Pacific fishermen's name 'silver marlin' perfectly described the vibrant colors of black marlin in the hot tropical currents. These marlin, with their vibrant warm-water colors, were not originally recognized as the same fish as the slate, drab, colder-water marlin.

In varying degrees, billfish sometimes show bronze tones, neon colors, or very little color, adding further to the difficulty of identification. Even the color of the stripes varies. Sometimes stripes show on billfish that are usually non-striped. These stripes, so evident on some billfish in life, may disappear by the time the fish is

weighed, so anglers wonder whether their eyes are deceiving them and scientists then question the angler's color observations.

Awareness of these problems makes it easy to understand the queries of practical and practicing fishermen. The arguments go on and there is room for further confusion, particularly in the Atlantic, where some of the great Indo-Pacific Ocean wanderers ignore the neat borders envisaged for them. On the ocean there are no borders, and Japanese longline fishermen, the masters of the high seas, have even recorded black marlin from Cuban waters.

Standard scientific measurements assist scientists with their identification keys to separate species. These can include length or characteristics of fins and proportions that may vary as the fish gets bigger and heavier.

It is now generally accepted by scientists that in the Indian and Pacific Oceans there are six billfish species.

They are:

- Broadbill swordfish (*Xiphias gladius*) Linnaeus 1758
- Sailfish (*Istiophorus*) Shaw & Nodder 1792
- Short-nose spearfish (*Tetrapturus angustirostris*) Tanaka 1915
- Three marlin: blue (*Makaira mazara*) Jordan & Snyder 1901; black *Makaira indica*) Cuvier 1832; striped (*Tetrapterus audax*) Phillipi 1887.

In the Atlantic and Caribbean the species are:

- Blue marlin (*Makaira nigricans*) Lacapede 1802
- White marlin (*Tetrapturus albidus*) Poey 1860
- Sailfish (*Istiophorus albicans*) Latereille 1804
- Long-nose spearfish (*Tetrapturus belone*) Robins & de Sylva 1963
- Mediterranean spearfish (*Tetrapturus belone*) Rafinesque 1810.

It is important to realize the variations in body shape and proportions that come with age and condition. Photographs of fish on a weigh station

◀ The action and luminous colors of this hooked Atlantic blue marlin at St Thomas, Virgin Islands, show why it is so keenly sought by sportfishermen.
Photo: Darrell Jones

or even on the deck with some fins depressed do not give a real impression of body thickness, or make it easy to see that billfish (other than broadbill and, to a lesser extent, blue marlin) are oval, not round, in body shape. Sailfish are even more flatsided and so weigh less — much less than the weight they appear when seen side on. Only full adult sailfish have appreciable girth. When photographing, pull all fins so that they show, taking care that the hands do not show in the photographs.

While it is fairly easy to identify the broadbill swordfish, the sailfish and the spearfish, it is much harder to correctly identify the marlins, particularly as juvenile and full adults. Black marlin, for instance, can normally be identified by their immovable pectoral fins, but this does not apply to black marlin of less than around 55 kg (120 lb). At

◀ This classic greyhounding photograph of striped marlin at Bay of Islands, New Zealand, has captured the imagination of fishermen for more than fifty years.
Photo: Tudor Collins

this weight or less it is often possible to move the pectoral fins of black marlin alongside the body, but they will not lie flat as the pectorals of white, blue and striped marlin will.

For this reason, observing the shape of the pectorals is just as important as observing their folding characteristics — sometimes rigor mortis can create a false impression. Black marlin pectorals are aerofoil and sickle-shaped, whereas other marlin have pectorals that are flat, more evenly tapered and less sickle-shaped. Fully adult striped marlin heavier than 140 kg (300 lb) resemble blue marlin in body shape and proportions, thus adding to the confusion.

The dorsal and anal fins of all marlin, sailfish and spearfish fold down into streamlining grooves. Broadbill swordfish in excess of 24 kg (50 lb) have immovable fins. At less than this weight they may be movable to some degree.

The shape of tails assists in identification. Sailfish tails are veed, blue and black marlin tails are symmetrically sickle, while striped marlin tails are straight edged and angled at the tips. Familiarity with the shape and weight of bills and the mandible (lower jaw) also helps in correct identification. It is better to accurately identify a fish than simply hope the naming is correct for record claims.

The difficulties of identification in onshore weighing stations are multiplied when the billfish are performing actively in their natural environment and changing their color from beautiful and vivid neon blues and silver to bronze or more subdued colors.

▲ A small black marlin turns a kawa kawa bait to swallow it headfirst.
Photo: Mike Kenyon

A Key to Billfish Identification

The following will help you to identify billfish, even when they are only briefly alongside the boat for tag and release. The shape of the dorsal and the length and diameter of the bill are important characteristics to look for. It is much better to release a billfish, even if you're not sure of your identification, rather than to gaff and kill it just to find out what it is.

What to look for

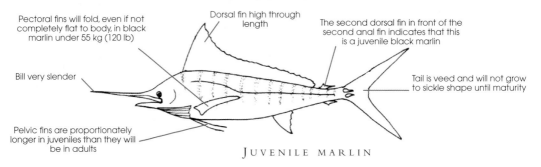

Pectoral fins will fold, even if not completely flat to body, in black marlin under 55 kg (120 lb)

Dorsal fin high through length

The second dorsal fin in front of the second anal fin indicates that this is a juvenile black marlin

Bill very slender

Tail is veed and will not grow to sickle shape until maturity

Pelvic fins are proportionately longer in juveniles than they will be in adults

JUVENILE MARLIN

BROADBILL
(Worldwide, Atlantic and Indo-Pacific)

Long, flat, oval jaw; fins immovable in adults; first dorsal high, same shape as upper lobe of tail; body compressed into flat keel at junction of body and tail.

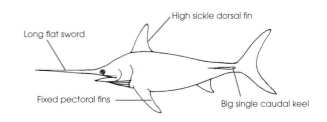

High sickle dorsal fin

Long flat sword

Fixed pectoral fins

Big single caudal keel

SAILFISH
(Atlantic, Indo-Pacific)

Slender, round bill; straight mandible (lower jaw); very high dorsal (almost the length of the body); dorsal highest in middle; tail slightly veed; pectoral fins very long, lateral line clearly visible.

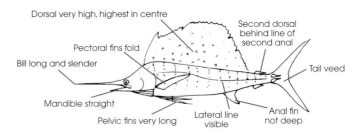

Dorsal very high, highest in centre

Second dorsal behind line of second anal

Pectoral fins fold

Bill long and slender

Tail veed

Mandible straight

Pelvic fins very long

Lateral line visible

Anal fin not deep

WHITE MARLIN
(Atlantic)

Slender, round bill; straight mandible (lower jaw); dorsal high and rounded, tapers to rear from ninth ray onwards; anus close to anal fin, less than half depth of anal fin; second dorsal slightly backward of start of second anal; lateral line visible.

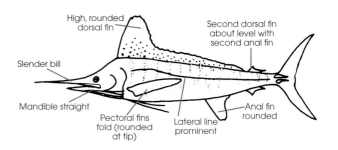

High, rounded dorsal fin

Second dorsal fin about level with second anal fin

Slender bill

Mandible straight

Pectoral fins fold (rounded at tip)

Lateral line prominent

Anal fin rounded

BLACK MARLIN
(INDO-PACIFIC)

Heavy, round bill; down-curved, heavy mandible (lower jaw); low, rounded dorsal less than half body depth; pectoral fins curved and aerofoil in section, fixed in black marlin more than 55 kg (120 lb); second dorsal *in front* of start of second anal fin; anal fin depth about equal to height of dorsal; tail semicircular; single lateral line visible in most weights, particularly juveniles and jumbo size marlin.

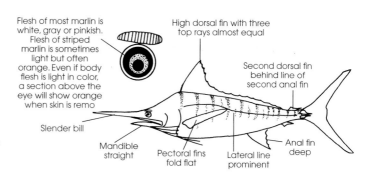

Dorsal fin low, not pointed

Short, heavy bill

Second dorsal fin in front of second anal fin

Mandible curved and hooked

Anal fin not deep

Pectoral fins fixed in marlin in excess of 55 kg (120 lb); will move but will not fold flat at under this weight

Lateral line visible

STRIPED MARLIN
(INDO-PACIFIC)

Slender, round bill; long, straight mandible (lower jaw); high dorsal, first three high rays almost equal height; dorsal about equal to body depth, not so obvious when larger than 120 kg (264 lb); pectoral fins tapered and flat; second dorsal behind start of second anal fin (anal fin deep); tail slightly veed, cut away at tips of both lobes of tail; flesh above eye shows eye when skin is removed; single lateral line clearly visible.

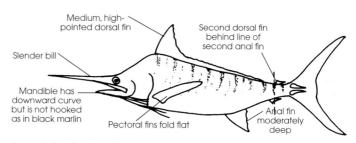

Flesh of most marlin is white, gray or pinkish. Flesh of striped marlin is sometimes light but often orange. Even if body flesh is light in color, a section above the eye will show orange when skin is remo

High dorsal fin with three top rays almost equal

Second dorsal fin behind line of second anal fin

Slender bill

Mandible straight

Pectoral fins fold flat

Lateral line prominent

Anal fin deep

BLUE MARLIN
(ATLANTIC, INDO-PACIFIC)

Moderately heavy, round bill; slightly curved mandible (lower jaw); medium high dorsal; pointed dorsal about three-quarters of body depth; pectoral fins tapered and flat; second dorsal behind line of start of second anal fin; anal fin medium depth; tail strongly semicircular; lateral line not visible in adults. Atlantic blue marlin have as many as three or more chain links. Pacific blue marlin have single chain link and partially single lateral line.

Medium, high-pointed dorsal fin

Second dorsal fin behind line of second anal fin

Slender bill

Mandible has downward curve but is not hooked as in black marlin

Pectoral fins fold flat

Anal fin moderately deep

ATLANTIC Lateral line chain-like with three or more chain links; often visible only when skin section is removed or skin has scales removed

INDO-PACIFIC Lateral line in single chain; often visible only when skin section is removed or skin has scales removed

SHORT-NOSE SPEARFISH
(INDO-PACIFIC)

Very short, round bill not much longer than straight mandible (lower jaw); dorsal long and high, highest at front, rounded at tail; short pectoral; anus separated from anal fin by approximately length of depth of anal fin; tail veed.

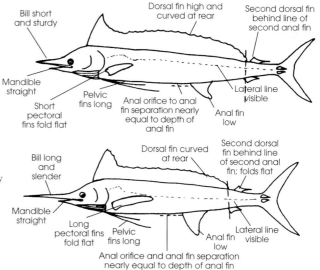

Bill short and sturdy

Dorsal fin high and curved at rear

Second dorsal fin behind line of second anal fin

Mandible straight

Short pectoral fins fold flat

Pelvic fins long

Anal orifice to anal fin separation nearly equal to depth of anal fin

Anal fin low

Lateral line visible

LONG-NOSE SPEARFISH
(ATLANTIC)

Slender, round bill; straight mandible (lower jaw); from 15th ray dorsal long and high, rounded at rear, highest at front; short back to tail; rounded pectoral; tail veed.

Bill long and slender

Dorsal fin curved at rear

Second dorsal fin behind line of second anal fin; folds flat

Mandible straight

Long pectoral fins fold flat

Pelvic fins long

Anal fin low

Lateral line visible

Anal orifice and anal fin separation nearly equal to depth of anal fin

FINDING AND CATCHING BILLFISH

MARLIN

Ernest Hemingway and Zane Grey are rigthly regarded by their millions of readers as great authors. They were also fishermen and their works influenced generations of anglers. For fishermen, three words of Zane Grey never fail to start the adrenalin rushing, making them relive the action. Those words are: 'There he is!' But the words should really be 'There SHE is'. Zane Grey was always after the biggest and heaviest of the fishes, and in marlin they are the females.

Those three words mean much to every marlin fisherman. They bring back in memory the following wavery, shadowy, brown shape that suddenly lights up and dons vibrant colors as it viciously slashes at bait or lure or fades away into the blue depths without a strike. They bring back memories of sickle tails riding the ocean swells or cruising slowly on top with the tail and sometimes an erect dorsal fin slicing the surface ahead of the tail, giving a guide as to the size and species of the fish.

No fish creates more excitement than marlin; no other fish has gained more respect, is instinctively

Mike Lerner congratulates a happy Ernest ▶
Hemingway on his Bimini blue marlin.
Photo: IGFA — Lerner Expedition

◀ Even a small striped Marlin leaves a hole in the water as it jumps. *Photo: James Watt*

thought of for tag and release and is more important to the economy of recreational fishing ports, fishing destinations and sportfishing generally.

In the Atlantic the feisty white marlin — the jumping jack — and the superfast, supertough, Atlantic blue marlin, in all sizes from midget to monster, are the two species that have created industries of boat building, bait catching, tackle manufacturing, magazine publishing, accommodation, travel, taxidermy, photography and even fishing clothing and fishermen's polarizing glasses.

In the Pacific and Indian oceans, three marlin species create and support such industries. The Pacific blue marlin, the black marlin and the striped marlin are all top fish. As in the Atlantic, the widespread ocean-wandering blues are exciting fish in all sizes, from lightweight aggressive, needle-billed speedsters to the perfectly proportioned, maximum-size female giants. These are the heaviest and biggest of all the marlins recorded commer-

cially. They seem to be even bigger and heavier than their Atlantic relatives.

The striped marlin, the Indo-Pacific cousin of the Atlantic white marlin, is the smallest and lightest of the three Pacific species, growing to a maximum of around 250 kg (550 lb). If the striped marlin is the Grand National competitor of the marlins and the blue marlin the Champion Cup and Derby winner, the third Pacific marlin, the black, is the angry rhinoceros of the ocean. It is found in rocky coastline waters right along the cliffs and headlands as well as in the expected marlin waters, the deep water. Some black marlin become local fish and stay in an area even when the water cools to lower than the usual minimum temperature for this species.

Marlin are known to migrate or wander over long distances, and many of the Pacific black marlin have been proven by tag and release and subsequent recaptures to have called Australia home. Microscopic larval black marlin have been taken in Bongo nets and other plankton trawls outside the Outer Reefs near Lizard Island. They substantiate reports of black marlin sighted spawning in the Great Barrier Reef area of the Coral Sea.

It seems logical that after a year or two in those waters the black marlin begin their migrations. Marlin tagged in the Cairns–Lizard Island fishery have been recovered from a 180 degree radius of their breeding area: south along Australia's east coast and to New Zealand, north and east around Papua New Guinea and east at least as far as Kiribas, south of Hawaii. Small black marlin tagged off New South Wales have been recovered almost back at the latitude in which most of the tagging of the adults has been carried out. In the Great Barrier Reef fishery, more than 90 per cent of the marlin hooked are released to continue their life cycle and give a worthwhile number of tags and releases for data on migration and growth.

Tagging in the Atlantic and eastern Pacific and at Kona in Hawaii also shows that all marlin species wander and migrate and appear to have regular schedules to return. Many of the recaptures are a year or annual cycle after the point of capture and tag and release.

The Tuna Club at Avalon, Santa Catalina was founded after Dr C. F. Holder landed a 92 kg (200 lb) bluefin tuna in June 1898. The emphasis at the Tuna Club changed from tuna to marlin as the great schools of surface-feeding tuna gradually disappeared and anglers tasted the excitement and challenge of fishing for marlin worldwide. Ernest Llewellyn caught the first marlin, a striped, on rod and reel in 1903. This first fish of 57 kg (125 lb) opened up a new world of sportfishing that spread to warm waters in most parts of our globe.

Australia was the scene of the first black marlin capture on rod and reel when Dr Mark Lidwell successfully landed a small black marlin of around 36 kg (80 lb) at Seal Rocks near Port Stephens in 1910. The skeleton of this 190 cm (6 ft 3½ in) marlin is in the Australian Museum. Marlin have formed the basis of the exciting sportfishing

industry in all oceans wherever the warm, clean ocean waters and other natural environmental factors and access combine to bring man and great fish together. The continuing refinement of fishing tackle is in itself recognition of the stamina, speed and tenacity of marlin; they are indeed VIFs (Very Important Fish).

Marlin, particularly Indo-Pacific black and striped marlin, are taken in water as shallow as 9.2 meters (5 fathoms) close inshore as well as their expected wide offshore environment of 55 meters (30 fathoms) and out over the ocean's depths.

It seems hard to believe that black and striped marlin up to 90 kg (200 lb) have been taken by anglers with live bait from rocky headlands. The combination of shape of headlands, deep water close in, and the warm water of the tropical ocean currents pushed by current and wind right inshore opens up a whole new challenge for land-based gamefishing. In this type of fishing there is no chance of rocks 'backing up' to assist line recovery.

The marlin's usual environments are reefs, peaks and canyons in water deeper than 55 meters (30 fathoms), out to the 180 meter (100 fathom) drop-off from the continental shelf and other deeper edges and drop-offs. These bottom features are most productive and are home for the bait schools, which are attracted by the food plankton in the upwellings. The combination of these bottom features with temperature differences, warm current edges and upwellings produce the marlin 'hot spots'.

WHERE TO FIND MARLIN

Billfish hunt right into the coastline, as proven by rod and reel captures of black marlin, striped marlin and sailfish onshore from the rocky headlands in Australia and South Africa. Success in boat fishing usually comes in offshore water of 55 meters (30 fathoms) or deeper. In most areas other than Cairns, where the big blacks feed and congregate along the outside reefs, the heaviest marlin are generally caught over

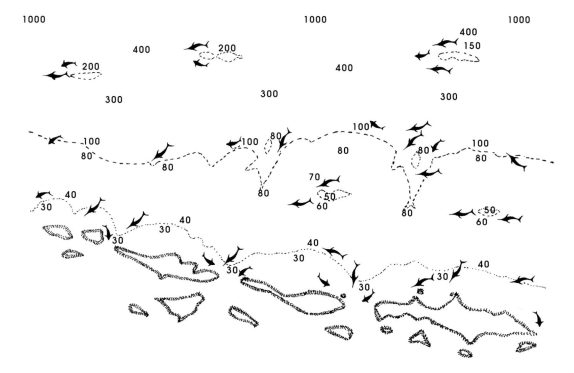

▲ Where the fish should be, outside the reefs.

ridges in depths of 55 meters (30 fathoms) or more, with 180 meters (100 fathoms) an important depth for striped, black and blue marlin along the continental shelf and its canyons.

Marlin fisheries are associated with some of the most beautiful islands and land areas in the world. Hawaii, Puerto Rico, Australia's Great Barrier Reef, the Bahamas, the Virgin Islands, New Zealand, Florida and Mexico would be popular tourist destinations even without their great marlin fisheries. These and other less photogenic marlin fishing areas owe much to the attractions of these great fish.

All marlin species can be fished with a variety of methods. Some methods are more productive than others in particular hot spots. Because of their preferred temperature ranges, the best marlin fishing occurs during the warm months. There are, however, some year-round, twelve-month fisheries sustained by warm currents and water temperatures.

The marlin lunar timetable varies from fishery to fishery. It is interesting to assess the best fishing

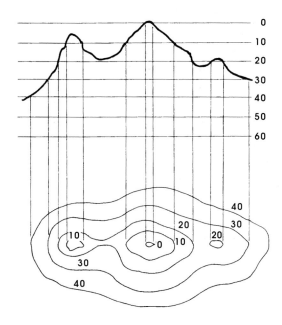

▲ To gain an understanding of where the fish should be, translate the soundings on a chart to a vertical profile; join up the soundings of equal depth to establish contours.

▲ Blue marlin hooked on a lure rips up the surface at Kona, Hawaii. *Photo: Mike Kenyon*

periods not only by season or month, but by moon phase. Captain Laurie Woodbridge, the dean of the Cairns–Lizard Island charter fleet, while stressing the importance of the word 'generally' in regard to moon phases, says that for the Cairns–Great Barrier Reef waters, 'Four days after the full moon you will see more black marlin than any other day in the month. Yes, right in the middle of the waning moon, there they are . . . Even though you get this flurry of action on the wane, it is generally believed that the first quarter to the full and last quarter to the new are good fishing periods offshore'.

Laurie Woodbridge stresses the importance of keeping records and studying the tide and moon when the big fish and great numbers of black marlin are present. Keeping a diary and studying it will show that fish numbers tend to fall into a definite pattern through the year, and over the years in each area. In writing about marlin fishing off Cuba, Ernest Hemingway said, 'Marlin seem to feed best after the first quarter through to the full moon, to drop off during the last quarter. They usually drop off in their feeding for a day or so when the moon is full.' Great

Atlantic captains would have known and expected optimum results at certain moon phases and times in various areas. The great New Zealand captains Francis Arlidge, Jim Whitelaw, Pat Edmonds and Snooks Fuller knew the peak times for their home waters, as do captains all round the world. No doubt this is one of the reasons why it is said, and generally seems true, that 10 per cent of the fishermen catch 90 per cent of the fish.

Despite the expected peaks of activity, much of the best, most pleasant and productive fishing takes place in non-peak times and at times when there are lower wind speeds. It often seems to blow harder at the time of spring tides, particularly those of the full moon.

In Hawaii and many other parts of the world it is believed that the best time to fish for marlin is in the week of the dark phase of the moon, particularly on days when there are at least two (and preferably three) tide changes in the fishing day. This theory is based on the logic that marlin will feed actively during the day if restricted by darkness in their night hunt. Graph reproductions of the data kept by the Hawaiian International Billfish Association show the high incidence of strikes, even in the deepest of water, coinciding with the top or bottom of the tidal change.

There are of course other natural factors that account for marlin activity and successful fishing. The water temperatures that warrant trolling fall in a known range for billfish, tuna and other pelagics — 15°C–30°C (59°F–86°F). It is a waste of time, fuel and money to fish when water temperatures are below the minimum acceptable to the billfish, but out on the ocean there is only one rule: there is no such thing as 'one way' or 'always', and great fish have been found and taken when they should not have been there. These are fish that have apparently diverted from their normal wandering pattern to become local residents.

Best results come with trolling over known reefs, canyons and crevasses and along the 180 meter (100 fathom) or deeper shelf drop-offs. Even in depths of 360 meters (200 fathoms) most action and

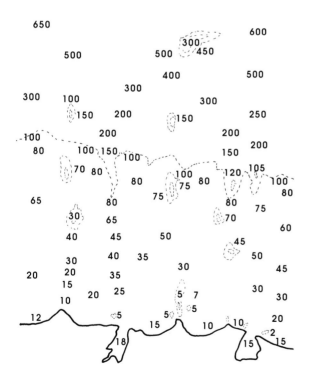

▲ Typical reef canyons where fish should be found.

success comes at the top and bottom of the tide changes. Other factors influencing where to troll are the presence of bait schools, current lines, temperature edges, current upwellings, weed and flotsam lines, sea kelp clumps, logs, manmade FADS (Fish Aggregating Devices) and any natural havens for bait fish. Like other marine animals, marlin kill and eat fish in great quantities, so the appearance and position of bait schools is important.

Logically, much successful fishing is done in proximity to the bait schools. Skipjack tuna, yellowfin tuna, small bluefin and other tunas, mullet, garfish (ballyhoo), mackerels of all types and sizes from kingfish and tanguigue to the small striped, common mackerel of the world's oceans, pilchards and other small fish species are the dominant bait sources. In New Zealand, kahawai and trevally in their countless numbers and schools are the natural prey for the hungry marlin. It is logical to use live or dead baits of the same species on which marlin are feeding. Constant watchfulness of sea and sky for activity will show the presence of bait schools. Schools of squid are not always obvious unless recorded on depth sounders and sonar, yet they are an important factor in the presence and time frame for marlin. One of the advantages of running a depth sounder or fathometer when trolling is the location of deep-swimming bait species and, in fact, many baits do indicate a prime fishing area even though nothing is showing on the surface to hint at this.

When operated by experienced crew, color sounders will indicate the type as well as the depth of bait schools. The giant pelagic billfishes feed not only on the bait fish usually found near the surface, but also on reef-dwelling species on the ocean bottom. Small sharks, broadbill swordfish and small marlin are all grist to the mill of this speedy peak predator, which uses its bill as a club and a spear for gaining food. Many marlin use their bills to stun their prey, then swallow it headfirst. Occasionally, fish (particularly small tuna) taken from the throat and stomach of captured marlin clearly show having been speared.

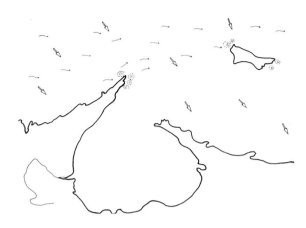

▲ Shore formations attract big fish in warm currents, bringing the action right inshore.

In some fisheries the time of day can be important in the strike rate. For instance, off the Great Barrier Reef most action seems to come after 2.30 in the afternoon, although many mornings are also productive. In most areas it seems that strikes and action will come at any time through the day, and depend on factors other than time of day.

It is now widely accepted that the productive times and areas to fish natural baits are when and where the great gamefish are in concentration for various natural reasons. Of course lures will also produce billfish and tuna in these concentrations or pack conditions. Conversely, it is widely accepted that lure fishing often produces results when the billfish are scattered and travelling in very deep water or feeding well below the surface. Experienced, dedicated, successful bait skippers and crews will change to artificials in areas and at times when their experience and judgment indicate that it will be most productive.

FISHING FOR MARLIN FROM BOATS

Marlin are caught from boats by the following methods:

- Trolling with dead natural baits
- Trolling with live natural baits
- Drifting with live or dead baits
- Fishing at anchor with live or dead baits
- Trolling with lures
- Casting live or dead baits

TROLLING WITH DEAD NATURAL BAITS

The traditional worldwide method for taking marlin since Ernest Llewellyn's first marlin capture in 1903 was by trolling with dead natural baits — lures are the method of the 1990s. These are rigged

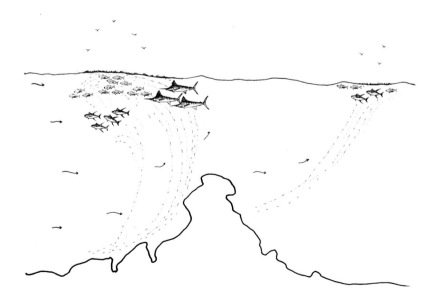

Fish should congregate ▶ upcurrent of higher bottom formations of reefs and peaks. In fast currents fish congregate where the current returns to the surface downstream of bottom projections in a second upwelling.

◄ Marlin usually feed at the rear of a bait school.

in such away that they skip or swim naturally. That first striped marlin and many marlin since caught around the world fell to the attraction of flying fish. In Florida the skilled skippers and crews learned how to rig baits from mullet and their local garfish (ballyhoo). Their skill was introduced to potential marlin areas with baits rigged additionally on bonefish, small tuna and mackerel species. In New Zealand, kahawai were the number one bait. In Australia prior to the evolution of the Great Barrier Reef marlin fishery, bonito, yellowtail kingfish, mullet and garfish (ballyhoo) were the logical baits. Skipjack, bonito and small-toothed mackerel are the chosen baits in South American waters. In the prolific fisheries of Cabo San Lucas, flying fish are the number one bait choice. The successful marlin areas of Venezuela and Costa Rica are fished with the full range of baits, from small mullet to skipjack and the local toothed mackerels.

The Atlantic coast of the USA has a big population of eels, so it is logical that much of the

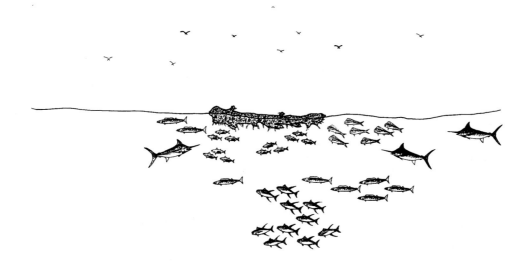

▲ Floating logs and smaller pieces of flotsam attract bait in the warm currents.

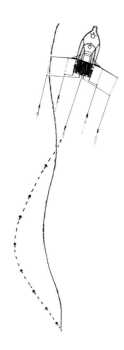

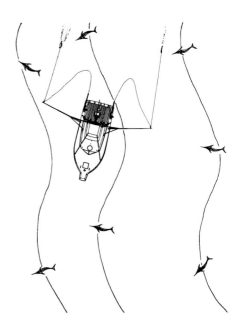

▲ Productive zig-zag trolling in response to current or temperature variations.

▲ Marlin usually swim down swell so boats should troll along the swells.

success in the active and prolific marlin fisheries of Atlantic City, Cape Hatteras and other major ports has come from eel baits. Eels were also reproduced

▲ Amberjack and yellowtail both take big baits intended for billfish. *Photo: Peter Goadby*

in plastic or soft rubber so anglers could troll eel baits even if natural eels were unavailable.

In all the marlin fisheries around the world, local pelagic fish of various sizes from 500 g (1 lb) in the green chub mackerels, along with sardines, scad, and goggle eyes, yellowtail scad that school so prolifically, through to the big baits such as skipjack and other small tuna species up to about 3 kg (7 lb), are regarded as ideal skipping baits and filleted strip baits. The development of the Cairns–Lizard Island black marlin fishery was part of the world trend towards the trolling of big (up to at least 10 kg or 22 lb) natural baits as a skipping or splashing bait. This was a natural development not only because of the availability of fish of this size and the action when rigged for trolling, but because of the size of the marlin being sought.

Giant blue marlin are taken on natural baits as well as lures in many hot spots. In the Atlantic, the east coast of the USA, Walker's Cay, Puerto Rico, the Virgin Islands, the Ivory Coast of Africa and the Azores produce fish from all methods. This is also the case in the Indian Ocean grounds of Mauritius and

Western Australia and in the Pacific Ocean locations of Australia's east coast, New Zealand, Micronesia and the Polynesian islands, Hawaii and Mexico, where fishing methods are mixed, particularly between lures and live baits. The general world trend for marlin is trolled lures or slow-trolled live bait.

The number of lines trolled with baits varies between heavy and light tackle. With medium and heavy tackle it is usual to troll only two baits, generally from outriggers. On lighter lines, four or even more small natural baits may be trolled in conjunction with a teaser. These small baits are often rigged with plastic squid, plastic skirted jigs, lure skirts or feather lures over the head of the bait. Strip baits cut from tunas, mahi mahi (dolphin fish), mackerels and wahoo are also popular and successful rigs, particularly for small billfish when rigged with plastic squid, hexheads or feather lures.

Moldcraft and other plastic squid and soft head pushers are ideal in hookless teaser daisy chains. Top skippers such as Hooker's Skip Smith and Peter Wright, who seek light tackle billfish records

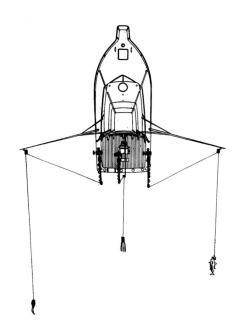

▲ Automatic drop back is sometimes impractical, particularly in high winds. Some people prefer minimum drop back on water and in the air with the angler giving and timing the drop back.

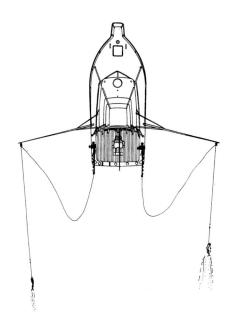

▲ Automatic drop back often assists billfish hookup rate when only two baits are being trolled in calm water.

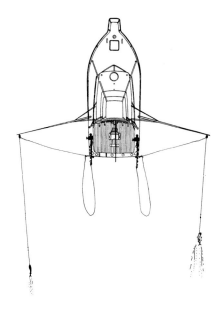

▲ Line drop back for high winds. Line back to black or Aftco clip on transom. Line is twisted to hold in clip, but could also be overbound with dental floss to make a holding loop.

around the world for their anglers, may not troll natural baits or hooked lures until a marlin raises and follows the trolled teasers. The rigged and ready bait or lure on the chosen tackle category is then trolled in position alongside the teaser that has raised the fish so the hooked offering will be struck and give a chance for a hook-up. The teasers may be brought in as soon as the baits are in position so the fish's interest will be directed only at the bait.

The rigged baits trolled on heavy tackle for big fish are generally a tuna or mackerel-type fish rigged as a skipping bait with hook on top or just in front of the head on the left outrigger, plus a much smaller swimming bait of some kind of mackerel or mullet on the right outrigger. The swimming bait is trolled further behind the boat than the skipping bait.

The action and depth at which swimming baits are trolled is often improved by rigging a ball or oval

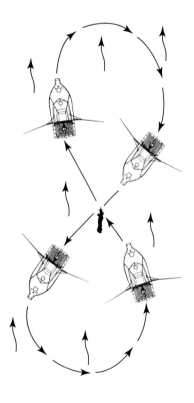

▲ A productive trolling pattern around a log or weed mat: a figure of eight going with the current, not across it.

sinker on the leader loop under the head. Skipping baits are towed about 30 m (100 ft), and swimming baits about 40 m (130 ft) behind the boat, depending to some degree on size and sea conditions. Baits should be rigged so they do not spin, not only because of the unnatural appearance, but because of the extensive damage that can be done to lines. See also Points for Successful Bait Trolling, page 89.

THE HOOK-UP

Florida captain Bill Hatch provided the key to deliberate and successful angling for billfish. Through keen observation and understanding of their feeding action, this great captain realized that billfish generally hit their prey to stun it, and then pick it up to swallow headfirst. Examination of stomach contents and observation of feeding habits to this day support his original deductions. Captain Hatch instructed his anglers to give 'drop back' (that is, to allow the line to run freely from the spool with only enough drag to prevent an overrun) for at least a count of ten. At this time, if a pause indicated that the marlin or other billfish had taken the bait to swallow it headfirst, the angler would increase his drag and immediately strike and, with luck, hook the fish. With this knowledge, his anglers were able to catch what had previously been rarely or accidentally hooked billfish. Bill Hatch's drop back technique is now used with slight variations in bait trolling right around the world. Recognition of the need and benefit of the drop back also assisted in live bait and dead bait fishing on the drift, slow trolling or at anchor.

In the Cairns–Lizard Island fishery, as in some others, when fishing only two lines, depending on wind conditions, line is allowed to trail along the surface of the water to act as an automatic drop back. Some skippers gun the boat to help anglers hook up immediately the bag of line becomes taut and line is running from the reel. Others prefer the angler to judge when to strike with the advice of captain and crew. They wait until the fish is

TROLLING BAITS

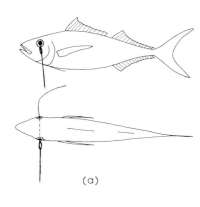

(a)

(b)

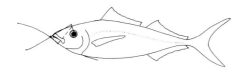

(c)

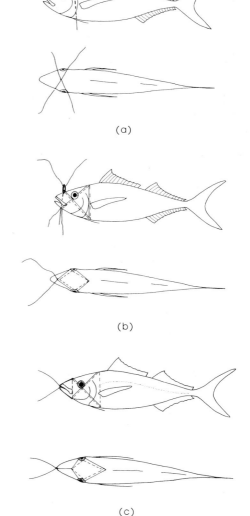

(a)

(b)

(c)

BRIDLE RIG FOR TROLLING DEAD BAITS

(a) Thread through top of eyes.

(b) Knot ends over eyes. Push thread down through
head, top to bottom. Cut groove in lip.

(c) Tie with surgeon's knot. Closed mouth gives
two threads for towing bridle and for tying
close to mouth.

HALTER RIG FOR BAITS WITH HOOK IN FRONT OF NOSE

(a) Double cord through needle eye. Push
needle down through back with two equal
lengths. This gives four ends.

(b) Take two lines and knot over eye, then push
needle through from top of head. There are
now two threads at top of head, two at lower.

(c) Knot over mouth ready for half-hitches onto hook.

TROLLING BAITS

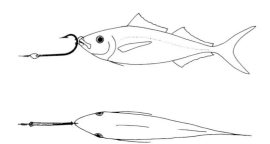

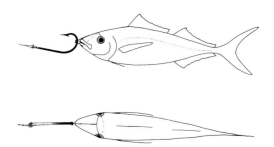

RIG FOR LIVE OR (USUALLY) DEAD TROLLING
If live, leave mouth open with slack 3–4.5 cm
(1–1½ in) bridle. For 'quickie' rig, the hook could
be placed through jaw as in Catalina rig.

OLD BAY OF ISLANDS TROLLING RIG
Trolling dead fish with 3–4.5 cm (1–1½ in) bridle
through mouth and eyes.

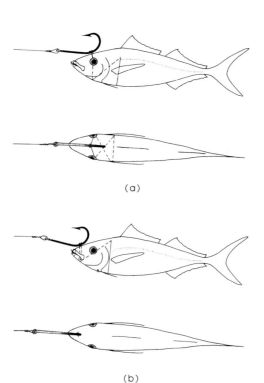

(a)

(b)

(a)

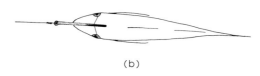

(b)

SIMILAR RIG FOR DEAD BAITS
(a) Mouth sewn closed.
(b) Hook tied on nose instead of eye (Cairns
    variation). These can also be rigged with
    second hook towards tail.

BIMINI OR PANAMA TROLLING RIG FOR LIVE BAIT
(a) Needle with slot eye ready on hook for live
    bait trolling.
(b) Live bait trolling: open mouth. Dead bait
    trolling: mouth closed. Bridle 1.5–3 cm (½–1 in).

TROLLING BAITS

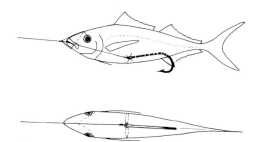

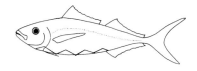

CABO BLANCO TROLLING RIG
Two-hook trolling rig with hooks in belly. Sometimes the backbone is removed.

HOW TO CLOSE INCISIONS IN TROLLING RIGS
Herringbone stitching is used to sew up cut belly or back. Care must be taken to allow space around hook to allow natural movement without hook being sewn tight. The gills as well as the mouth of the bait should be sewn tightly closed to restrict water entry.

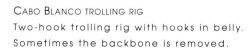

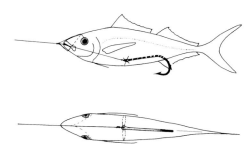

BLUE MARLIN TROLLING RIG
Single-hook rig, sometimes with backbone removed. Bridle through body as well as mouth is an aid on bigger baits.

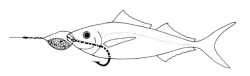

SWIMMING RIG WITH HEAD SINKER (TROLLING)
When trolling a dead fish with the backbone removed or broken, leader is passed through the eye of the hook and an oval sinker is used to make the bait run deeper and to vary the action.

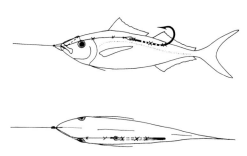

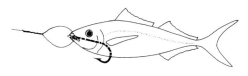

TROPICAL MARLIN TROLLING RIG
To allow a short drop back, which may be beneficial when trolling dead fish (where the gamefish may take the baits from the rear and swallow quickly), the leader can be bound with dental tape to facilitate non-slip tying of towing bridle. The dental tape stops slip and makes sure the pull is on the head. A practical rig where wahoo and other razor gang fish mutilate marlin baits.

SWIMMING DEAD FISH
The leader is passed through the eye of the hook. Mouth is sewn shut and leader has a big loop to enable the bait to be turned. The backbone can be completely removed and the body, including the tail, split.

definitely running with the bait and thus give more time before hook-up. Both methods are effective but the latter is generally more beneficial, particularly if the marlin are not feeding voraciously and may be striking at the bait to kill for some reason other than the dictates of hunger.

Angling history credits Captains Bill Hatch and Charlie Thompson of Florida with the development and refinements of the drop back. It is not known who commenced the evolution of teasing and the fast cranking back of a bait if a hook-up does not occur on a strike.

Despite printed references to the benefits of teasing, some skippers and anglers still prefer the ultra-cautious technique of long drop back with virtually no drag. Some feel there is benefit in even pulling line by hand from the reel into the water without drag so the marlin can take and swallow its stunned prey naturally. The marlin is not struck by the angler, with or without the boat going ahead, until minutes have passed, minutes that seem like hours. After a pause, the fish pulls line freely from the reel and the marlin is struck. This is an exciting, although nerve-racking, method of drop back or hook-up.

Generally however, the current thinking is to rig for a quick hook-up. Then, if the marlin drops the bait or just hits but does not take it, teasing by winding the bait quickly back towards the boat will change a placid fish swimming away to an excited predator chasing, slashing and taking its 'stunned' food. Both Kip Farrington and Ernest Hemingway refer to this teasing in their writings, yet it was not often practiced until recent years. There is no doubt that the teasing technique is almost as important for success as the drop back. Some of the great marlin captures have been made after a marlin has taken or at least struck at the bait and swum away as often as three times. The key to the marlin returning to the bait is the quick retrieval of line on to the reel or the angler pulling by hand to give the bait, or what is left of it, the appearance of escaping.

The savage return of a marlin to bait remnants or only a part of the bait head, or to an otherwise bare hook for a second, third or fourth strike is difficult to explain if natural baits truly look natural to the fish. The similar violent and related strikes that are made at soft and hard plastic lures indicate that marlin and tuna may hunt and feed in response to vibrations received along the lateral line, and in response to what they seem to be hunting by sight or by vibration rather than by their sense of smell.

TROLLING WITH LIVE NATURAL BAITS

This method is successful, particularly when the baits are trolled around the bait schools from which they were caught, or with pre-caught baits from the boat bait tank. Live baits are also effective where there is an upwelling and where the sea bed configuration of reef, ridge or canyon creates a locality worthy of spending time in slow trolling. Baits are pulled about 30–40 m (100–130 ft) behind the boat.

Boat speed for live bait fishing is the slowest of all trolling methods, with a top speed of around 4 knots. Skipjack tuna are the most popular and successful of live baits around the world, although the little tuna and kawa kawa (mackerel tuna) are also prime species. In New Zealand, because the kahawai and trevally are the usual bait school species, success comes from trolling these species, particularly kahawai.

In California, Mexico, Australia and many other areas, chub mackerel, scad and goggle eyes are ideal live baits and can be cast to tailing and finning marlin. The benefits of these small live baits are their suitability for smaller size and weight hooks, which suit lighter leaders and smaller marlin.

Many anglers and skippers prefer that the line trolling the live bait be held by the angler who is to take the strike. The benefit is that the angler can actually feel and advise of any panic of the bait, and of even the most gentle tap from a billfish when it stuns the bait and takes it. The angler should be able to tell the skipper exactly how bait and quarry are interacting.

Others prefer to fish with the line with the live bait held lightly in an outrigger clip halfway up the outrigger. This enables the angler to be in the

Fast Strike Bait Trolling

Action of Fish

- Fast crash strike (may hook itself on strike)
- May chase other bait
- Runs fast (does not pause to swallow bait; this has been done on initial strike)
- Jumps, runs fast

Action of Fisherman

- Reel alarm click ratchet is on, with drag lightly set
- Angler transfers rod to chair with captain's agreement to lock up to strike
- Imperative to bring second bait inboard immediately
- Harness hooked on
- If captain knows marlin position, he runs boat towards fish or backs up to minimize loss of line
- Boat runs the fish or is backed up as marlin position dictates

Slow Strike Bait Trolling

Action of Fish

- Attracted to the baits by boat, baits or vibration of other hooked fish
- Surveys baits as prospective meal
- Hits bait to kill, or grabs bait
- Takes bait in mouth, swims off slowly
- Swallows bait during pause
- Swims on faster than before
- Jumps, runs very fast or panics in an effort to be rid of the hook
- Struggles against hooking, line drag and forward way of the boat
- Jumps or runs fast and sounds after hooking

Action of Fisherman

- Reel alarm click ratchet is 'on'. Set drag lightly.
- Watch baits for movement or quick 'hits'
- Be ready to work baits gently and to replace with fresh or live baits if necessary
- Exercise care to prevent overrun and at the same time be alert to feed line to fish that are very shy (as marlin may be in temperate waters). Sometimes it is necessary to gently retrieve line to keep contact with the fish and its movements
- Bring in other outfits. If anchored, crew quietly drop dan buoy on anchor line so that the boat can be maneuvered
- Keep all weight off the line. The angler should strike after a short time, say a count of five
- Three or four sharp lifts of the rod with the boat going fast ahead should be enough to set the hook firmly
- Strike immediately, with the boat going ahead
- Ease drag a little so rod can be placed in chair gimbal
- The boat can be backed up and when the fish slows down the boat can be maneuvered to recover line

▲ Small black marlin make tough light-tackle opponents at Port Stephens, Australia. *Photo: Peter Goadby.*

(Alf) Stevenson at Cairns. We had taken a yellowfin about 10 kg (20 lb) and quickly rigged it. A deck hose kept it alive and oxygenated until we reached the deep water, then it went over for what we believed must be a sure strike for Alf.

Nothing happened, so Alf said, 'It's our last day, put out a skip bait for yourself as well!' So out went an ox eye herring — small tarpon bait on my 60 kg (130 lb) outfit. A few minutes later, even though the big live bait restricted possible trolling speed and the dead bait was flopping in what was to us an unnatural manner at that speed, we had truly unforgettable action. Two big black marlin came up behind the bait. They ignored the panicky live yellowfin bait as they zeroed in on the skipping bait. The smaller marlin struck and took that flopping bait. That marlin weighed 517 kg (1137 lb), and was only the seventh marlin more than 454.5 kg (1000 lb) taken in Australia. Some captains, such as Bobby Brown, Bart Miller and Geoff Ferguson, are consistently successful with live baits.

DRIFTING WITH LIVE OR DEAD BAITS

Success while drifting or at anchor generally comes when the techniques are used over or along ledges or reefs, around bait schools and in other areas where marlin should logically be. One advantage of this is that other fishing can be carried out at the same time as the lines are out for marlin. Fishing can be carried out on the bottom for snapper and other species with bait or jigs, as well as for tuna, amberjack and yellowtail kingfish. In Florida, Tommy Gifford and other innovative skippers combined all of this with running a live bait for marlin and sailfish from a fishing kite. With the right wind conditions this method can be very effective, and the kite bait can be used to tease an interested billfish into action.

It is important when fishing with a float while at anchor or drifting that the float used be rigged lightly so that it will break away immediately on the strike and not spook the marlin. Only apply enough drag through the reel to prevent an overrun in the event of a fast strike.

shade, cool and presumably alert. It ensures the skipper the benefit of a drop back with only a light hold on the line, whereas an inexperienced or buck-fever angler may hold the line too hard, strike too soon or pull the bait away from the fish. As with dead bait fishing, marlin should be given time to turn the bait and swallow it headfirst before striking to set the hook. The strike drag should be set at between 25 and 33.3 per cent of the line class breaking strain. During trolling, whether held by hand or in the outrigger clip, the drag should be set at just enough to prevent an overrun from a crash strike.

Dead baits or even a lure or two trolled right on the surface can add to the effectiveness of trolling live bait, even at the slow speed of live baiting. I first became aware of this when fishing with Sir William

If mako sharks are expected in the fishing area, the light float line should be 70–100 cm (2–3 ft) in length to minimize chance of cutoffs from makos that attack the balloon or other float.

The hook-up technique is similar to that in slow trolling with live bait, but if you are at anchor it is imperative to slip the anchor line. Successful anglers use a long drop back time to allow any fish that has taken the bait plenty of time without drag before striking. They let the line run freely from the reel until there is a pause, then allow a count of at least five before striking the fish. This is hard on anglers' nerves, but critical in the hook-up. If the taut line starts heading to the surface, indicating a fish ready to jump before the angler has struck, the fish has felt something is wrong and is racing to the surface to rid itself of the bait fish. If this happens you still have a good chance of a hook-up — immediately strike hard and often until the fish is hooked or jumps and throws the bait or runs away from the boat. Depending on conditions and on the number of outfits that can be used, drifting baits should be from 10 m (30 ft) on the surface to down around 100 m (30 ft).

Many marlin hooked while fishing at anchor or drift are hooked either on big dead baits on heavy leaders rigged for sharks or on small live baits rigged on monofilament leaders for tuna. These contrasting leaders add to the challenge, and to the need for expert crew.

While fishing at anchor, the dan buoy float on the anchor line must be ready to slip overboard so the boat can be maneuvered and the marlin played clear of this obstruction.

Marlin are taken commercially drifting at night, though this technique is rarely practiced recreationally. The difference in success rate is naturally related to the number of baited hooks that can be fished.

Marlin weighing over 455 kg (1000 lb) have been caught from boats 6 m (20 ft) in size, through to the traditional sophisticated battle wagons. There are some benefits in fishing from small boats, particularly for those fishing short stand-up outfits or with chairs in the bow.

CASTING LIVE OR DEAD BAITS

The innovative sportfishermen of California realized that when striped marlin were swimming slowly on the surface or appearing to sun themselves, they would not always react to trolled dead baits or lures no matter how skillfully these were rigged or presented. Days of probable frustration were turned into days to remember by the casting of live mackerel, sardines or other live bait to striped marlin and broadbill visibly swimming along the surface. This technique naturally spread to Mexico's Cabo San Lucas and is now an important part of the success of their year-round fishing. It has led to the development of new types of rods and reels that are more suitable for casting these lightweight baits than conventional trolling rods are. When trolling tackle was used for casting, the line could be coiled on deck or in a bucket or other smooth container, and the live bait leader thrown by hand in front of the surface-swimming marlin. Some boats now have live bait tanks forward as well as in the cockpit.

Once the marlin takes the bait, the fish is struck quickly because the small size of the cast baits enables the marlin to swallow it at the time of the strike. If bigger baits are used, longer pause and longer drop back are further factors in a successful hook-up.

The technique of trolling while searching for billfish on which to cast live baits is exciting, but the real excitement comes when tailing fish are seen. The angler then goes to the bow, or in some cases casts from the cockpit, endeavoring to place the live bait in a position where it will be taken by the marlin. Co-operation and communication between angler and crew are important.

Sometimes the cruising marlin are found near bait schools, and crew or other anglers can fish for fresh live baits on the spot with small feather and skin multiple-bait catching rigs. These will provide fresh and lively baits of the size and species that the marlin may be ready to feed upon. The skipper, from his position on the bridge, has the best visibility and should clearly direct angler and crew to the position of the marlin the boat is working. The bow of the boat is 12 o'clock and the transom 6 o'clock.

The rods evolved for live bait casting have lighter, more flexible tips than trolling rods, although much the same butt power. The reels take advantage of space-age materials, being lighter in weight in the spool, and generally improve casting ability with the light baits. This flexibility at the tip not only facilitates casting, but reduces the overall length of the rod.

The presentation of the bait is usually best done from the bow, although chances often come at other positions around the boat. If hooked from the bow, it is fought from there until the angler can walk to the cockpit. In small boats the marlin may be played from the bow. In ideal circumstances, the marlin is cast to in the 4 o'clock to 8 o'clock positions with the angler already in the cockpit.

The sight of marlin cruising on the surface is worth the day at sea. The hook-up and fight followed by tag and release is an extra bonus. Southern California and Baja provide the ideal surface conditions for live bait casting. One day out from Palmilla on Baja around the edge of the fabulous Gordo Bank we counted 40 tailing striped marlin, a memorable sight to anglers from the western Pacific but routine in this fabulous eastern Pacific fishbowl.

FISHING FOR MARLIN ON THE DRIFT OR AT ANCHOR

Marlin fishing is now often equated with surface or near-surface trolling. The obvious results of commercial longliners, native fishermen of past and present and sportfishermen are often ignored. Statistics show that many of the world's biggest marlin, as well as the vast majority of marlin taken, are on commercial longlines.

The take by commercial longliners and flaglines (short longlines) puts tremendous pressure on the stocks and survival of billfish. This pressure reflects not only the efficiency but real potential of drifting or fishing at anchor where the billfish are or should be.

Fishing in these modes always had a special attraction for pioneer sporting fishermen. In each area they visited indigenous fishermen were already regularly going out to sea in canoes or small boats and returning with marlin and tuna. In his expeditions to many parts of the world, Michael Lerner spent hours, even days, fishing with the drifting method and baits at depths fished by the local fishermen.

Of course the longliners and flagliners have an advantage over recreational fishermen in terms of the sheer number of hooks and baits used. Japanese fishing papers and international investigation have shown that marlin are target species for longliners as well as being the oft-quoted 'incidental' catch when tuna fishing.

Recent research with electronic tags has high-lighted the importance of 73 metres (40 fathoms) in the cruising and hunting life of marlin. They spend much of their time at this depth, so it is logical to drift with baits down deep or to fish at anchor with baits deep.

In the great New Zealand striped marlin fishery, the boats often stop for lunch while the skipper 'boils the billy'. This time is not wasted as baits are fished down deep in what is often the quiet part of the day. At Mayor Island, a great part of the fishing day is spent in drifting because of the possibility of big thresher sharks. Not surprisingly many of the marlin hooked are not the expected striped, but the heavier blue or black marlin.

One of the great benefits of this non-trolling fishery is that it gives anglers every opportunity for a smorgasbord of species in all weights. Giant tuna, mid-size tuna, plus all the sharks and the oceanic gamefish are potential opponents. If sharks are unwelcome opponents, the use of monofilament leaders gives every chance of cutoffs. Unfortunately, monofilament is also easily cut by wahoo, which would be welcome strangers.

Every oceanic species is potentially available with this method. Chances of action can be improved dramatically by the use of chum (berley).

DRIFTING AND ANCHOR BAITS

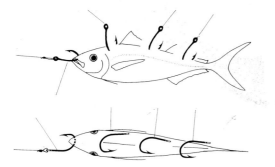

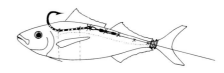

(a)

LIVE BAIT RIGS FOR DRIFTING AND AT ANCHOR
For use with chub mackerel and goggle eye (scad) as well as bigger fish species. Position of hooks depends on the current and depth required.

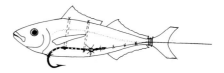

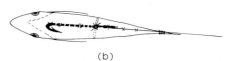

(b)

(a)

DEAD FISH FOR DRIFTING AND AT ANCHOR
Hook point must be kept clean and eye of hook tied very firmly. Leader must be tied very firmly at junction of tail and body.

(b)

CUBAN DRIFTING RIGS
(a) Fish rigged tail up (can also be rigged head up).
(b) Squid and fish combination.

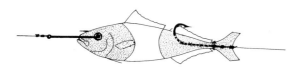

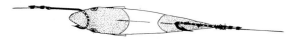

STRIP BAITS: DRIFTING OR AT ANCHOR
Fillets should be taper cut and rigged with heavy end at point of hook. Tie at hook eye to leader and bait must be very firm. The bait gives best results if the strip is not much longer than the hook.

CUT BAITS
Two drifting baits can be cut from one small tuna or other fish.

▲ The blue water ballet of a striped marlin at Palmilla, Baja California. *Photos: Peter Goadby.*

▲ Position of boat when angler is ready to cast to tailing or surface-cruising billfish.

The cubing of fillets and small fish adds to the effectiveness of fishing by this method.

One of the exciting features of this non-trolling method is that it can be sight-fishing. As chum works its attractant magic, fish of all species and size are lured to its source — the boat. The ocean around the boat can become a living fishbowl. Sometimes free-swimming hunting marlin cruise into sight before they attack the live, dead or strip baits. Sometimes sharks of all species, with attendant pilot fish and remora, provide silent, frightening sights at boatside. Sometimes tuna cruise majestically or zip and flash through the chum. Sometimes strikes come from baits set at favored depths, the fish peeling line from the spool slowly or at fantastic speeds before they are sighted.

Despite the speed they exhibit after being hooked, and the savagery they show when slashing at trolled baits or lures, marlin generally take the bait slowly and cautiously. Anglers must be alert to

movements of floats, of line coming slack or moving out a few feet. Marlin often hunt up-current, so a slack line or float moving against the current indicates action. Anglers must be watching the baits and floats, looking for fish, alert for unusual indicators. Vigilance and alertness are hard to maintain, with sometimes the only visible action being the regular distribution of chum and the appearance of a few apparently disinterested birds.

The caution of marlin dictates that reel brakes, ratchets and clicks on reels should be set just enough to prevent an overrun in case of a speed strike. Anglers must be alert to switch click or ratchet off and ease the drag and pull line by hand from the reel to the fish. Often the angler will feed line without weight on the fish at all. Often line will need to be recovered back on to the spool to minimize the chance of the marlin swimming across loose line in the water, until the swallowing pause and faster swimoff indicate that it is time to try to set the hook. Of course if the fish speeds up

and heads for the surface, the angler should strike hard and quickly to try and ensure hook-up before the fish can throw the hook by jumping. Marlin hooked at drift or anchor are fought as if hooked in trolling.

Marlin usually take baits slowly and cautiously, in contrast to the power they exhibit later. Once a bait is taken, all the other lines in the water are brought inboard while the angler concentrates on his strike and hook-up. The fighting technique is the same as for marlin hooked while trolling. The marlin has the advantage that it may be heading down into the depths at the time when it is being hooked. Marlin often fight deep and sometimes do not zip back to the surface. More often, though, marlin hooked by all methods will head for the surface and reach for the sky. Sometimes the size and species of the opponent are not known until it is right at boatside for gaffing or tag and release. Whether kept or released, they are an angler's dream fish.

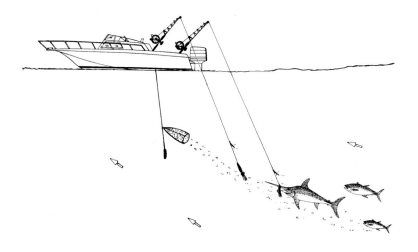

◀ Hawaiian fishermen continue to practice the traditional Ika Shibi style of fishing in which small pieces of chum are wrapped in an open-ended cloth bag around which is rolled a stone- or lead sinker-weighted chum line. The rolled line is held by the chum drop line while it is lowered to the desired depth then, when the drop line is jerked sharply, the rolls of chum line come free, the bag opens and the chum sinks and scatters to attract fish. This is carried out every 20 minutes until the nearby baits are taken.

Points for successful fishing for marlin on drift or at anchor:

- Set drag and ratchet just hard enough to prevent an overrun.
- Put floats on light breaking lines.
- Anglers and crew should be alert to fish and bird activity and line or float movement.
- The fish that has taken the bait unseen can be of any size and species.
- Be careful to prevent overrun before hookup.
- Immediately the cockpit is clear, gaffs, gloves, wire cutters and tag pole must be ready for use.
- Remember that even though marlin are sought as the opponent, the hook-up could have been on marlin, shark or tuna, so it is important to be ready with a range of gaffs and tail ropes — just in case.
- In the event of double strike, double hook-up on separate fish, try to assess which fish is smaller (more likely to be taken quickly), or which fish is hooked on heavier tackle. Fight this fish hard from the chair or standing up, then go for the other fish.
- Minimize the chance of marlin taking more than one bait, as a fish that is hooked or entangled on more than one line is not eligible for a record according to the published IGFA rules.

- It is beneficial if the skipper checks regularly with binoculars from bridge or tower, checking for fin, surface activity and bird activity.
- If depth and circumstances allow, jig or fish with other tackle to catch other fish. Remember, the vibration of smaller live fish being caught will attract other fish.
- Spincasting to schooling fish such as small tuna in the chum trail will add to activity and attraction.
- Check with sounder that drift is maintaining wanted depth and whether big fish are between the boat and the sea bed.
- A sea anchor may be useful to improve the angle and rate of drift.

Anchor fishing naturally has many links with drift fishing.

- Again, it is important to fish where the fish should be. The boat should be positioned on reefs and peaks so the baits are along the edges of canyons and drop-offs of the reefs.
- Have the anchor line rigged and ready with a dan buoy so that the anchor line can be dropped immediately there is a run or strike from a marlin. The boat can be maneuvered or the current used so boat, fish and line are clear of this obstruction.

If the fish hooked is jumping or running towards the boat, the skipper guns his motors to move the boat away from the fish and help keep the line tight. This action minimizes the chance of the fish charging into the boat and the possibility of it jumping with mouth open towards the boat and throwing the hook. If the fish is running away from the boat, peeling line at frightening speed from the spool, the boat should be backed up as fast as fish and boat ability dictate.

Once the marlin has settled down, many skippers and anglers prefer to change from backing up with the leader coming over the body and tail to running the fish so it is resisting the pull of the line and reel drag with its head and muscles. Skippers will maneuver the boat not only to keep the marlin working against the drag and the boat, but to change the direction and depth in which the fish is heading. Most hooked marlin run towards the deep water. In some cases, particularly on rough days, they run in the direction they were already travelling.

Constant pressure with no let-up or slack will see changes in the fish's swimming pattern and direction. When they are tired, they sometimes circle in the manner of tuna. Even though angler, skipper and boat can all contribute to the minimizing of belly in the line from an apparently straight-running fish, a belly of some size will occur; it may feel as if the fish has come free before the line again comes tight. Some successful anglers in Panama have developed a technique of deliberately creating a line belly to assist in tiring the fish, but more generally, and particularly with light tackle on fast fish, the loop or belly is kept as narrow as possible.

When fishing light tackle, it is usual to drop the rod tip when the fish is jumping, in order to prevent breakage. To minimize the chance of breakoff on medium and light tackle and with giant fish it is imperative, particularly with lines of little stretch, to back the drag off (in some cases right back to free spool) when a jumping fish quickly changes direction. The fish may be travelling on the surface at a speed in excess of 48 km/h (30 mph), and the weight of the belly of line will quickly cause a breakoff.

When line is running through the water under tension, it is more like line running around a solid than through clear liquid. One of the most thrilling

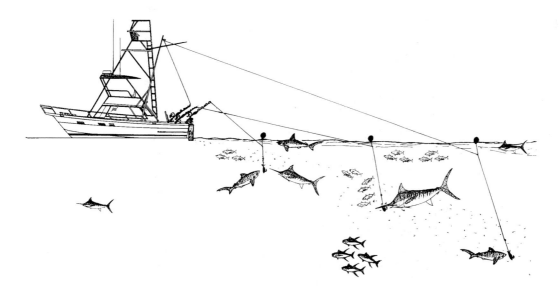

▲ When fishing on the drift or at anchor using chum various fish will respond to baits covering the whole water column.

sights in marlin fishing, apart from a jumping fish, is when a fast-running fish and the boat are in such a position that a column of spray jets from the surface from the line.

The constant and alert watching of baits and lures is an important factor in successful marlin fishing. There are many times when the action of a skipper or crew — teasing, or presenting a fresh or a live bait — will change a follower to a taker. Vigilance is what turns 'nothing' days into 'something' days.

Whether fishing baits or lures, the fighting technique is much the same. Once the strike occurs and the angler has the rod, other lines are brought in as part of clearing the cockpit for fighting space. It is most important to make sure the baits and lures are put right into the cabin or right forward in the cockpit. This is to prevent any chance of leaders going overboard or out the scuppers. If this happens, hooks can be pulled into crew's legs or feet and leaders can tangle around the propeller.

If a chair is used, a harness would be on the chair, ready for the angler or crew to attach the harness clips to the reel as the cockpit is being cleared either before or after the fish is hooked. With the marlin hooked and jumping or running, the skipper backs up to minimize line loss or to help in recovery while

gaffs, ropes, gloves, tag poles and wire cutters are made ready. Outrigger halyards are ofen taken from deck level to the flying bridge just in case, as black marlin or white marlin usually do a boatside jumping exhibition. So crew mobility, speed and balance are imperative in the cockpit.

TAKING THE LEADER ON MARLIN

Many marlin are lost right at the boatside before they can be gaffed or tagged and released. A great strain and responsibility rest with the crew members taking the leader or handling gaffs or tag poles.

With marlin, particularly black marlin, the leader man must be ready for the fish to jump. If a big fish jumps away from the boat, the leader man must release the wire to prevent dislocating any joints, going overboard, or breaking the leader. It is for this reason the angler winds the swivel to the rod tip, eases the drag, puts the ratchet or clock on and is ready with his left hand to prevent overrun and backlash.

Once the angler has the swivel to the rod tip or the leader in reach of the crew, the leader man takes hold and, without jerking or bullocking, pulls the leader so the marlin is within reach of the gaff or tag pole.

◄ Cozumal white marlin are ideal light tackle adversaries.
Photo: Gil Keech.

TAKING THE LEADER AND GAFFING

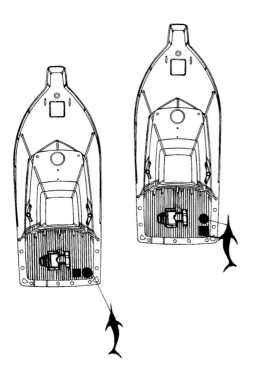

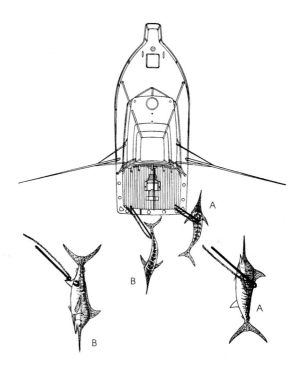

● Wireman or leader man

■ Gaffman or tag man

Gaff billfish for minimum chance of tearing in the shoulder (A) or the anal fin bone structure (B), *not* in the tail or stomach areas.

Gaffing should be done on the port side of the boat if crew are to work right-handed. The leader man takes the leader with the gaff man behind him then, as the fish is pulled into gaffing range, he moves forward so the gaff man can reach the fish at the shoulder. The same applies for tag and release but after tagging the fish the tag man cuts the leader behind the leader man or removes hooks if possible so the leader man can release the wire when he is ready and balanced.

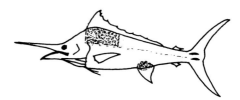

Billfish should preferably be gaffed in the shoulder muscle behind the dorsal or above the anal fin bone structure. They should never be gaffed in the tail area.

On light tackle where the monofilament leader and double are often joined by an improved Albright or Uniknot so the leader can be wound on to the reel, it is the angler who brings the fish boatside into gaff or tagging range. With this rig, the leader is usually in two pieces with the swivel or snap swivel joining the sections. The first section of 24 kg or 36 kg (53 lb or 79 lb) monofilament has 45 cm (18 in) of heavier monofilament or light piano wire or stainless single strand wire attached to a snap swivel. Once a fish is tagged, the crew takes a wrap of the monofilament and cuts or breaks the leader wire.

GAFFING MARLIN

Many of the early fishing writers stressed the logic of gaffing marlin near the tail region so that the fish's propeller could be lifted clear of the water. Most skippers and crews now prefer, if a fish is leading, to gaff it in or just behind the dorsal fin and as deep down the body as the gaff allows, where flesh and muscle minimize the possibility of gaff tearout.

If the marlin is not leading when the leader is taken and is still heading away from the boat which is backing up, some skilled crewmen reach out and place the gaff hook under the body immediately above the anal fin, in muscle and bony fin ray area — the only non-ripping area for a gaff on the underside of the fish. Once gaffed, a tail rope is often necessary to complete the catch. The marlin should be subdued with a billy or club to terminate the struggle. If the size of the fish or the transom door allows, the marlin can be slid inboard and fishing may continue.

In onshore marlin fishing and on long-range boats, long, flexible gaffs are used to hold and lift the fish clear of the water and onto the fishing platform. Naturally, two or three gaffs are required to lift the fish.

Marlin fishing is regarded as the pinnacle of saltwater sportsfishing. Anglers, skippers and crew thrill to the challenge of the crashing blind strikes with the fish clearing the surface like a jet at full throttle. A big fish clear in the air where a split second before there was nothing but unblemished sea and sky is unforgettable. There are strikes that give humans more time to see, to think and react: a following shadow is tipped by a dorsal fin above the surface, a bulge of water is pierced by a bill and sometimes a wide-open mouth. At other times the strike to kill the lure comes only after teasing a following fish with drop back and fast recovery. Sometimes the billfish, after raising every watcher's blood pressure and heart rate, drops down into the depths and disappears.

All marlin have the ability to peel line from the reel at blistering speed and to make the reel click scream above the rumble of the diesels, causing an instant surge of adrenalin for the fishermen. The power, size and speed of marlin as well as giant tuna have forced continuing changes and improvements in fishing tackle. All marlin create in fishermen an intense feeling of excitement, respect and admiration. No other fish mean as much to so many fishermen.

MARLIN FISHING ON TROLLED LURES

There is no dispute that marlin can be and are caught on live or dead baits, and always will be, but bait is not the only or necessarily the best way to attract action in all fishing areas. Data and experience show that there are times and areas where fishing is most productive from use of baits, and that there are times and areas when trolled lures are not only the most productive, but the best and sometimes virtually the only chance of success.

The boat speed at which lure fishing is practiced ensures that the lures and hooks are presented in front of the greatest possible number of fish. The inherent problems of availability of bait fish and skill and time in rigging and trolling speed can also inhibit fishing time and thus results from fishing with baits. In lure fishing, lures can be bought from a store or lure maker already rigged — ready to go fishing, ready for action, and ready for quick change or replacement.

▲ A striped marlin takes to the air off Baja California. *Photo: Peter Goadby.*

It sometimes takes years of effort in new and developing sport fisheries to pinpoint the exact times and places for fish action, so the trolling of lures to cover maximum territory and thus find the hot spots is most logical.

Once the data or times and places are known the natural baits may be the more productive, correct choice, but having been successfully established on artificials most fisheries continue to fish and develop with this method.

Take a rigged lure, add water of the correct temperature over a likely sea bed configuration and stand by for marlin action. Lure fishing is instant fishing.

The comment is sometimes made (by fishermen who do not practice or are not successful at lure fishing) that in nature the great ocean gamefish do not feed on plastic. They point out that fish and squid are found in fish stomachs, plastic is not. Despite this, the fact is that marlin of all sizes do strike hard and often at hard and soft plastic or metal-headed and colorfully skirted trolling lures.

The argument that the great saltwater gamefish do not eat plastic could apply equally to trout and salmon, which do not eat feathers, plastic or metal yet are usually taken on these materials in sport, or to the speedy toothy mackerels and wahoo which do not eat metal but are taken for commercial as well as recreational use on metal spoons, wood, plastic and feathers.

In both fresh and salt water, the evidence can be seen every day that the world's great and classic gamefish, despite their highly developed sight, do strike hard and often at a variety of lures. Sometimes a marlin will just strike with its bill at the head of the lure or on the leader ahead of the lure.

To change this pattern of strikes with zero hook-ups, zero fish at boat, some reduce the strike drag in trolling mode to just enough to prevent an overrun. This light initial drag gives the marlin the chance to turn the lure and get it where the hooks can take hold, instead of being pulled away from the striking fish. Trolling smaller lures often gives a more effective hook-up rate. Big lures certainly attract fish of all sizes, but many of the big lure strikes are not followed by hook-ups.

Another way to overcome the problem of shy marlin is to use an extra outrigger out from the bridge or tower and down the center line of the boat. Ideally a roller-type outrigger release is best for this shotgun rig. The lure from this center outrigger is trolled well back on wave nine or ten, specifically for shy and following marlin and for another chance at strike from a marlin that has struck and not hooked on one of the lures trolled closer to the boat. Unsuccessful trolling consumes time and money, so use of proven lure designs is most logical. There are many top makers.

Variations on the 'how-to' for success with lures have evolved in a number of areas, but generally the Hawaiian techniques and patterns remain the basics for success with offshore trolling lures anywhere in the world.

The basics of lure trolling are:

• Troll where the fish should be, because not even the best lures in a perfectly trolled pattern can produce action where the fish aren't. Knowledge of where the fish should be comes with experience and research. Keep a diary or log.

- Troll in a pattern of lures that suits the boat. Trial and experience will show what works best for each boat in terms of lure shape and trolling pattern. Variations come from the size and shape of the boat, its action in the sea, its wave wake, the angle of V in the hull, and even the boat propellers and power.
- Troll with lures of colors known to be successful. They should resemble the coloration of local bait fish or squid populations, and take into account the light conditions of the day. Put out a proven selection of light and dark color combinations.
- Troll with shapes to suit the water surface. A few designs work well and produce in all seas, but most are designed to be successful in either rough or smooth water.
- Troll each proven lure at the distance and on the wake wave that suits the lure. Work out which lures work best from outriggers, from the centre rigger, on flat lines or when pulled down even closer to the water with line releases of some kind.
- Troll a pattern of lures in which all lures work at their best at the same speed. Some lures that work well at higher speeds (12–15 knots) do not work well at 8–10 knots, the normal lure speed, and should be trolled only in a high-speed pattern.
- Troll the number of lures that common sense, crew and angler experience, speed, sea conditions, outriggers and rod holders indicate as practical. Most skippers troll four lures, some five or more with a shotgun lure far out. When travelling at higher speeds (more than 15 knots) it is usual to troll only two or three high-speed lures, usually those with bullet heads.
- Troll a proven wave pattern. If four lures are run, these are often placed on waves four, five, six and seven, or waves four, six, eight and nine or ten. If five are trolled, they may be on waves three, four, five, seven and eight, or even starting close in on two, or any combination back to wave nine or ten or even further. Some skippers troll a fifth lure, the shotgun lure, in the centre, well back

(at the tenth wave wake) instead of short. They troll other lures, outrigger and flat line, inside that long lure. The lure positions are often described as long outrigger, short outrigger, long flat and short flat.
- Troll from outrigger with stinger or tag lines or direct from outrigger halyard with outrigger clip. Troll short or close in, on flat lines from rod tip or pull lower down towards water surface with an outrigger clip.

Some lure riggers add either one or two strips from lure skirt material in gold or hot pink or yellow colors to the skirt combinations. Some fishermen prefer the tough, fairly stiff skirt materials such as Moldcraft or Newell. Some combine stiff and soft skirt materials, while some still prefer the original red or black rubber-and-upholstery fabric that was popular before soft plastic squid and skirts became readily available. In the Indo-Pacific, preference is shown towards the soft-squid Japanese and Sevenstrand type skirts. In the Atlantic, preference seems to be for the tougher, less stretchy, thicker skirt materials.

The importance of lures in the offshore fishing scene is demonstrated not only by growing numbers of successful lure captures, but by the number of already successful offshore fishermen who head back to Hawaii and fish the Kona Hawaiian Billfish Tournament and the Hawaiian International Billfish Tournament for more reason than just competition.

Apart from the pleasure of fishing in these prestigious tournaments, one of the prime reasons is to learn and relearn, to update on successful saltwater, deepwater lure fishing. Hawaii is the university of successful lure trolling for billfish. It was developed there and the Hawaiian technique is now the fastest growing and most successful method of fishing for marlin right around the world. Lure fishing is the ideal way to explore fishing grounds and define areas for potentially viable bases.

So running well-proven designs and color combinations is most productive. Lures from successful makers — Joe Yee, Gary Eoff, Marlin

Magic, Sadu, Rose, Lock Nut and Ho of Hawaii, Top Gun and Pakula of Australia, Murray Bros, R&S, C&H, Sevenstrand, Doornob, Schneider and Braid of the USA and Africa's Striker — are consistent fish takers in hard plastic, as are Frank Johnston's Moldcraft Lures of the USA. In soft plastic there are successful lure makers in most other fishing countries — Mexico, Papua New Guinea, Japan, Tahiti, Guam and New Zealand. Before the day's fishing it is sensible to check with the skippers and crews on charter or private boats to work out the best lure pattern.

The dark-colored skirt combinations — brown and pink, black and purple, dark green–light green–black over red, green and pink — can be used effectively with either dark- or light-colored heads, but are generally combined with dark heads. Lure fishermen in many countries believe it is beneficial to have one or two dark-colored or dark-colored-skirted lures in the trolling pattern. Their theory is that the dark lure head and skirt are easily seen from below, with lure and bubbles silhouetted against the light of the surface. Most feel it is very important also to have at least one clear lure head that flashes and shines from its inserts of pearl or tape, mirrors or stainless steel. Some successful lure fishermen include a metal or weighted plastic jet head or Doornob shape in their trolling pattern. These two lure designs are for faster trolling, and are particularly effective when trolled at 12–16 knots. Most kona head designs, whether scooped or pusher (non-scooped) or straight runners, work best at 8–10 knots. Knucklehead lures work well at slower speeds — as slow as bait trolling speeds (4–7 knots).

Some fishermen experience a problem with skirt material — particularly the softer squid-type skirts — becoming tangled around the hook. This problem can be prevented by cutting the skirts in such a way so they are shorter than the barb position on the hook. Some fishermen prefer their lure skirts to be cut dead even and square, others cut the material so it is tapered.

▲ A black marlin creates a mirror image in the water of the Great Barrier Reef. *Photo: Bob Bury.*

Many of the most successful color combinations are old faithfuls, designed with the colors of mahi mahi (dolphin fish), mackerel, tuna, saury, flying fish or other local natural food fish colors. Some successful combinations of reds and yellows do not seem to relate to nature's colors at all, but work because they may excite or annoy the big fish. Modern scientific papers report that even though fish cannot see colors in the same way as humans, they can distinguish them. This could be why some head and skirt color combinations have proven to be regularly effective.

Despite the success of fish and squid-type look-alike colors, there seems little doubt that the reason these lures bring a high strike and hook-up rate may not be their natural appearance to marlin or tuna, but their vibration, flash, sound, action and bubbles, all of which may trigger annoyance or curiosity.

Billfish have large, well-developed and effective eyes, so it is conjectured that even the best-rigged natural baits may not fool the fish. Some theorize that despite the natural smell, color and action of these fish baits, many of the strikes are triggered by some of the same factors that make lures effective.

The size of modern lures in a successful pattern usually ranges from a maximum of around 100 mm (4 inches) head length and 250 mm (10 inches) skirt length, with a trend towards smaller lures around 200 mm (9 inches). The long monster heads of years ago, which produced many strikes but gave a low proportion of hook-ups and fish at the boat, have declined in popularity and use. Every year in Hawaii, as in other fishing and even non-fishing areas, new shapes and color combinations are designed, tried and adopted or discarded. Perhaps even more than the fish they seek, lure fishermen are prey for new lures. They are convinced that this is the one, this is the special producer. Trolling with light tackle (less than 10 kg, or 22 lb) limits the maximum size of the lure and hooks that can be trolled sensibly and productively. The giant Atlantic blue marlin found at Madeira respond savagely to lures bigger than those customarily used in other fisheries.

OTHER DEVELOPMENTS IN MARLIN LURE TROLLING

Experienced fishermen often say, 'This is the only way to' or 'That is a waste of time and never works'. Every time it seems there is a tried and proven only way or a clearly defined example of 'don't do this, it won't work', someone comes along and tries and proves something different, something that is diametrically opposed but works successfully.

It seems only a few years ago that many fishermen believed there were no benefits in trolling one or more dead baits in conjunction with live baits. Similarly, there was an expressed belief that there were no benefits, in fact that it was counter-productive, to troll one or more lures while trolling live or dead baits at bait-trolling speed. Yet now it is known there are benefits in trolling one or more lures in conjunction with live bait, at live bait speeds of 3–4 knots or slower,

instead of their usual lure trolling speed of 8–10 knots. Marlin sometimes take the dead bait in preference to the live bait or take a lure that is swimming awkwardly at slow speed instead of the live or dead bait trolled enticingly at bait speed.

The traditional proven trolling method with lures, particularly for billfish, is to set strike drags hard (¼ to ⅓ of line class) and to gun the boat immediately to help set the hooks. A more recently developed method goes contrary to this previous advice. This newer technique, which is perhaps logical for Moldcraft and other soft-head lures, works also with hard-head lures on the conventional clear polyester, and other hard plastic lures. The technique is to troll at normal lure trolling speed, but instead of setting the hand strike drag and heavy rubber band or outrigger release hard, to troll with a weak setting on the outriggers and strike drag just enough to prevent overrun. This method is in line with the accepted natural bait drop back philosophy to give the billfish every opportunity to turn the lure in order to swallow it headfirst.

The logic of this method is obvious when the hook-up success on small kona heads and other trolling lures on light 4 kg (8 lb), 6 kg (12 lb), 8 kg (16 lb) and 10 kg (20 lb) line classes is considered. The success of lures on light tackle in hot spots as far apart as the Caribbean, Costa Rica and Australia is proven, so consideration of the light-hold, light-drag technique is worthwhile. Those who advocate and practice this light technique use it with both hard heads and soft heads, despite the often-expressed belief that marlin will not return to strike at a hard head if the hook-up was missed on the initial strike.

We know that sometimes marlin will strike a lure repeatedly before hooking up and that they can sometimes be triggered into returning to strike and kill after an unsuccessful hook-up. The teasing of the marlin and quick line recovery often turns a missed hook-up into a return strike, hook-up and marlin at the boat. The teasing technique has proven as successful with lures as with baits. Some who use the light-drag techniques run the line to a

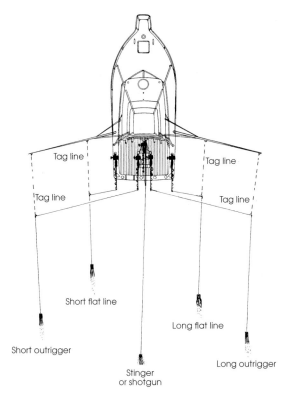

Tag line

Tag line

Tag line

Tag line

Short flat line

Long flat line

Short outrigger

Long outrigger

Stinger
or shotgun

▲ The 'W' trolling pattern with tag lines. The
inner lines could also be trolled flat from the
rod tip.

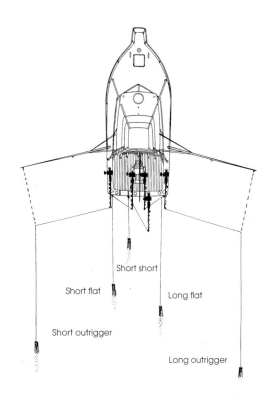

Short short

Short flat

Long flat

Short outrigger

Long outrigger

▲ The 'V' pattern. The short lines could be run from
rod tip instead of from the clip or line release
down on transom.

lightly set outrigger clip which holds it, as in bait fishing, and then troll a loop of line down to the water surfaces for an automatic drop back, giving the marlin every chance to turn the lure headfirst.

Sometimes the line is held lightly or through an outrigger release and tension held by the brake of the reel. In essence, the technique is related to bait rather than to conventional trolling technique with hard or soft head lures. This technique requires concentration, readiness to be right there immediately a strike occurs or there are billfish behind the lure. This is as in bait fishing and is a basic imperative for success in all trolling, though often not sufficiently taken into account in offshore trolling. This technique enhances the sign on the boat of skilled Panamanian Captain Louis Schmidt, an expert with baits: 'The price of a marlin is eternal vigilance'.

Most of the hot lure designs and sizes can be trolled on all line classes down to 15 kg (30 lb). The lines under the 15 kg (30 lb) class, which are ideal for smaller billfish, the school billfish and other similar pelagics, are successfully fished with smaller lures and sharp hooks. The hook sizes trolled in lures have reduced over the years. This is a result not only of experience, but of a general reduction in the length and diameter of lure heads. See also Points for Successful Lure Trolling, page 89

LAND-BASED MARLIN FISHING

Most fishermen associate their thoughts of gamefish, particularly of billfish and tuna, with fishing from boats. Boat handling, backing up and running the fish are all essential skills for taking big fish from boats. But in some parts of the world,

MARLIN LURES

HEAD COLORS

1. Transparent light blue with mirror, shell, reflective tape or stainless steel insert.
2. Transparent green or clear with green and yellow top or bottom strip with mirror, stainless steel or reflective tape insert.
3. Black or clear with black insert and pearl or reflective tape strips, or pepper and salt (black with crushed abalone, pearl or paua shell) or purple reflective insert.
4. White or clear or clear blue or green tint with white, pearl or abalone, stainless steel, paua shell or silver reflective insert.
5. White, clear, or clear tint, blue, green with silver, blue or green inserts with holes.

SKIRT COLORS

1. Light or dark blue outer skirt over dark green and gold or lime green. Pink or white over silver inner skirt.
2. Green with gold outer skirt and green with yellow, lime-green or silver inner skirt.
3. Black and silver outer skirt over green, pink, orange, lime-green or purple inner skirt. Black and silver outer skirt over purple and silver, red and silver inner skirt or black over pink.
4. Light blue outer skirt or other light color over pink, yellow, white or silver inner skirt.
5. Any light color combinations.

OTHER LURES WORTH HAVING:

6. Clear with stainless steel, mirror or tape insert with blue strip on top or bottom of lure.
7. Clear with white, silver, stainless steel, light green or pink reflective tape insert.

6. Light blue, white or silver outer skirt over light green or pink inner skirt.
7. Red over yellow, blue over white, green over yellow or gold, blue over silver, blue over pink, blue over green.

▲ A selection of lures suitable for marlin lure trolling. Left to right: Murray Bros, Joe Yee, Winfred Ho, C&H, R&S, Doornob, Pakula, Top Gun, Hypalon, Moldcraft.

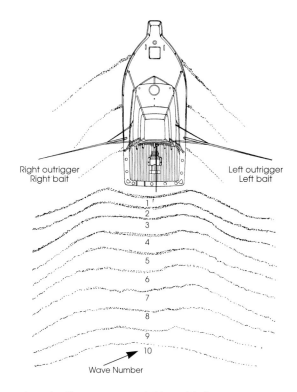

Wave Number

▲ Lure trolling — waves right and left.

▲ Efficient trolling in a small boat is practical even without outriggers, particularly if one set of side coverboard rod holders is slightly angled out.

Right outrigger
Right bait

Left outrigger
Left bait

1
2
3
4
5
6
7
8
9
10

billfish up to 90 kg (200 lb) are sought and taken from immovable fishing platforms — the rocks. In this fishing there is no benefit to be gained by

yelling, 'Back up, back up'. The only movement or change of angle comes when the fisherman changes position, and that has natural limitations!

◀ The tag pole is ready though the leader is again out of reach as the chair is pulled around the jumping black marlin.
Photo: Greg Edwards.

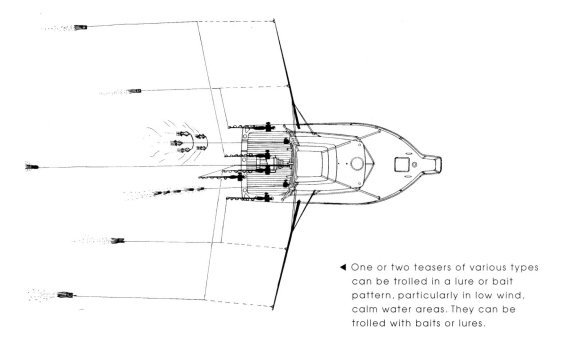

◄ One or two teasers of various types can be trolled in a lure or bait pattern, particularly in low wind, calm water areas. They can be trolled with baits or lures.

Traditionally, many species of gamefish have been taken by shorefishing methods or from jetties, bridges and other structures, as well as from boats. The quest for and successful capture of black and striped marlin and sailfish from the rocks is, however, a more recent development.

Land-based gamefishing is practiced in countries where environmental conditions combine to bring the fish in range of the shorebound fisherman instead of the fisherman having to travel long distances to sea looking for fish. What is needed is accessible rocky headland formations washed by an ocean current. The current must be of a temperature to carry the cherished gamefish, the rocks should drop off quickly in the ocean to a depth of at least 10 m (30 ft) — preferably deeper right along the rock formation. The best results are achieved when the wind and current are generally moving in the same direction, generating plankton-rich eddies and upwellings, the base for the life cycle of species usually associated with wide offshore waters. A few sections of the coastline in Australia, South Africa, Hawaii and New Zealand all have the natural features for successful land-based gamefishing. Many other countries have formations and currents and conditions that should be productive for those who want to fish offshore species without going offshore to rock and roll. The rock formations at the tip of Baja, California are just one such area.

Rods used for land-based gamefishing are usually around 2.5 m (8½ ft). They are light and flexible in the tip section and powerful in mid and butt sections. The light, flexible tip assists in the casting of live baits and is sensitive to the activity of the live bait when a big predator is in the vicinity. The power butt and mid section give the angler stick to meet the power of the big fish. They also give lift to help offset the weight and action of the fish when it is in proximity to rocks or gaffs. Special gaffs have been evolved to make gaffing and lifting up the rocks possible. For extreme heights, some of the gaffs are designed to slide down the line and leader with heavy cord attached. Others have long, flexible handles to reach from rock-fishing positions to the fish.

Although pioneering rock captures were made with star drag reels, the ready availability and reasonable price of lever drag reels of aluminum and other lightweight materials have encouraged fishermen to change to the most modern designs, in various brands. Both narrow and wide spool reels designed for 24 kg (50 lb) line are popular. The line used is generally 15 kg (30 lb) and 24 kg (50 lb). Surprisingly, many ocean gamefish hooked on the live baits do not head out to sea. Much of their swimming and jumping parallels the rocks in deeper water. Skilled pumping, hard effort and, of course, a slice of Lady Luck will bring the fish to within gaffing range. Then comes the long arduous climb, with assistance from other anglers, to bring the capture back to the top of the headland, to the waiting vehicle which will take the land-based gamefish prize to be weighed.

The southern section of the coastline in New South Wales, Australia, particularly inside Jervis Bay at the northern headland, is the locale for captures that defy the conventional fishing imagination — black and striped marlin in excess of 90 kg (200 lb) have joined the growing list of rock-caught species.

Western Australia added the concept of balloons blowing with the wind offshore to get their live baits out from cliffs. They added sailfish to the list of gamefish caught from the rocks as well as tanguigue (narrow-barred mackerel), cobia and other usually offshore species.

In Australia, thoughts of the challenge of really big fish from the rocks were triggered by the success of high-speed lure fishing from the headlands and cliff platforms. The change from the frantic activity of high-speed spinning, with its stress on reel gears, to drifting live baits in those waters where the current runs along the rocky headlands was a natural fishing evolution.

This fishing revolution appeals to those who climb cliffs and don't fish from boats for various reasons. These rock gamefishermen catch and carry their small live bait fish, and keep a few alive in a children's portable swimming pool. They often camp overnight on rock ledges so they will have precedence at the favored fishing location. They are often young, always enthusiastic.

How to increase safety when fishing from rocks

- Don't fish alone.
- Don't turn your back on the sea.
- Don't go down to the water to retrieve terminal tackle.
- Do watch your chosen fishing location for 15 minutes to make sure it's safe.
- Do be aware of tide changes and changes in the velocity and height of waves.
- Do wear safe footwear with non-slip soles.
- Do plan how to return to safety in case you fall into the sea.
- Do tell others where you are going to fish and when you expect to return.
- Do have a line and float ready for emergency use.
- Do gaff fish high above the wave level.
- Don't ever risk your life in the quest for fish; there's always another day.
- Do, above all, keep your cool.

SALTWATER FLY FISHING FOR MARLIN AND OTHER BILLFISH

IGFA world record rules, and the tournament rules adapted from them, state that the fly must be cast and presented from a dead boat. A dead boat is one which is not only out of gear but is also not moving. Billfish are to be raised to the boat by use of hookless teasers, which can be natural or artificial. Hookless Panama strips are often successful, as are teasers made of plastic squid or trolling lures. The angler must be ready for the billfish to come to the teaser(s) so that the crew or a fellow angler can keep the teaser active and moving when way comes off the boat and it comes to a stop. The angler can then cast his fly to the roused billfish which should now be ready for take and strike.

Hooks must be razor sharp to hook up in the bony bill or jaw. Once the billfish is hooked, great care is needed — the angler must exert maximum pressure, but be mindful of the tippet breaking

A Baja striped marlin shows how ▶ the species got its reputation for acrobatics.
Photo: Peter Goadby.

strain. He must be ready to bow to the fish then drop his rod tip to minimize the jumping power of the angry fish. Great boat handling skill is a key at all stages of the fight, up to and including the gaffing, which must be done only with fixed head gaffs. The use of flying gaffs, allowed in conventional fishing, is prohibited in saltwater fly fishing.

Despite their light weight, modern saltwater fly reels have smooth, powerful drags in sizes that suit all species, including billfish. For world record standards, the reels must be designed expressly for fly fishing. Extension butts of up to 15–24 cm (6–10 in) are allowed.

SAILFISH

Sailfish hold a unique place in the hearts and minds of fishermen. Their beauty and color live on in countless homes, offices, clubs and restaurants. They are the peacocks of the sea, with glorious colors and graceful winged bird shape.

They are a blend of marine savagery and efficiency in the way they hunt. The beauty and mystery of these acrobatic jumpers — whose muscles can propel their slender needle nose body

at a calculated 113 km/h (68 mph) — make them the light tackle fisherman's dream fish.

Sailfish have been the subject of thousands of magazine articles, chapters in fish books and a classic book, *The Sailfish, Swashbuckler of the Open Seas*, by Jim Bob Tinsley. Fishermen seeking sailfish have the privilege of seeing nature and evolution in action. They can gain, first hand, an answer to the standing question: 'Why do they have the sail? What is its use?'

Those who have been under way or drifted near these fish as they hunt and ball up their prey can see the answer. That apparently flimsy sail, supposedly balance destroying when upright, gives the slender-bodied sailfish the silhouette of a monster fish; in combination with the long-rayed pelvic fins, it increases the visible body depth by a factor of five.

Sailfish are an intriguing, challenging and at times annoying light tackle opponent in the world's tropical

▲ Typical saltwater fly for billfish.

waters. The dorsal fin sail adds mystique and uniqueness as well as beauty to this fish. This spectacular jumper offers everything sought in offshore fishing on light tackle, everything offered by its bigger billfish relatives. Sailfish add interest to any tournament or fishing even when other, bigger billfish are the hoped-for opponents. To their beauty, whether they are to be taken or tagged and released, can be added the visual benefit of looking bigger and heavier than they are. Sailfish work in schools and respond to every fishing method, yet at times are particularly frustrating and difficult to hook.

Part of the excitement with sails is that they are often sighted, worked and teased while, at other times, blind striking at live or dead trolled baits is the only indication of their presence. Schools of these ideal light tackle opponents are pinpointed not only by the traditional bird and bait association, but by free-jumping fish or one of the ocean's most striking and intriguing sights: sailfish cruising with sail up and set clear of the surface.

Free-jumping sailfish in association with balled bait in calm, clear water give fishermen the opportunity to see these fish hunting co-operatively. It is a privilege to witness natural activity and feeding in nature's fishbowl — the hunters and the hunted, all part of nature's fabric.

The apparently random free-jumping sailfish are part of an organized, ruthless, co-operative feeding pattern. The jumpers, like most ocean-feeding predators, work anti-clockwise. This surface jumping with sail down and often landing flat helps ball up the bait fish into tight masses.

The surface indicators of the free-jumping sails are repeated into the depths by other sails, again circling anti-clockwise, with sails fully extended and long pelvic fins fully down so each fish looks like a massive butterfly. Sailfish do not generally rush into and monster the bait ball they have patiently created. Instead, they gently take their prey from the outside of the column of bait in their circling.

WHERE TO FIND SAILFISH

Sailfish are expected in tropical waters, although they do sometimes appear far from expected locations after riding the warm current. In the Caribbean and some other locales, tag and release has shown that they migrate over long distances from Florida to at least Venezuela.

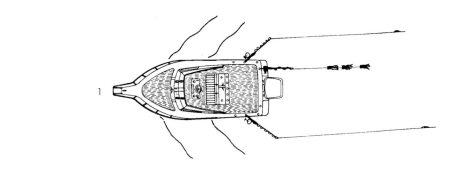

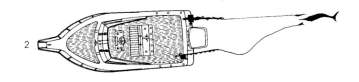

▲ Saltwater flyfishing. 1. Billfish can be raised by trolling Panama strips or other hookless baits, teased. 2. Boat must be stationary, not under way, while fly is cast.

Tag and release results in Australia show that the sailfish schools are local populations. These locals do not move long distances north and south. The recognized populations and their hot spots may be separated by as little as 160 km (100 miles). Sailfish are even found in coastal waters that may be distinctly brownish, discolored by heavy inflow of fresh water from major river systems.

They are often found over sandy as well as reefy sea beds in association with the bait schools which may be down deep. Echo sounder and sonar can show the position of the small fish schools on which they feed. These may be goggle eye, yellowtail, the wavy striped greenback chub mackerel or puffer fish (sea toads) and ballyhoo (garfish).

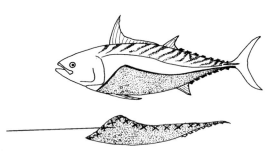

▲ Successful billfish teasers are made from belly strips of small tuna and other bait fish. They can be trolled and maneuvered on a long rod, such as a surf rod.

Thinking skippers often catch live bait from schools of the bait species at sea. They use them immediately and productively for deep slow trolling or drifting or for casting near the bait schools.

At certain times sailfish are found around coral reefs and sand cays with reefs, as well as in the passes, channels and outside edge of the outer reefs where warm currents are close inshore.

FISHING FOR SAILFISH

The hook-up of sailfish on the troll was a challenge that, once solved, opened the door to successful trolling for all billfish species. Captain Bill Hatch of Miami is credited with the concept and introduction of the drop back in trolling for sailfish. One of his crew was the equally legendary Tommy Gifford. The development of outriggers by Captain Tommy Gifford helped not only the improved action and position of trolled baits, but the effectiveness of drop back. Fishing for sailfish also influenced rigging technique and the development of trolled baits, both whole fish and strips. Subsequently, live bait fishing evolved, with kites introduced to the east coast by Harlan Major, followed by live bait fishing around the bait schools at Stuart and Palm Beach, Florida.

Live bait fishing for sailfish evolved in two ways, with bait fish taken from inshore

▲ An Atlantic sailfish at Cozumel, Mexico.
Photo: Gil Keech.

and with those caught offshore where the sailfish were feeding. Those taken offshore were captured by cast nets, a technique used off Stuart and Palm Beach.

Light tackle is synonymous with sailfish right around the world. This tropical aerial acrobat is taken on all types of tackle. They can be cast to, fished from anchor or drift, and trolled with live baits, dead baits and lures. The sight of the slender bill and distinctive sail is thrilling, whether deliberately fished for or as an incidental strike and hook-up. Sailfish are exciting fish.

They are ideal antagonists for beginners in offshore fishing. On balanced tackle their spectacular activity creates interest, plus a desire to continue and fish for bigger billfish. Memories are easily made with sailfish, even with the modern trend to tag and release. Whether the angler's billfish is tagged and released or just released, he or she can still have a trophy of the day's fishing and a superb 'fish' by simply giving the approximate weight and dimensions of the fish to a taxidermist — in these days of fiberglass and skin mounts, the taxidermist can supply a mount in glowing living colors.

Pacific sailfish are bigger, heavier and even more colorful than their Atlantic cousins. Sailfish were identified in Picos' *Naturalis Braziliae*, published in Holland in 1648. The Indo-Pacific sails were recorded by Bernard and Valentjin, and a stuffed sailfish from the Indian Ocean was taken to London, where it remains in the British Museum. The biggest in the Atlantic seem to be found off central Africa. There was once a belief that some of the big sailfish in this area may be Indo-Pacific sailfish that have straggled around the Cape of Good Hope and into the Atlantic, as have the occasional black marlin, striped marlin or southern bluefin.

Sailfish are usually trolled for with live or dead natural baits. Like other billfish species, they are often most active when the wind chops the surface and they can ride down the swells. Polarizing sunglasses give angler and crew the opportunity to see the strike. Often birds and surface activity with balled-

up bait indicates the likely presence of sailfish. Sometimes the bait and sails are down deep, revealed by echo sounder or sonar; sometimes the slender tail slicing down the swell shows the presence of the fish. Sometimes there is no indication of the fish until suddenly one or more slender, wavery shapes move up to the baits, a slender bill slashes down on the head of the bait, and the line comes clear of the outrigger clip and runs slowly from the spool. Often the pause of sailfish turning and swallowing the bait is almost undetectable.

Some fishermen believe a count of five to ten from the time of the fish hitting the bait to the angler striking will provide a hook-up, whether the strike is on flat line or outrigger line; others play it by ear and strike when they feel the sailfish has swallowed the bait. The modern trend of running a small feather or plastic jig or plastic skirt over the head of the natural bait aids the strike and hook-up rate, as it adds excitement and toughness to the bait and, by teasing, increases the angler's chances after the initial strike.

Ballyhoo (garfish), small mullet, flying fish, green chub mackerel, goggle eye, yellowtail scad and strip baits are the most successful trolled natural baits. Goggle eye, yellowtail scad and green chub mackerel are productive as both live and dead baits. Sailfish also take small kona heads, knuckleheads and other plastic head and skirted lures, as well as wooden and plastic minnow-type lures. They sometimes unexpectedly take big kona heads trolled for marlin and tuna, adding welcome variety to any day's fishing. Live baits are sometimes trolled, but more often fished drifting and casting into and around the schools of balled-up bait. Particularly at Stuart and Palm Beach in Florida, ballyhoo (garfish) are sometimes taken by cast nets in the balled-up bait schools to be used on the spot. Live baits of various kinds, particularly goggle eye and mackerel, are taken out from shore for each day's fishing in live bait tanks that are now important and necessary equipment on boats seeking sailfish.

◀ A Pacific sailfish lifts itself clear of the water in Costa Rica.
Photo: Darrell Jones.

In eastern Australia and some other successful fishing areas, live baits are cast on heavy spinning rods into the bait schools worked by the feeding sailfish.

The spinning rods are used to deliver the small, live baits to strategic positions right in front of the circling predators, alongside and into the bait schools, to swim and drift with the baits. Other live baits may be cast by hand on slack line from trolling rods to supplement those cast on spinning rods.

Even if the live baits are not taken while the bait and sailfish are active on the surface, they may be taken down deeper if the drift with deep swimming baits is allowed to continue. Use of the echo sounder and sonar will confirm the presence of live bait under the boat, even when it is not showing on the surface. Fresh live bait can often be

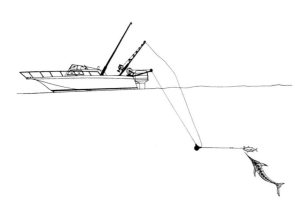

▲ Deep trollers, such as PENN Trollers, are productive with live bait and lures, particularly where they can be worked around structures and bait schools.

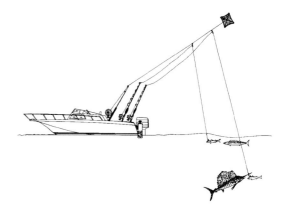

▲ Kite fishing: Two live baits can be fished from one kite. A lightweight outrigger clip, clothes peg and paper clip or ring allow positioning of baits and quick release.

◀ A Pacific sailfish flies clear
at top speed.
Photo: Darrell Jones.

caught from these same schools, giving anglers an even better chance. Sometimes, however, even when bait is visible, best results come with trolled baits. Every day can be different.

Fishing kites are used off the Florida Keys, particularly off the drop-off of the reefs outside Islamorada, Marathon and Key West, to produce sailfish strikes when other methods are not successful. Fishing with live or dead baits from a kite, particularly with baits of blue runners or other live bait, gives great results with sailfish and marlin.

Live bait drifting and casting have allowed many more fishermen to enjoy and experience the thrill of fishing for sailfish. There is, however, something very special about angling for these 'swashbucklers of the sea' in the classical manner — trolling carefully prepared and rigged natural or strip baits.

Occasionally, particularly in calm weather, sailfish, either singly or in small schools of three or more, will cruise on the surface with sails raised. This is a thrilling and treasured sight and gives an excellent chance of a strike. These are often bigger fish than those found in the usual school and conditions. While the slender sailfish epitomizes the symmetry, beauty and colors of the billfish, it can also exhibit the smashing savagery and dedication to feeding and killing that is equally synonymous with billfish. The smashing and killing power are multiplied dramatically with size in the other billfish.

Sailfish are an ideal challenge for anglers using saltwater fly tacking before trying their skill on the more powerful marlin.

Teasers run in conjunction with a trolled bait pattern continue to be popular. Some crews run

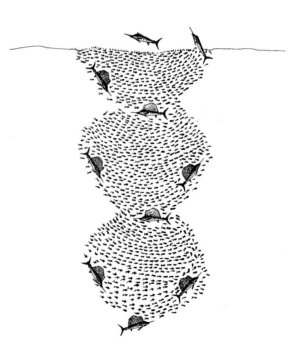

▲ Sailfish ball the bait school. One will work the surface by jumping anti-clockwise in a tight circle with tail and fins folded. Others will circle below the surface at various levels with dorsal and pelvic fins fully extended.

▲ Chum creates an oil pattern on the surface, sinks into the mid water region, is seen and then can sink deeper.

one or two strings of bubble-creating splashing lures such as pushers with or without jet holes, others prefer a daisy chain or coathanger spread of Moldcraft or similar soft plastic squid. Plastic teasers

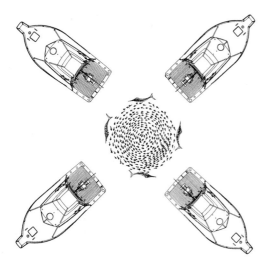

▲ This is a safe way to work billfish with cast lures, or live bait on a ball of bait fish, when more than one boat is involved.

and natural teasers, particularly the Panama strip, run without hooks, are successful in raising sailfish as well as other billfish to the boat, where fly fishermen can cast their saltwater flies. Fishing rules stress that the way must be off the boat. Teased sails will chase the Panama strips or other teasers maneuvered by the crew or other anglers to maintain billfish interest.

At 40 kg (88 lb), the body thickness and depth of the sailfish increase markedly. From this weight upwards they increase in power and toughness while still retaining their active, acrobatic performance. Despite the dramatic increase in power of big sailfish, they are always popular anglers' goals at any weight on any light tackle class.

Sailfishing is often done with leaders combining monofilament and light single-strand wire jointed with a snap swivel. The monofilament may be 24 kg (50 lb) or 37 kg (80 lb). The wire is light, so that after tagging for release the mate can take and hold his wraps of the leader to break the light wire. If the fish is quiet, he may take the bill to retrieve the hook as

▲ Costa Rican sailfish combine barrel rolls and a balancing act with more conventional tactics.
Photo: Darrell Jones.

well as to hold the sailfish — the forward way of the boat quickly aids re-oxygenation.

Light tackle leaders around 2.9–3 m (8–9 ft) are very practical because they are long enough to clear the average-sized fish. Gaffing or tagging can then be done by one other person without the necessity of the leader being taken in hand and the fish being lost through the added pressure.

SPEARFISH

Spearfish are the least known of the world's billfish. The two species of most importance to anglers are the long-billed spearfish of the Atlantic and the short-billed spearfish of the Indo-Pacific Oceans. There is another relatively short-billed spearfish, the Mediterranean spearfish. Unfortunately, none of these spearfish grow to the weights of the other billfish. However, despite their small size, they strike at lures intended for bigger billfish. Angler interest in the 'Spear Chucker', as it is familiarly called in

Hawaii, is spasmodic. The vivid coloration, eating quality, and only occasional catch sparks real interest in them when caught.

They are an incidental catch in many warm-water trolling sport fisheries. It is a pity that there are not specific fishery areas and methods for them, so these smallest of billfish could be sought on tackle balanced to their weight. Spearfish give a good account of themselves when fought on light tackle, with splashing jumps and a long run.

The short-billed spearfish is difficult to confuse with any of the other Indo-Pacific billfish. The only possibility would be confusion with a broken-billed juvenile striped marlin. However, a quick check of distance between the anal opening and the anal fin is a distinguishing feature; in spearfish they are widely separated whereas in the other billfish they are close together.

Big long-billed spearfish of the Atlantic can be confused with white marlin. In the long-billed spearfish the second dorsal fin is closer to the tail than the second anal fin, the reverse of the positions on the white marlin, and the dorsal is curved at the rear instead of tapering straight. Once the fish is out of the water and into the cockpit, a clear difference can be measured. In the long-billed spearfish, the anal opening is nearly the depth of the anal fin, whereas in white marlin it is closer than halfway along the body.

Hawaii consistently produces more short-nosed spearfish than any other known area. Despite the relatively small size of the Atlantic and Pacific spearfish, comparatively few fishermen have taken or tagged these fish and completed a full hand of world billfish brought to boat.

It would be interesting to know whether any boat has, in the Pacific, the Atlantic or the Caribbean, ever brought in or tagged all the billfish available in those oceans in any one day. In fact, few boats would have caught all available billfish in their watery world in a season. It is ironic that the smallest species, which seem to be a link between the mackerels and billfish, are the least prolific in anglers' catches.

TROLLING BAITS FOR SMALLER BILLFISH

(a)

(b)

(c)

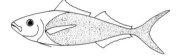

(d)

(e)

TYPICAL STRIP BAITS FOR TROLLING

(a) Belly strip (short) for trolling.
(b) Belly strip (long) for trolling with swimming tail to vary action.
(c) Side strip bait from mullet or other small fish.
(d) Panama strip — top edges are sewn together in position.
(e) Strip bait held with safety pin in wire.

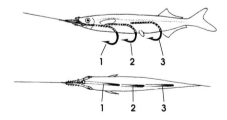

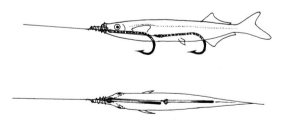

SINGLE HOOK BALLYHOO (GARFISH) TROLLING RIG
The hook can be below or from the side in any of the three positions shown. Hook position depends on size of bait and type of fish sought. Break the bill off short and bind leader to stump of bill to hold and close mouth.

BALLYHOO (GARFISH) TWO-HOOK TROLLING RIG
Break the bill off short. Hooks can be: (a) one up one down; (b) both in from side; (c) two down.

BROADBILL SWORDFISH

The red silk kite fluttered above the surface, incongruous and seemingly out of place against the remoteness of sea and sky. The kite height and direction were regulated by a great fisherman, Captain Geo. Farnsworth, as he used it to bring a bait enticingly into position in front of the fish swimming with dorsal and tail clear of the surface.

Captain Farnsworth's angler was hopeful of success because of the successful teamwork developed with his captain. No one had yet caught one of these fish on rod and reel. The kite they used had successfully presented baits that hooked and caught bluefin tuna while other skippers and anglers wondered how they did it and went fishless. Now they were baiting the broad-sworded gladiator of the sea from that fragile red silk kite.

The rest of that day made angling history. William Boschen, who is credited with the design and concept of the world's first star drag reel, called by maker Vom Hofe the 'B'Ocean', landed that broadbill and so became doubly enshrined as a first prize winner. The year was 1913. Boschen fought his first broadbill, of 162 kg (358 lb), without benefit of harness or chair, from a small, single motor launch.

Swordfish have been recorded in Greek and Roman writings. The scientific name *Xiphias gladius* comes from both Greek and Latin, both words meaning 'sword'. In 350 BC Aristotle called them 'broadbill'.

▲ Pacific spearfish at Kona, Hawaii regularly take lures trolled for bigger billfish. *Photo: Jacquie Acheson.*

Broadbill are still regarded as saltwater angling's greatest prize, even though their capture has been made a little easier and more widespread through the development of night-time drift fishing.

◄ Baby short-nose spearfish have long bills and bear little resemblance to adults. *Photo: courtesy Dr David Grobecker, PORF.*

▲ Captain Doug Osborn watches intently as Michael Lerner fights a Chilean broadbill. Gaffs are at the ready on the coverboard.
Photo: IGFA—Lerner Expedition.

Broadbill characteristically cruise on the surface in a few areas of ocean, apparently to re-oxygenate. They are exasperating to bait, hook and fight as well as to locate, even on calm days.

They are tough opponents, combining some of the best and the most difficult characteristics exhibited by marlin, tuna and sharks. To these, add the special factors of soft mouth, soft skin and tissue. Combined, these difficulties negate modern technique and powerful tackle, so that even when a bait is taken and a hook-up effected there is still the

problem of pulled hooks, a problem exacerbated by the power of angler and tackle. These difficulties remain, whether broadbill are fished in the classic hunting method of sight fishing — requiring perhaps the greatest dedication and single-mindedness of any sportfishing — or by the more recent night-time drifting of live baits which, along with the long established dead bait presentations, is sometimes successful.

One of the highlights of my fishing has been the opportunity to fish for and bait broadbill in California using the classic method of seeking, spotting and presenting the bait in daylight. Florida's successful development of night fishing by drifting the canyons and other likely broadbill hot spots, pioneered by the Webb brothers, produces broadbill for those prepared to fish in often difficult and uncomfortable conditions. Night-time drifting offers the greatest chance of success with these fighters in Australia, New Zealand, Hawaii, Venezuela and other areas where broadbill do not commonly cruise on the surface. Each method requires skill, preparation, hard work, vigilance and concentration. Each gives fishermen a chance to tangle with the greatest gamefish. It is unfortunate for anglers that there are relatively few known areas in the world where broadbill can be consistently visually fished on the surface. Chile, the locality for many broadbill records over the years, is still producing great fish taken by the classic method of searching, sighting and presenting baits.

Ted Naftzger, who has taken more broadbill by sight fishing than any other angler in world angling history and has proved a master on all tackle classes for all marlin and giant tunas, rates broadbill as the ultimate challenge. Ted is an incredibly accurate judge of just how much pressure to apply to the limit of the line breaking strain, and has an uncanny understanding of what the fish is doing. He could have weighed many more and bigger broadbill than he has by fishing with the benefits of IGFA rules. Instead, as a past president of the Tuna Club of Avalon, he fishes Tuna Club rules. When fishing in

California, Ted fishes to the Tuna Club tackle regulations, even though he knows the shorter leader of 4.5 m (15 ft) increases the difficulty of capture. IFGA rules allow maximum leader of 9 m (30 ft) and 12 m (40 ft) combined in double and leader. Anglers should always fish to IGFA rules in case of a potential world record catch.

WHERE TO FIND BROADBILL

Broadbill range from tropical to cool waters worldwide. The few known places where they regularly cruise on the surface include California, Baja, north-east USA and of course Chile, Peru and Ecuador.

They are usually deepwater fish, expected in 110 meters (60 fathoms) and deeper, although they have been sighted feeding on school fish right alongside beaches and rocky headlands. Study of Japanese longline data and commercial catches should give the times and places.

Best results usually come fishing canyons along the 185 meter (100 fathom) drop-off, and the edges of deepwater banks and features on the sea bed. Success in night fishing is often associated with areas known as productive longline grounds.

SIGHT FISHING WITH DEAD AND/OR LIVE NATURAL BAITS

Daylight fishing for broadbill means hunting, with all on board looking for the distinctive sickle fins. Eyes scan and search ceaselessly from tower, bridge and deck level. Binoculars are a great help for long-range identification, just as they are with tailing marlin. Birds and bait action and water color changes — just in case broadbill are associated with these indicators — are more readily observed. One of the frustrations for broadbill fishermen, and something that proves their dedication and single-mindedness, is that they must deliberately bypass and ignore tailing marlin that would surely take a bait or lure and bring some action in the day. They know that if they are distracted and spend time accepting the chance for marlin action instead of searching for broadbill, they may miss their chance at their objective.

Preparation for broadbill starts with meticulous checking of tackle to be used. The reel brake should be super smooth. On heavy tackle — 37 kg (80 lb) and 60 kg (130 lb) — the brake must be set to give no more than 10 kg (22 lb). On lighter tackle, one-quarter to one-third of line class should be set. The 10 kg (22 lb) maximum will minimize the chance of pulled hooks.

Baits of two or three kinds must be rigged on the monofilament leaders with razor-sharp hooks. Squid are the number one bait, the others being pelagic fish common in the area to be fished. Barracuda, skipjack tuna and mackerel may be successful if the squid are not taken after four or five presentations to the slowly moving fish. Rigged and spare squid should be packed in plastic bags so they do not come into contact with ice or fresh water — these will discolor the baits and they will not present naturally.

Once at sea, the combination of keen eyes, binoculars, the choice of likely areas and experience will give an angler the best chance to bait a broadbill.

Most broadbill fishermen prefer to bait a fish while it is swimming straight and at a constant cruising speed, rather than while it is changing direction and speed and circling. Once the fish is sighted, the boat speed is dropped until steerage is just maintained. The engine revolution should not be further varied until the fish has taken or slashed at the bait. All noises, including voices and vibration, must be minimized until hook-up time.

It is important to position the bait carefully so it can be seen by the broadbill, keeping in mind the position of its eyes and vision along the sword. Live bait is most effective.

Many fishermen try to run the bait about 70 meters (80 yards) behind the boat. They have another 35–40 meters (40–45 yards) of slack line on the water ready as a drop back from rod tip to where the line is held. Many are reluctant to use outriggers and outrigger clips, but some successful broadbill crews do it with the line held from the flying bridge.

Some skippers try to keep the boat up-sun of the fish while presenting the bait so they and the angler can see as clearly as possible what the fish is doing. Although some skippers and anglers believe it does not upset the fish, most will try to avoid putting boat wake across the cruising fish as they position the bait.

The bait should be passed slowly in front of the broadbill, about 60 cm (2 ft) under the surface. It should pass within 6 m (20 ft) of the big fish. Many skippers do not want the bait to break the surface. After several passes at this depth, the bait can be given more line so it runs deeper — the broadbill may be further under the surface, even if lost from sight. It may pick up a sinking bait where it was last seen.

In his books, Kip Farrington stressed that the line should not be retrieved, even for a short distance (to gain better positioning), while near a cruising broadbill.

When a bait is taken or struck by the sword, the motors should be pulled out of gear, ready for the angler's or skipper's decision to strike to set the hook or hooks. Broadbill baits are often rigged with two hooks to give better chance of a solid hook-up.

The action of broadbill taking a bait can be anywhere between a gentle tap and a violent, savage slash. The angler's strike should, if possible, be made after the pause that comes with the big fish swallowing the bait. The pause that follows the swallow and swim-on for broadbill may be longer than that with marlin and sharks. A slow count of five after the resumption of swimming should be sufficient. Sometimes, after taking the bait, the broadbill will immediately rush towards the surface. In this case the angler should strike immediately. At other times, whether line is taken smoothly or with a series of jerks, 60 meters (65 yards) of line out from the reel should provide every chance. Above all, anglers should be patient — they should be thinking, trying to feel exactly what the fish is doing, keeping in touch with the fish before committing to the strike.

At all times during the fight, the effect of reel brake with decreasing spool diameter and bag and drag of line in the water must be considered. If there is a bag or long length of line out, the angler must ease the reel brake to minimize the pull on the hooks and maximize the chances of the hooks staying in place. Once line is recovered and the line is shortened and leads straight to the broadbill, the brake can be returned to its previous level.

It is important to keep working the fish, to give it no respite. Backing up, running the fish and planing the fish should all be directed at bringing fish and boat close together. The circling maneuver that so often works on marlin, sharks and other fish may be counter-productive with broadbill; it could increase line drag and the ratio of pulled hooks.

SIGHT FISHING WITH CAST LIVE BAITS

Anglers in California and Mexico often cast a live bait on lighter tackle from the bow of the boat to the surface-cruising fish. Some boats have a pulpit and an additional live bait tank forward, so anglers can readily fish live bait for striped marlin and broadbill. Experienced fishermen like to have two casting anglers and tackle ready to cast the live bait to broadbill in these circumstances. The first mackerel in the water will often race back to the boat to the protection of the hull as it is chased by the broadbill. A second bait presented to the broadbill, as it tries to monster the first bait but can't reach it because of the boat hull, will sometimes be readily taken.

The problems with broadbill, once they are found, baited and hooked, are not only their fighting characteristics, whether deep or on the surface, but also the frustrating proportion of pulled hooks.

In his 1883 *History of Swordfish* published in Washington DC by the Government Printer, George Brown Goode referred to the number and size of the broadbill off Chile and Peru. Despite modern fishing pressure, these waters are again providing record captures.

There is no doubt that one of the most magnificent fish ever taken is Lou Marron's 60 kg (130 lb) class broadbill of 536.5 kg (1182 lb). The superb cast of this fish in the clubhouse of the Rod and Reel Club of Miami ensures that it is never forgotten; it also offers a challenge for someone to catch a bigger broadbill. They created awareness and excitement centuries before their quest by rod and reel anglers. They were known and recognized many centuries before marlin, sailfish and spearfish were identified. They were taken by drifting at night, by the Mediterranean traps and by those who fished with harpoons centuries before the modern slaughter by longlines and drift nets.

Dr C. F. Holder, who triggered the formation of gamefish clubs and rules and ethics, was a fisherman whose interest in big fish preceded his sportfishing. Long before he caught his milestone tuna at Avalon, Santa Catalina, California, he was interested enough in broadbill to take a trip on a harpoon sloop from Woods Hole to search out beyond Block Island. That trip was successful, bringing back three broadbill. One of the harpooned broadbill was 3 m (9.5 ft) long. Holder wrote, 'Though I have frequently caught sharks that measured 13 ft [4 m] I never saw one that equalled the strength of this formidable creature'. Appropriately, it was William Boschen, a member of the Tuna Club Dr Holder founded, who captured the first broadbill with rod and reel.

DRIFTING AT NIGHT WITH LIVE OR DEAD BAITS

In many waters broadbill do not surface cruise in daylight, which would give anglers a chance to see and bait them. There are often better odds in fishing out wide and deep at night. While heading out early in the morning to fish, the Webb brothers of Miami realized that commercial fishermen, many of whom had learned the techniques in their original home, Cuba, were heading back to port with broadbill captures. The Webbs applied this night-drifting technique to sportfishing in the areas where broadbill should be. They added the benefits

of cyalume light sticks to their fishing, with the result that a successful sport fishery was created. Unfortunately, the value of the fish caught triggered a commercial fishery and after a few short, successful seasons there was a frightening decline in stock from longline overfishing right along the USA's Atlantic coast. Now the stocks have also been drastically reduced in other parts of the world, not only by longlining but by the cursed driftnet fishing.

Night sportfishing for any species is quite different from fishing in daylight. Every difficulty is magnified. The horizon is not defined, the sounds and effects of wind and waves are magnified, the level of danger is dramatically increased. Suddenly the difficulties of holding position over the bottom and regulating depths of bait — difficulties that are present but relatively small in daylight — are magnified. A continuous watch for ships and other boats is necessary. The night-time activity of sharks, particularly high-flying makos, adds to the challenge and danger at boatside.

One of the joys of night-time fishing, apart from the chance of broadbill, is simply being part of another, different world. The fishing lights in and over the surface attract and show sea creatures not often seen in daylight. Squid and small fish move right into the top water levels at night. Squid can often be caught to provide fresh live baits and replace those eaten by other squid or fish. Out and below the lights, the environment is truly 'eat or be eaten'. Action comes from various shark species, particularly makos, blues and threshers, oil fish, opah (moonfish) or one of the big tunas, plus any other deep-water species that come towards the surface in the evening (as the food chain rises) and sink back to the depths as the morning approaches. Night-fishing broadbill crews may experience the thrill of makos, jumping as high or higher than the flying bridge. Razor-sharp curved teeth, black eye and blue and silvery white body show dramatically in the lights. The use of monofilament leader minimizes the shark catch and time of involvement, but often (particularly when it is not wanted) the sharks don't cut off; they fight right to the boat.

At night, as in the daytime, broadbill strike in varying ways. There may be a smashing blockbuster that tears line from the reel and shakes the rod in its rod holder, chair or cover board while the line disappears at blinding speed, or a gentle, almost imperceptible take. Sometimes squid or fish will be belted and slashed while the line slowly rolls from the spool. There is then the swallowing pause and faster follow-on, giving the angler the chance to strike. At night-time broadbill often race towards the surface to jump or run once they or the angler has effected a hook-up.

The cold blue or green glowing light stick provides a possible big fish attractant when affixed to the leader or concealed in the bait. On the leader they are important markers for visually positioning the leader and fish, assisting boat maneuvering in darkness.

Some night-time broadbill fishermen prefer to fish in the dark of the moon, working on the belief that the fish will come even closer to the surface; others prefer the full moon. The amount of moonlight on any night should be taken into account, along with the current and the sea conditions, in determining the depth of the baits. It is difficult to fish with more than three lines, so baits should be positioned and sometimes weighted to cover the productive depths.

Sea anchors can be used to help control the rate of drift and to make the boat action more comfortable. Sometimes natural conditions dictate drifting with only two lines. Depths of bait vary from 10 m (32 ft) to 90 m (300 ft). Lead weights on light breakaway thread can be used to help keep the bait at the chosen depth. Plastic bottles, polystyrene foam blocks and balloons can be used as floats, again with lightweight breakaway threads. The light breakaway threads are a must so that the bait will be free, not resisting pull or swallowing by the fish. Heavy resistance alerts the fish, which then usually does not proceed with taking the bait.

Downriggers with the release set very light are also sometimes used to hold the bait down deep.

There are differing opinions as to when to strike for hook-up, as hook pulling is always foremost in fishermen's minds. Some set the reel drag at the maximum strike they will be using (10 kg or 22 lb) on heavy tackle, particularly when using curved point hook models such as those used commercially on handlines and some longlines, particularly in Hawaii. Others keep the brake light, as they would for sharks or marlin in drift fishing; they are prepared to let the fish take the bait and move away with it slowly, then wait for the pause to swallow and to swim away again before striking to set the hook. If the broadbill races towards the surface before being struck by the angler it should be struck immediately, as the fish is either hooked or aware of an object and trying to be rid of it by jumping and throwing it clear.

TAKING THE LEADER

Another crisis point with broadbill, as with so many other fish, is when the leader is in reach and in hand. It should be agreed by angler, skipper and crew alike whether the leader man is to pull as hard as the leader will allow or handle it carefully, at about the same pressure exerted by the angler during the fight. Both the maximum muscle and the kid glove technique have strong advocates, with results to support their contentions. My personal preference is in-between — be careful not to provoke a quiet fish, but use as much power as the leader will take on an active fish to give a shot with gaff or tag when the leader is in hand. Agreement on the plan for handling the leader is imperative.

GAFFING BROADBILL

Because of the soft flesh of broadbill, the gaff or gaffs must be placed to ensure maximum bite over the body. Just behind the dorsal fin and into the shoulder is usually best. A tail rope will secure the catch until a meat hook can be slipped through the lower jaw so the prize fish can be brought on board.

TROLLING BAITS

BALLYHOO (GARFISH) TROLLING RIG
Ballyhoo (garfish) with small pusher type lure
for sailfish.

VENEZUELAN TROLLING RIG
Whole small fish with vinyl replica or feather.

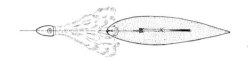

HEMINGWAY TROLLING RIG
Strip with small feather or vinyl replica. Lures
will sit right down on head of strip or bait fish.

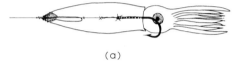

(a)

DRIFTING AT NIGHT

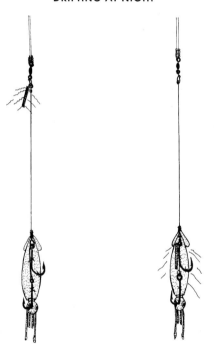

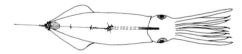

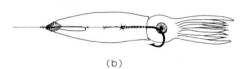

(b)

TROLLING — DRIFTING
(a) Double-hook squid.
(b) Single-hook squid The multi-pull bridle is
    identical in these two squid-trolling rigs.

CYALUME LIGHTS
Cyalume lights are helpful when attached to the
top of the leader as they show the postion of
the bait, attract fish and, during the fight, show the
position of the leader. They can be inserted inside
rigged squid, as in the diagram on the right.

FIGHTING THE BILLFISH

The pioneers of billfishing learnt the hard way. Anglers, captains and crew had to develop skills and knowledge together, through experience. While the pioneer days may be behind us we will never cease to learn and experiment, always seeking a better way.

Success comes from concentration, co-operation, communication and experience. Much of the angler's enjoyment and success comes from having an understanding of what the other members of the team, the equipment and the fish are doing. In most fights between angler and big fish, there are times when heat and hurt force the angler to query if it is all worth it. The power and endurance of billfish show why they are such great predators. There are times when, despite the comfort of easing up, the angler must remember that the next fish may be just as tough, just as dogged, and that similar effort and hurt will be expended and endured in fighting the next fish.

There are two particularly critical times when fish can be lost, with or without angler error. These periods are on the hook-up and first run, and then when the fish is close to capture. Fish may be lost, hooks thrown, lines broken or the fisherman may endure any of the other circumstances that cause loss. Sometimes, whatever can go wrong will go wrong.

◀ Jacquie Acheson catches the fleeting color changes of Jerry Dunaway's grander black.
Photo: Jacquie Acheson.

The problem on the first run, with and without jumps, is not only that the maximum dynamic power of the fish causes an adrenalin rush for the fisherman, but that it is also a dangerous time for line breaks or overrun birds' nests. Generally, on this run, the angler must remember that as the length of line reduces on the reel spool the diameter of spooled line is smaller, so the reel brake on the line automatically increases. The high rate of fish loss close to capture is caused by an increase in the size of the hole made by the hook, the change in angle of pull on the hook, and the chance of line break as line with minimum stretch leads straight from rod to fish.

American angler and author Harlan Major demonstrated in the classic *Salt Water Fishing Tackle* that a reel spool of 15 cm (6 in) set up with reel brake of 14 kg (30 lb) will increase to 21 kg (45 lb) when the line spool diameter has reduced to 10 cm (4 in), and 42 kg (90 lb) when the diameter has reduced to 5 cm (2 in). He also showed a diagram of the result of pulling the linen line used at that time through water. He found that 375 meters (300 yards) of 10 kg (22 lb) test would break at 15 knots, even without reel brake or fish, and that 365 meters (400 yards) of 15 kg (30 lb) line would break at 12 knots.

This automatic brake increase on the line clearly makes impossible the often-made statement: 'I had the brake set on full drag on strike and the fish peeled off all the line, spooled me.' All this proves is that the brake was not set high to start with, as, rather than being spooled, the line must have broken with less than one-third of the line from the spool.

Modern strike drags are generally set at one-quarter on light tackle to one-third on heavy tackle of the line class used on balanced tackle. Listed below are brake recommendations that have proved successful over the years and through the tackle changes. Experienced fishermen often work well above the fighting brake outlined here when the fish and fight allow.

It is a revelation to work with aggressive anglers such as Ted Naftzger, a master on all line classes, as he uses his brake, working harness unclipped, while recovering line on 24 kg (53 lb) and upwards, using the harness when the fish is fighting deep. Ted's experience goes back to days fishing with Tommy Gifford for all the great ocean gamefish. He often fishes 24 kg (53 lb) and 15 kg (33 lb) and lighter on marlin, even giant blacks. IGFA vice-president Jack Anderson, on the other hand, when fishing on 60 kg (130 lb) for giant black marlin, sets the strike brake at 25 kg (55 lb) and keeps the brake in this position, fully aware of the automatic increase in drag as line reduces on the reel spool. Both of these master

anglers will move at sunset to full drag, when the double line is on the reel, while being ready to instantly ease back if the double leaves the reel. On light tackle with a big jumping fish, particularly one that changes direction, Ted will instantly ease the brake almost back to free spool.

Modern tackle development techniques and balanced tackle generally use stiffer and more powerful rods, particularly in the tackle classes from 10 kg (22 lb) upwards. Associated with this is the modern philosophy of working the fish hard in attacking in order to burn the fish out. The philosophy is more 'pop or stop' rather than sitting or standing with a big drag line in the water, hoping the fish will tire of dragging this bag of line through the water.

In all these strike and fighting schedules, consideration must be given to the speed, position and activity of the fish. Common sense as well as experience dictates that there are times when it is imperative to ease up a little on the fighting drag. At times there is no need to pump at all, simply a need to wind as fast as humanly possible to lay line evenly on the reel. When pumping, short, rocking pumps are most effective. They keep the fish moving, ideally up and towards the boat.

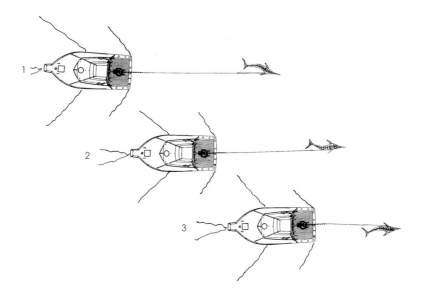

◀ Backing up is a successful technique for recovering line and closing with fish.

It is important to think about what the fish is doing. Some fish swim in circles through different depths. While the fish is on the up-swim of its circling, line is gained. On the down-swim of its circling, line is lost. It is characteristic of billfish to head to deep water and into the direction of the wind and the current.

Anglers who understand what the fish is doing take advantage of the fish circling to pressure, to pump and recover on the up circle and hold hard and evenly on the down. The position of maximum disadvantage to the fisherman is when the fish is down straight under the boat. Planing the fish is the best way to beat this and other Mexican stand-offs.

Two basic angling philosophies are used in bringing fish to gaff. One way is by attack. Attacking fishermen use a quick action of the rod, a quick lift and line recovery, even though some jerkiness or whip is transmitted to the fish. This technique is often used with soft and slow-action rods. Anglers of the other fishing philosophy tend to the 'leading' rather than the 'driving' method. They employ a constant smooth action of lift and recovery. The smooth technique suits quick-taper, quick-action rods that will lift a fish. Though the pressure is even and constant, the pumping can still be done in quick and short sweeps. Kip Farrington wrote that short pumps bothered and beat a fish more than the long ones.

The tempo of the fight should be controlled and dictated by the angler. The fish gets more benefit from a pause than the angler because its rate of recovery from fatigue is much faster. So keep the pressure on the fish.

Fishermen who lead and control their fish try to keep to one side of it, so that it is swimming with the muscles on one side working harder than on the other. When the fish changes direction the boat should be maneuvered so that the angle of pull stays the same. The constant pull away at one side tires the fish speedily. Fast 'backing up' is often used for quick marlin captures.

Many successful captains and anglers believe in keeping close to a hooked fish so that there is only a short length of line on which it can maneuver, sound or jump. Long lengths of line in the water give the fish a chance to jump against a bag of line or cross over the line, cut it and break free. Synthetic lines do not exert the same drag and friction as were given by the old linen lines, so there is less advantage now in having a long length of line in the water.

The fisherman, with the help of the skipper, tries to avoid the stand-off, a stalemate between the opponents with neither gaining or losing line nor changing relative position. This situation, in fact, quickly wins an advantage for the fish, for the constant wear and tear of the fight carried on along a short length of line gradually and then quickly causes line weakness and eventually a breakoff. To change this losing pattern a vigorous attacking technique, such as planing the fish to a shallower level or circling against the fish, may be necessary. Line is lost from the reel spool initially during these maneuvers but the angle of fighting, of lift, gradually becomes more favorable to the fisherman. When a stubborn fighter is forced from where it wants to stay, the advantage is the fisherman's, but the lifting pressure must be maintained. The planing or circling maneuver often has to be repeated time after time until the fish finally gives in. Repeated circling or reverse circling by the boat is often the key to success against deep fighting billfish.

In prolific waters, sharks present an added hazard by attacking and mutilating hooked fish, so every minute the fight continues is another minute during which mutilation becomes likely. It is nothing short of amazing how sharks shadow and wait on a tiring fish, the strong wolves of the sea waiting on weakening marine giants. Landing, keeping on top of the fish and beating the stand-off in a short time is the only way of defeating the fish and circumventing the sharks.

Marlin tend to run straighter on their fights than the deep fighters and quickly try to head towards deep water after they finish their surface performance. To beat them, boat and angler must work as a team after the fish's first heart-stopping

IGFA LINE CLASS	LINE CLASS		SAFE STRIKE DRAG		FIGHTING DRAG	
US CUSTOMARY LB	ACTUAL LB	KG	LB	KG	LB	KG
2	2.20	1	1/3	.15	1/3–1/2	.25
4	4.40	2	3/4	.34	3/4–1	.50
8	8.88	4	1 1/2	.68	1 1/2–1 3/4	.75
12	13.22	6	2 3/4	1.25	2 3/4–3	1–1.50
16	17.63	8	3 3/4	1.70	3 3/5–4 1/4	1.75–2
20	22.04	10	5	2.27	5–6	2.25–2.75
30	33.06	15	7 1/2	3.40	7 1/2–8 1/4	3.25–3.75
50	52.91	24	13	6	13–16	6–8
80	81.57	37	22	10	22–27	11–13
130	133.27	60	45–55	20–25	55–80	25–36.5

acrobatics. The boat should be kept away to one side — the up-current side is easiest — while the angler keeps working, lifting, leading and forcing the billfish to change direction, to come back to the top.

Many experienced anglers and captains prefer to fight their fish right behind the stern with the fish working against maximum reel drag. They believe the fish tires quickest against the drag and boat. Line is recovered by running along the line, by circling, by pumping and by planing.

Planing and keeping the boat to one side of the fish both help to offset the tactics of billfish that roll in the leader. Most skippers like to keep on the deepwater side of the hooked fish to influence it to run back towards shallower and easier water. The bottom-sounding runs are not so effective in shallow water, and there is a better chance of pumping and lifting up an exhausted or dead fish.

Most top fishermen try to bring their fish to the boat as speedily as possible. The shorter the fight, the less time for failure of equipment or for the hook to tear out or any of the hundred things that can work against the angler. Their philosophy is: if the fish is to be lost, then make it 'lost' quickly and so have time to try again. The fish that is worked hard and evenly will be beaten more often and more quickly than the fish in between. The landing, the gaffing and tail roping of 'green' fish is, of course, much more difficult than it is with played out fish. Big fish can often be outfought or

outmaneuvered and outsmarted before they wake up. If crews are ready to gaff whenever they come into the boat, success often follows 'giving it a go'.

When using heavy tackle, a harness is necessary in order to gain maximum benefit from the fighting chair. A variety of chair harnesses are available: seat harnesses (monster buckets), kidney harnesses and combined kidney/shoulder harnesses.

Stand-up fighting, particularly on 15 kg (30 lb) and 24 kg (50 lb) with short rods, also requires the use of harnesses and fighting belts. Anglers sometimes use 37 kg (80 lb) tackle in stand-up fighting, even though super strength and fitness is essential to benefit from the stronger line class.

Good anglers, fast anglers, are those with a smooth, quick pumping action, whether they fish with a hardset brake or lighter drag and thumb the line. The good angler and his tackle appear to be one entity: the rod and reel are part of the fisherman, visible extensions of his body in the same way that a top-flight tennis player is so much at home with a racquet that it seems to be a continuation of his arm. So, too, with the great golfers or equestrians. An experienced balanced horse rider is at one with his mount, co-ordinated and in time, and so it is with fishing: co-ordination, concentration and timing, with no one set of muscles straining but the whole body and tackle balanced and working together naturally in fluid motion of pressure and line recovery.

▲ Scott Levin of *Hooker* is ready to wire this black marlin. *Photo: Jacquie Acheson.*

prevent a bunch-up. The pump is repeated again and again, dozens or hundreds of times, during a long, tough fight. With the extra brake exerted by the downward pressure of the thumb the fisherman lifts the rod smoothly, usually to the vertical position, then drops it down quickly, almost horizontally. At the same time, the line regained by the lift is quickly reeled on to the spool. Sometimes only a few centimeters (inches) are recovered, sometimes meters (feet); once the fish weakens, more line can be recovered with each pump. With shoulder harnesses, pumping action tends to be longer and more sweeping. This is one of the reasons why shoulder harnesses are generally used on light tackle where lifting is combined with holding pressure while the fish runs against the lightly set brake.

A harness assists on all tackle from 6 kg (12 lb) upwards, and is particularly helpful in long fights against strong fish. A harness may not be needed for small fish, but if fish are to be 'walked' on a drifting or anchored boat the harness makes the work easier and safer.

▲ A 147 kg (325 lb) blue marlin dogs the *Pescador* as the crew take the leader for angler Ralph Christiansen Jnr. *Photo: Captain Bill Harrison.*

The pumping line recovery action is uncomplicated, requiring only a little practice to smooth the action and give power fishing, with or without harness. The drag or brake is set so that the spool will turn and allow line to run out at less than the breaking strain. Extra braking power on light tackle can be exerted by using the left thumb to press the line down against the rod foregrip. If the fish runs strongly, the thumb can be lifted instantly. Some successful heavy-tackle fishermen use the left hand to press against the side of the reel spool to apply extra resistance. Others have been known to hold the line high from the rod with a firm grip of the left hand and almost pull the line back on to the spool.

When the line is being wound in, the fisherman's left hand should lay it evenly along the spool to

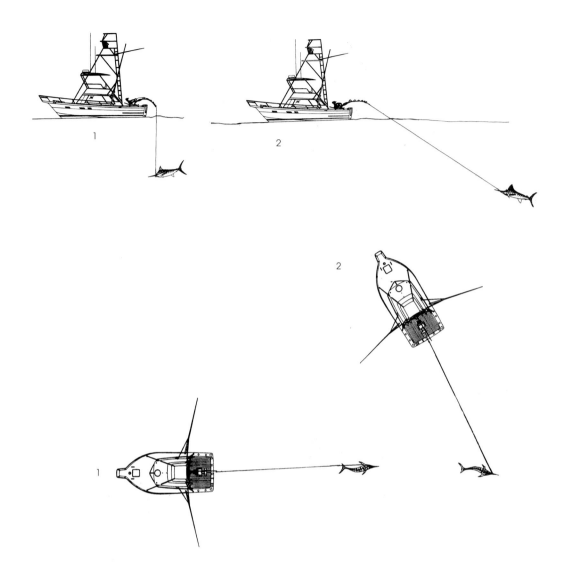

A harness allows the weight of fishing gear and fish to be taken evenly on the fisherman's back muscles. It eliminates the need for a death-like cramping grip with the lifting hand and arm. A harness also makes it more natural and balanced because unless the line is laid on evenly, it will bunch up and then collapse or may jam against the reel seat or bars on the reel. Sometimes it seems as if the ideal angler should have five hands to do everything: to pump, to prevent sideways twist, to wind, to adjust brake as line spool diameter alters and to lay the line evenly. The harness is also a necessity for billfishing with single or multiple strikes.

If maximum braking power is to be maintained, the experienced angler will occasionally alter the brake by using the star drag or lever; novice anglers should set the brake and then leave it alone.

People often talk of luck in fishing. Sure, there is luck. Fish often act out of character and make mistakes — and these are often the record fish. But usually luck evens out, particularly with those who fish over a long period of years. My personal assessment of the ingredients in consistent successful fishing is: 30 per cent complete preparation by anglers, captain and crew of gear, boat and fishing plan; 20 per cent balanced tackle so that angler and

▲ Planing the fish: if a fish is dogging down deep and won't lift and come closer, running the boat forward will improve the angle so that the fish comes closer to the surface. Some skippers circle as well as back up once the fish has come to a higher level in the water. The three steps are illustrated: 1.Dogging down deep; 2. Improving the angle; 3. With improved line angle the fish is closer to the surface to be 'backed up' on or circled to recover line. 4. The fish is shorter on the line and closer to the surface in this operation.

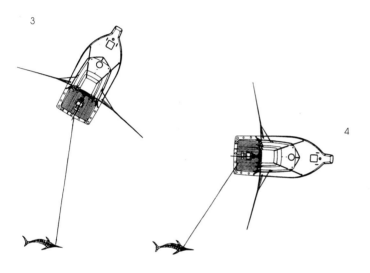

◄ Technique of changing from position of back up to running the fish at improved angle to 'lead' the fish on one side.

crew have a visual indication of the fish's actions; 20 per cent skill of captain and crew in rigging baits, fighting and landing fish; 20 per cent skill of angler in handling his tackle and working in with the other team members; and 10 per cent luck. Experience comes into the first four categories. Experienced fishermen and crews know almost instinctively what they should be doing and what the fish is doing. Practice on boat and on shore will help the novice to gain the smooth technique of polished fishermen.

The best way to learn how much weight is being applied at the hook is to pull with balanced tackle against spring scales with rod bent, as if you have a fish on. The setting of strike drag against a spring scale is important, not only for strike, but for fighting. Setting the drag with rod in the angle that it will bend during the fight is logical although many pull straight from the reel.

Despite this setting against the scale, common sense must also be applied; the brake plates will heat up as the temperature increases during the day. Regular checking by pulling line against the brake will ensure that the brake is practical in that position for the line class.

It is important to hold the rod firmly down in the rod holder with one hand while pulling with the other so the pull against the spool does not lift the rod from the holder and overboard. This applies when drifting or trolling, as a sticky drag can lift a rod clear of the rod holder in the twinkling of an eye, even though the drag is theoretically set just hard enough to prevent an overrun on a fast strike from the fish.

When pumping, keep the rod tip up as the rod is designed to be a spring as well as a lever. In stand-up fishing, whether the rod tip is short as in the 'short stroker' or of conventional length, positive results come from short, quick attacking pumps. Stand-up fishing is growing in popularity with both lengths of rod tips.

It is important for each angler to find and to practice a style that suits the individual build, strength and experience. Stand-up fishing requires a high level of fitness. Many anglers, even when fishing with 15 kg (30 lb) tackle, quickly come to appreciate the assistance of fighting or fishing chairs.

Serious advocates of fishing with short stroker rods, such as Marsha Bierman, often have an exercise regime to maintain maximum fitness for their fishing. Generally, the ultimate benefit of fighting with short rods is associated with much practice and fitness

exercising. Some anglers believe the short rod tips are of benefit with line classes up to 15 kg (30 lb). Others believe they benefit on lines of 24 kg (50 lb) and 37 kg (80 lb). Even the most experienced fishermen benefit from onshore pumping practice to ready themselves for their hoped for offshore activity.

The mouths of most fish are hard, so consideration must be given to the all-important strike to try to set the hook. On trolling and even bait casting and spinning tackle, the hook-up can be made by increasing the drag and lifting the rod tip up and to the side two or three times. On fly tackle the strike is often made by the angler pulling the line rather than lifting the flexible rod tip. Care must be taken to prevent breakoffs with jumping fish. Lowering the rod tip, bowing to the fish and easing the drag all assist in preventing the sickening sensation of broken line.

The technique of pumping to control the fish, lift the fish and recover line is perhaps carried to the ultimate by experienced heavy tackle anglers in fighting chairs.

With heavy tackle, pumping is a combination of a rowing and a sliding action. The angler slides forward or is pulled forward by the fish and may even lower the rod tip a little, then drives back with

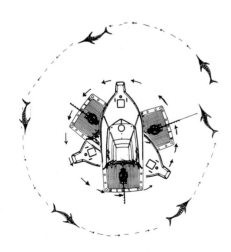

▲ The boat, particularly if equipped with twin motors, can turn inside the circling fish as it is brought close. The fish is usually closest to the surface on the left side of the circle.

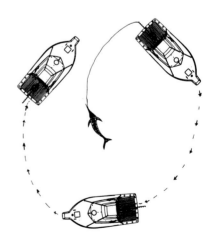

▲ The Port Stephens circling method works well on billfish dogging down deep and is particularly useful if the angler is using a single-speed reel.

the power of legs and back while the left hand lays the line recovered by the winding of his right on to the spool. Often the only way to hold, stop the fish and recover line is when the angler is lifted to his feet out of the chair by the force of the fish. Confidence and balance on the chair's footrest allows the harnessed fisherman to use his body weight and leg strength to return to the chair seat.

Fit, experienced heavy-tackle fishermen often fight repeatedly in this position with left hand pressing down hard on the reel frame and spool. Sometimes the right hand is used on the rod holder frame or armrest to steady on these lifts. This tactic often makes anglers wish that the rod butt were pinned to the gimbal or for a safety line to ensure they could not be completely lifted from the chair and overboard if the reel brake grabs or is set too hard. It is at this time and when taking the rod and reel from rod holder without assistance, while the line is running out fast and the fish jumping and hooked, that the angler must be most careful — ready to ease the brake if necessary, but conscious always of the danger and problem of an overrun. On light tackle an overrun and line jam is expensive and annoying; on heavy tackle it is dangerous and even more expensive.

Line friction, that is line drag caused by long lengths of line and loops in the water, is a problem on lines of all weights. The heavier the breaking strain the greater the friction, but also the less chance of breakoff even with big loops in the water. With the light line class there is much more possibility of this causing breakoff, even without the action of fish or boat. Milton D. Shedd of AFTCO expanded and confirmed Harlan Major's work on reel brake increase with reduction of line of spool and his reports on line friction and speed, although Harlan Major's reports dealt with linen lines. Milton Shedd's data provided information and further thought-starters on the need to back off as line disappears from the spool and to minimize bag of line in the water and the shape of the loops. The position of boat and fish, and the line breaking effect, he described as 'side-cutting' friction. The complications come from multiple loops in the water and the habit of fish, particularly marlin, to change direction and depth in their activity. The rod tip is a visual indicator as well as a lever and a spring, so experienced anglers use this indicator as well as experience and gut feel.

Important factors when fighting a billfish:

- Ability to move safely on rolling boat.
- Knowledge of all the gear that is used. Check drag and deflection.
- Know from the bend of the rod whether more or less brake should be applied.
- Check drag against scales for strike and fighting positions.
- Drop the rod tip down when fish jumps or lunges but minimize slack line.

- Ease off drag when the line sings in breeze.
- Most anglers increase drag once fish settles down after first run.
- Remember as line shortens and fish comes closer, there is less line to stretch and act as a shock absorber. Be ready to ease as fish or sea dictate.
- Ease drag to give a hooked fish a chance to escape a shark, or if a fish takes a long run.
- If doubled line is used, the drag can be increased once the double is on the spool.
- Ease drag if the fish pulls the double off again.
- During light-tackle 'stand-up' fighting, it is often easier to fight and land the fish from the bow if this is safe and low enough for gaffing.
- When two or more fish are being fought at the same time, anglers must be ready to ease drags immediately if lines cross, to facilitate uncrossing and prevent cutoffs — the 'tuna two-step'.
- Angler and captain must be in agreement on the tactics to be used. Communicate.
- Be prepared to vary tactics.
- Watch position of boat in relation to fish.
- Skipper and angler should try to minimize bags or loops in line.
- Exercise for fitness, and practice with the tackle used — heavy, light, sitting down or stand-up with short or long rods.
- Have a harness and if necessary a rod belt to suit the tackle used.
- Be alert to ease pressure on jumping fish.
- Keep concentrating.

Fighting activity will vary with the following factors:

- Angler familiarity with tackle to be used.
- The fish itself: whether it is male or female, its condition (healthy, ready to spawn, at its peak or rundown, having recently spawned), and its mood (fighting mad, hungry or unaware that it is in trouble).
- Where and how the fish is hooked — shallow, deep, or foul.
- The angler: his condition (fit or tired), his mood (fighting mad or placid), his mental attitude (bright,

'on the ball', determined to win, or with his mind on other things besides landing the fish).
- The condition of the boat, gear and crew.
- Weather and sea conditions.
- Water depth and currents, reef obstacles.
- The shark problem — the possibility of mutilated fish.
- The presence of other fish that might cut the line.
- The time of day. A hook-up early in the day leaves plenty of time in daylight; a hook-up late in the day puts pressure on the angler.
- Mistakes on the part of the fish; luck or a choked fish.

In ultra-light fishing for big fish the angler should:

- Bow to the jumping fish i.e., lean body and tackle towards the fish as it jumps to ease the strain on the fragile line.
- Regularly check leaders for cuts or rubs, and, after landing each fish, replace top section of line regularly.
- Rod, reel and line should be balanced tackle.
- Be patient.
- Cast lures in front of the fish or work across in front of its likely track. Do not cast behind and pull forward.
- The shock tippet of Sevalon or heavy monofilament helps cutoffs from sharp teeth or gill covers.
- Retrieve flies or lures slowly, unless the fish that is being hunted is swimming very fast. Cast directly to one fish, even when others are in range.
- The fish must be worked hard and as evenly as possible on ultra-light, just as on other tackle categories.
- Maneuver the boat so it is between the fish and any obstruction.
- The strip retrieve for line is used in saltwater fly fishing until hook-up. The line is dropped to the bottom of the boat or casting platform on the bow and dropped on the water when casting and wading.

Noise must be kept to a minimum and the lure should be brought in very close before being lifted clear of the water for the next cast.

Points for successful bait trolling:

- Sharp hooks.
- Insure the line will come free from the outrigger with minimum weight in relation to bait and sea.
- The angler should be ready to take the strike, to tease or to drop back to the following fish.
- Baits should be changed if not working properly, or if stale.
- Baits should be supple and not waterlogged.
- Troll baits in a pattern so the boat can be maneuvered without tangles.
- A variety of bait species should be used in the fishing pattern.
- If a fish takes the bait be ready to feed line, so that a shy fish will swallow the bait, not drop it.
- Harness and gloves should be close by, in known positions, ready to use.
- If a billfish drops a bait after striking, jig the bait to tease the fish back to strike.
- Binoculars are useful for spotting tailing billfish and bird activities.
- A soft vinyl psychotail over the head of a natural bait makes it last longer in trolling, and allows it to be trolled faster, particularly on light tackle.
- Skipper and angler must be agreed on the method each favors, and reach firm agreement on how the fish is to be hooked and fought before any action takes place.

Points for successful drift and anchor fishing:

- Sharp hooks.
- Baits must be regularly checked for damage.
- Some lines may need weights or sinkers to get baits to the wished-for level.
- Look for fins or fish working on or near the surface.
- Check drags often so that they are not set too hard.
- Use click as warning and overrun preventer.
- Replace tired baits with fresh, active ones.

- Throw over live, unhooked and discarded bait fish occasionally.
- Make sure lines have not tangled.
- Cover all water levels from within 2 m (6½ ft) of bottom of reef to surface with live or dead baits.
- Attach a dan buoy to the anchor line so that it can be slipped if a hooked fish has to be chased.
- If fish are sighted but not striking baits, try decreasing hook and leader size.
- If shifting position, keep chum trail unbroken.
- Always chum regularly to keep trail unbroken.

Points for successful lure trolling:

- Sharp hooks.
- Experiment with a new lure in a proven pattern of successful lures.
- Troll the lures to cover a range of depth, some on the surface, some below the surface.
- Troll a variety in a non-tangling V or W pattern.
- The angler should always be ready for action.
- Choose lures with action and color to suit the day. Change lures as the day progresses, if success has not come on the first pattern used.
- The angler should be ready to tease a following marlin or to free spool back into the marlin's mouth if it is following with mouth open but not striking.
- Be ready to speed up to add to the excitement of following fish.
- Gun the boat to set the hook, then ease the drag once the hook is driven in so that the angler can take the rod from the holder to the chair, in accordance with IGFA rules.
- Troll each lure where it is known to be most effective.
- If two hooks are to be used, make sure this is done in accordance with the IGFA rule which prohibits the use of a dangling or swinging hook.
- Skipper, crew and angler must reach agreement on how the fish is to be hooked and fought before any action takes place.
- The angler and crew should be aware in a two-hook rig of the angles planned in the hook position.

THE BILLFISHING BOAT

Super boats are synonymous with the quest for super fish. The requirements of billfishing have dictated the development of many boating improvements which are now embodied in all types of power boats.

The boats that create the greatest interest at boat shows and marinas are the blue water fishing boats, the boats with a purpose. The sight of a big fishing boat conjures images of the lonely blue of the warm currents — the fisherman, a boat, scattered birds, and the restless sea and fish. Some visualize themselves on smaller, fully equipped boats (under 7 m, or about 22 ft), far out to sea or fishing around the shore and the estuaries, the homes of the fighting species.

It takes more than dreams to turn a boat into a fishing boat, though. Some stock boats can become good fishing boats even though they were not designed or built specifically for that purpose. Despite manufacturers' claims, there are boats that, even with the addition of the best fishing equipment, still cannot become good fishing boats. They may look like fishing boats, but do not perfectly fulfill the special demands of fishing.

Then there are the custom-built or semi-stock boats of various sizes, designed and built for fishermen. These proven boats have a special feel

◀ The *Rybovich Sea Genie II* runs through the rising sun at Kona, Hawaii. *Photo: Peter Goadby.*

as well as performance; they can be easily maintained to keep on fishing.

There are various other boats, sometimes one-offs, built for fishing. These boats can have specialist hulls, such as Hawaii's famous Haole Sampan.

If prospective buyers are serious about fishing they will find it more practical, more pleasant, less frustrating and safer to go for proven custom-built boats for which experience, purpose and tradition have been directed towards the search for and handling of fish. This applies to boats of any size. There is nothing worse than fishing in a boat which has a design and build that resist, rather than help, fishing. The addition of outriggers, a chair and electronic equipment does not miraculously transform a boat into a sportfishing boat that can be easily and safely worked. A great fishing boat is built around fishing needs, rather than the fishing needs being resolved by additions or alterations. Naturally, cost is a consideration, but so too are performance, safety and the knowledge that when fish are found, the boat will perform as it should.

The features that make a good fishing boat are:

- Twin motors for maneuvering, although some great boats, such as Merritt, have single motors and specific steering systems.
- Design and construction that allow fast running in tough conditions when going forward, and a similar performance when backing up if the

The prowess of Captain ▶ George Bransford made the name *Sea Baby* justly famous. Here *Sea Baby II*, skippered by Captain Laurie Woodbridge, runs back after a day at No. 10 Ribbon. *Photo: Peter Goadby.*

propellers and rudders are under the hull. Boats with outboards and outdrives naturally do not perform as well when going backwards as they do when going forwards, but they do have advantages. Outboards and outdrives are practical for many smaller fishing craft.

- A hull design that, in addition to performing safely in tough conditions when going forward or backing up, has sufficient strength without unnecessary weight so that it provides the range dictated by fishing needs.
- A working cockpit that facilitates safe and practical handling of fish, rigging baits and lures.
- The necessary electronic fish finders, and navigation and communication equipment.
- Good visibility.
- Comfort for angler, skipper and crew.

The logical way of ensuring these features is to:

- Check out and if possible actually ride a similar boat in fishing conditions, preferably when fish are being caught. Other sea trials are often not totally relevant to actual fishing conditions.
- Check the speed, fuel performance and range under operating load to ensure that the performance you need can be achieved.

- Check visibility while under way, particularly from the skipper's position.
- Check that the boat will run fairly dry and the hull lays spray down as much as possible. There is nothing more frustrating, annoying and damaging to essential electronic equipment, fishing gear and tempers than boats that are wet from spray blown by the breeze.
- Check that backing up is true and straight. Some boats will not track straight, and others generate so much vibration that the boat appears to be, and may in fact be, damaging itself.
- Make sure that the cockpit or fishing area is free of leader-catching obstructions. Trim tabs on the boat should be able to be folded flat against the transom for backing up and so that leader can be taken, and wire pulled and released with minimum chance of tangling and jamming on obstructions.
- If the boat has a transom door, make sure this is practical — that it will allow the entry of big fish. The bottom of the transom door should be very close, around 25 cm (10 in) above the water line when the boat is at rest. A transom door is often a compromise. Those who work the cockpit prefer one that opens out, so the water pressure in backing up keeps it pushed closed naturally.

Inwards-opening doors have water pressure trying to force them open. Transom doors that are not cut through the transom coverboard i.e., that open only through the transom, are best for fishing as this eliminates cuts or slots in the coverboard which might catch and jam the leader when the fish is alongside for gaffing or tagging. There are natural advantages in loading and unloading with transom doors that open through the transom coverboard — this is a matter to be decided by use and practicality. If the transom door opens through the coverboard, the height of the door opening is determined automatically. However, if the door opens through the transom but not the coverboard, in boats over 10 m (30 ft), the transom door (to take most fish) should be 100 cm x 66 cm (3 ft x 2 ft), depending on the width of the transom and its shape.

- The stanchion for the fighting chair should be 1.2 m (4 ft) from the inside of the coverboard. This allows room for the crew to work aft of the chair, even with the footrest extended for a tall angler. The rod tip, when bent, should clear cockpit corners; big boats may benefit from a gooseneck stanchion.

- For safety and the easy working of fish, the cockpit and transom coverboard height should be between 65 cm and 75 cm (25 in–29 in). Anything shallower than 65 cm can increase danger; deeper than 75 cm makes it difficult to reach water and fish. The seat of the chair should be 5–7 cm (2–3 in) lower than that of the transom, although some skippers and anglers prefer the height of the chair to be level or even above the coverboard, to give maximum height on pumps and help in clearing the corner of the cockpit. The seat of the chair is then about 60–70 cm (24–27 in) above the cockpit deck.

- The cockpit should have room for the fighting chair if heavy tackle is fished.

- The coverboards should be clear of line- or leader-catching obstructions. Cleats for gaff mooring ropes should be permanently fixed and immovable, not just screwed in position. They should allow room for more than one strong gaff rope and be readily accessible and workable.

- In addition to the cleats aft for moorings and the tying off of gaff rope, there are great benefits in installing a cleat or half cleat at the forward end of the cockpit. This makes it easy to hold a fish close to the boatside, with head and body held forward, after the first gaff is in position. Placing additional gaffs, if necessary, and a tail rope, is also easy.

- The cockpit should either have a through-the-bottom (under the cockpit deck) live bait tank, or a tank in the cockpit with circulated water, plus bait boxes, bait rigging, a bench with drawers for knives, needles and threads, files and other terminal tackle and necessary equipment below the work area.

- Deck hose for washing away fish slime or cooling the decks.

- The bait rigging work area should be under the flying bridge overhang, for protection from the sun and spray and, preferably, clear of obstruction by the cockpit bridge ladder. The placing of the ladder is always a problem as it takes valuable space and must facilitate quick transfer from bridge to cockpit. An upright ladder at or near the middle of the cockpit is generally a practical compromise. Safety rails on the rear and unprotected area of the side of the flying bridge are necessary for safety and for rod holders for fishing and stowage during a fight. Some boats have the bridge ladder recessed into the flying bridge; others have entry through a hatch.

- The flying bridge should be dry when the boat is running, even in fishing areas with high winds. Wet (spray-throwing) hull designs and conditions make clear plastic roll-up flying bridge curtains necessary. Despite the hoped-for clarity, these curtains do inhibit visibility to some degree. They should be kept out of the way during fishing and used only as needed, when the boat is travelling at speed. Even while travelling, it may be possible to have one side or part of the forward bridge open for maximum visbility in order to spot obstacles, water color changes, weed lines, bait schools, birds and fish tailing or travelling with fins and tails clear of the surface.

- The electronics on the bridge should be in the driest positions possible within practical limits of visibility and use. Again, this is a reason to use curtains.

- The height of the bridge controls is ideally around 90 cm (3 ft) and the wheel 5–7 cm (2–3 in) lower to be comfortable against the skipper's back when backing up. Most top skippers prefer rack and pinion steering, which turns from hard port to hard starboard in two and a half to three turns. Many prefer gear and throttle levers in one; others prefer separate gear and throttle controls.

- The flying bridge helmsman's chair should turn to allow lure and bait watching by the skipper, and to ensure forward visibility. It should allow for the wheel and controls to be reached comfortably when travelling. The distance between the helmsman's chair and the bridge console should allow the skipper to stand facing the stern during the fight and within easy reach of the controls behind. This position should give full visibility of the angler, chair and working crew at all stages of the fight.

- Dials should be easily read. Some captains follow aircraft practice and place visible tape on the gauge glass for quick recognition of where the needles should be.

- Audible alarms to supplement dial gauges.

- Lights for fighting a fish at night should be mounted at two levels: one set under the coverboard in the cockpit for visibility when working there, and another set (quartz halogen is ideal) on the flying bridge or flying bridge top to aid visibility when fighting and gaffing.

- Many boats now have controls only on the flying bridge and tower — others have cockpit and wheelhouse controls, in addition to bridge and tower.

- Stowage of rods, gaffs and other tackle is always a problem. A narrow projection on the open cockpit sides with a space of about 7 cm (3 in) above the cockpit deck gives the leader man extra safety (toeholds are necessary under this projection). This also assists with the coverboard in keeping distance from gaffs racked on the cockpit side. Rods and reels can be stowed and assembled on the saloon ceiling and cockpit overhangs. On most boats this is the only area available, and the only area where there is the required air circulation. In these positions they are ready for use instead of lying unassembled and out of sight in lockers. Fishermen also generally feel the rods and reels are attractive as well as essential, and take pleasure in being able to see them. It is practical to stow flying gaffs under side coverboards or upright against one side of the rear of the flying bridge. All gaffs should have hose or tubing or other safety covers over the points.

- Mooring lines, meat hooks, tail and other ropes can be stowed under the cockpit floor, as can much of the other boat equipment and spares.

- All cockpit floor hatches should have deep practical gutters to catch water that would otherwise run into the bilges. It is surprising how much water comes into the cockpit when the boat is backing up hard. For this reason the self-draining cockpit scuppers should have self-closing flaps and water ingress through the transom door should be minimized.

- Whether the engines are partly in the cockpit, as in Raymond Hunt designs, or, as more generally, under the saloon floor, there must be ready and immediate access to motors and pumps. It is beneficial to have at least one automatic pump in each hull compartment. Indicator lights on the bridge console show the skipper when any of these pumps are on and if there is need for

▲ The famous Hawaiian boat *Malia*, skippered by Henry Chee, the man who developed the trolling lure known as the Henry Chee pusher.
Photo: Peter Goadby.

centimeters (an inch or so) above his pulpit to give extra foot grip when casting or fishing from the bow.

- Rails around the cockpit are a nuisance when handling fish at boatside.
- Controls should be in the middle line of the flying bridge to allow clear vision of the chair, and are easiest to use in fight and in close maneuvering in port.
- In boats of all sizes, all surfaces that might be walked on should be non-slip. High gloss varnishes, paints and gel coats that can cause slipping are a big no-no on fishing boats. If the cockpit deck or forward decks are painted, add sand or some other non-slip material to the paint surface. Teak is an ideal cockpit, side and transom coverboard material.
- The tuna tower with full controls, which is a Rybovich refinement (as well as the balanced fighting chair and transom door adopted in other custom and production game boats), is of benefit not only for spotting fish and water color changes and other surface indications, but for safe navigating in reef waters. Visibility is greatly enhanced from a tower. Despite the bouncy conditions on Australia's Great Barrier Reef, captains such as Peter Wright and Dennis Wallace spend most of their fishing day in their lonely perch high above the water.
- The cockpit and transom coverboard should have more than enough rod holders, with two on the fighting chair, to allow all methods of fishing. Rod holders on side and bow rails are useful in fishing from anchor or on the drift and in walk-around fishing.
- Many boats are equipped with a row of rocket launchers at the rear of the flying bridge to hold extra rods and reels. These should be spaced to prevent contact and rubbing of the tackle.
- Outriggers are now generally built from aluminum or fiberglass.
- Dry bamboo is ideal for temporary outriggers.
- Live bait tanks, whether built-in or plastic, other

emergency action or for checks of hoses and pumps. On some boats access to the hoses and pumps is difficult, requiring the removal of semi-fixtures. This inhibits access not only for the necessary regular services and checks, but for emergency access into hot spaces as well.

- The expansion and growing awareness of stand-up fishing, that is, anglers walking around the boat with fish on the hook instead of the boat being maneuvered, has increased the need for safety rails from the rear of the saloon or the start of the cabin and around the bow. Charley Davis of southern California has an additional rail in stainless steel pipe running a few

◄ The winter surf on Oahu, Hawaii's north shore, dramatically shows the need for care and seamanship as *Marion B* returns to Haleiwai.
Photo: Jim Witten.

add-ons and tuna tubes are part of today's fishing equipment.

- Bait carrying can be a problem on billfishing boats. Those equipped with refrigeration can hold the main stock of big baits and swimmers frozen, as well as the rigged baits ready for a day's fishing.

THE ELECTRONIC FISHERMAN

Modern offshore sportfishing boats are equipped with so much electronic fish-finding and positioning equipment that perhaps the flying bridge should be renamed the flight deck. The miracles of miniaturization, of the silicon chip and practical waterproofing, mean that even small, open boats can be equipped with low-voltage, low-drain navigating, positioning and fish-finding equipment to give results that only a few short years ago were available only on the biggest, most complete commercial fishing boats. Electronic equipment that was once a major investment is now most reasonable, allowing boats to be equipped with a complete set of electronic equipment for less than the cost of just one piece of equipment a few years ago.

Modern equipment gives visual readings in color, in clearly read LCD digital, and on recording paper. Much of the equipment has built-in audio alarms to warn of shallow water, temperature changes and pre-set times. Some of the electronic aids to fishing are beneficial in safety at sea.

A boat working offshore needs to be equipped with at least the following:

- Echo sounder — color, black and white, paper recording, flashing light, LCD digital, or a combination of these.
- Sea water thermometer.
- Two-way radio with bands and frequencies to suit the operating area.

For the sake of efficiency, saving time and simply better and more productive fishing, add these:

- Bottom-scanning sonar that gives a much wider coverage of the sea bed than an echo sounder or fathometer.
- Color sounder — fishermen derive untold benefits once they are familiar with reading the unit of color sounders. Modern sounders will

automatically adjust the depth scale and gain. Manufacturers are already preparing GPS (Global Positioning Systems) additions that will facilitate return to a previous fishing area.

- GPS satellite navigation equipment gives the position of the boat, the distance covered, the distance to be covered, the real boat speed, the effect of current plus the ability to return the boat to any desired position (even that of previous fishing), as well as continuous positioning.

- Electronic charts — these will benefit fishermen with chart plotters, because they will give clear data on screen at the control station instead of from paper charts. Where Loran transmission is available, it gives positive positioning. The same situation applies to Decca, however neither

system is available worldwide. As GPS is further developed it will give the benefits of Loran, Decca and SatNav (Satellite Navigation or Transit System), with added benefits of simplicity and compactness.

- Color and daylight scanning radar have now replaced the early radar. Radar is available at long range, depending on model and height above the water. Sixteen to 32 nautical-mile range is sufficient for most boats in side scanning and parabola profile.

- Modern radar GPS navigators, Loran and depth sounders can be interphased to provide a tremendous range of practical navigation and fishing data. These capabilities can be enhanced by split screen and zoom features. Sea water temperature is given at surface and depth.

- Radios with multiple frequencies are necessary for offshore boats of every size. There is a large choice of ship-to-ship and ship-to-shore tranceivers that operate within a wide band of frequencies and range from SSB to powerful shorter range models. An operating radio (VHF is the most widely used) is a must for safety at sea. A mobile phone is not an acceptable replacement.

- GPS with readout is already available in a hand-held size that operates on AA alkaline dry batteries or a boat power supply to give:

> 50 waypoints
>
> Latitude/longitude
>
> Range and bearing to destination
>
> Speed and course over ground
>
> Time to go and ETA
>
> Cross-track error
>
> Velocity and distance made good

- Modern equipment and screens combine many functions previously provided by much other electronic equipment. Some equipment now gives course plotter, multiple course origin, destination and present position at the press of

▲ Ted Naftzger's Rybovich spends many hours at sea off southern California singlemindedly scouring the seas for broadbill swordfish. *Photo: Greg Edwards.*

▲ A Buddy Davis game boat, *Cormorant*, at Hawaii. *Photo: Peter Goadby.*

buttons. Other equipment gives depth, speed, elapsed distance, sea temperature, elapsed time, plus a three-dimensional view of the sea bed. Some equipment features multiple-purpose split screens of dual frequency with a range of up to eight functions and zoom capability for closer definitions.

• Automatic pilots continue to be improved in positive simplicity as well as being more 'sea kindly'.

• Electronic compasses are now available.

• Big boats now have options for on-board fax and weather fax.

• Boat thermometers give not only surface temperature readings, but for drift fishing purposes some also give deepwater readings showing the thermoclines and sub-surface temperatures where the fish should be. Modern equipment works at higher boat speeds.

It is obvious that to have any practical and safety benefit, this equipment must be in accurate operating condition. It is important that boat owners or operators know where and when to obtain regular and emergency servicing since it is particularly frustrating to need a piece of equipment and be denied its use. Electronic equipment that is not in working condition is worthless junk that can create problems. It is patently absurd and dangerous to overload the electrical capacity of a boat by installing electrical equipment without assessing whether the system and installation will cope. It is equally important to remember that, whether waterproofed or not, the electronic equipment should be protected from heat and water while still being in a practical position where it is easily readable and operable.

The problem of exposure is naturally greater on small boats than big boats, so the wise buyer chooses equipment by keeping in mind where it is to be used. It is safer and more sensible to spend a few more dollars to obtain top-quality equipment designed and manufactured for the small- or big-boat environment in which it will operate.

The best equipment, properly serviced, needs one other factor to perform as it should. That factor is the operator. It is imperative that the owner/operator understand what the equipment should and will provide. To do this he must know how it operates. Unfortunately, much equipment on boats is not utilized, simply because of insufficient training or practice or because service and operation manuals have not been read.

One of the great benefits of modern technology is that boat electronics can be interfaced with one another as long as there are interface outlets. Split-screen echo sounders can be interfaced with navigation electronics and will show a color picture of fish, bait and structures, water temperature and position with SatNav, GPS or Loran to give location for a future return to the fish's position. Radar can be combined with other electronics to show land, other boats, buoys and openings. Screens should be as big as is practical so they can be easily and quickly scanned to gain the needed data. There is a growing trend towards equipment that has several uses. It is particularly beneficial to have the boat track plotter visible on the same split screen as depth. Other settings give speed, temperature, bearing, way points, distance travelled and distance to travel to destination.

The development of electronics is evident in one piece of equipment — the eight-color screen which shows depth in feet/fathoms/metres, zoom, navigation mode, A scope, plotter, tracer, four full screens, 11 split screens, temperature drifting, temperature graph, boat speed, four alarms, and reducer and Navaid inputs.

EPIRBs, the emergency beacons that should always be carried offshore, are now received by satellites as well as aircraft and emergency services.

◀ Despite the boat's name, *Osprey*, Palm Beach pelicans are happy to hitch a ride in hope of a meal.
Photo: Peter Goadby.

◀ *Hooker* is carried on its mother ship's deck (*The Madam*) in a floating pull-on cradle.
Photo: Jacquie Acheson.

MOTHER SHIPS AND LONG-RANGE BOATS

The concept of living aboard boats that are too big and unmaneuverable for gamefishing and then fishing from boats that are too small to travel long distances and to live aboard has long been part of the sportfishing scene in salt water. Much of the pioneering exploratory fishing of the 1920s and 1930s was made possible by the combination of the big boat and the small boat.

Mother ships again came to the fore in the 1970s on the Great Barrier Reef in Australia, where motor yachts, sailing yachts, cruise catamarans and specially designed catamarans became floating motels and fuel docks for specialized gamefishing boats. These mobile bases moved along the anchorages of the reef to enable game boats to fish off the reefs and openings where the marlin were active, instead of being limited to island or shore bases where the marlin might be out of day range. These mother ships were serviced by fuel and supply barges with passenger transit by sea plane.

Three modern mother ship fishing boat operations have captured fishermen's imaginations and envy with their long-distance operations. Jim Jenks' 26 m (85 ft) *Ocean Pacific* and 10 m (32 ft)

Innovator were specially built as a combination. Jim Edminton's 30 m (100 ft) *El Zorro* was a Californian long-range boat, and her game boat, *El Zorro II*, was a specially modified 10 m (32 ft) open gamefishing boat, complete with tower. Jerry Dunaway, the owner of the most successful G & S 13 m (43 ft) game boat, *Hooker*, chose a 25 m (83 ft) oilfield work and crew boat as his mother ship. He continued and surpassed the Thomases' humor in name combination by naming his mother ship *The Madam*. These three combinations all carry the fishing boat on board, as does the 70 m (220 ft) *Kirsula* with her 10 m (32 ft) *Hatteras*. *Quest*, another converted oilfield work boat, carries three fishing boats, including an 11.5 m (38 ft) tower boat; it also has a helicopter.

Other mother ships tow the fishing machines — Paul Caughlan's *Mustique/Kanahoe* combination on the Great Barrier Reef and western Pacific opt for the towing option. Extra surveillance day and night is provided by closed circuit television, also used for the engine room watch.

The success of these operations and their skilled skippers and crew is demonstrated by the capture and release records, including at least one grander black marlin on the GBR for each combination. *Hooker*, skippered by Skip Smith, has run up an incredible tally of men's and women's IGFA world records, the most by any boat in angling history.

Long-range live-aboard boats of 30–40 m (100–130 ft) have also made important and highly visible contributions to the sportfishing scene from southern California to Mexico's spectacular offshore islands and sometimes to the Galapagos. These boats are the live-aboard platforms for spectacular wahoo and yellowfin fishing in particular. Fish are caught in stand-up fishing; during the daytime, anglers must be practiced in the 'Tuna Two Step' or 'Wahoo Waltz' to avoid line breaking, crossovers and tangles.

The trend towards bigger boats is generally evident in modern offshore fishing. Gamefishing cruisers of 17 m (55 ft) were once regarded as around the biggest practical fighting-chair gamefishing boats. Some of the recent boats, both stock and custom built, are in excess of 21 m (70 ft), a length once considered long enough and big enough to carry and service smaller boats from which to fish. The size and characteristics of boats change with the needs of modern fishing.

THE SMALL BOAT FISHERMAN

In the mini-battle wagons — boats under 7 m (22 ft) — the same needs are present, but fulfillment of them is even more difficult. Yet despite their size small boats can provide incredible captures, fishing both offshore as well as inshore. Many of these boats show the benefit of experience, ingenuity and thoughtful building, with minimum unnecessary weight and maximum fishability, strength and performance.

The capacity of small boats to carry fuel, chum (berley), equipment, tackle and people is of course limited, but despite this they fish most successfully and enjoyably in competition with bigger boats. Techniques have been developed by the small boat fishermen that make them competitive with bigger boats, and in some ways they have benefits rather than disadvantages for actual fishing. Obvious benefits are that even on light tackle the small boat is a float that acts as a drag and can be towed by the fish. This minimizes the chance of shock line

◀ The long range Californian vessels that fish Baja, California, take Striped Marlin as well as Yellowfin and Wahoo.
Photo: Peter Goadby.

breakage. These boats are maneuverable and, with center console and stand-up fishing, anglers can move around with the fish and have minimal chance of transom corner and hitting-the-hull problems.

Outboard and outdrive motors can be a problem when the fish is close and at gaff, or when trying to back up. Despite this they are very practical, and small boat skippers take advantage of their quick maneuvering capability to spin and run the fish in a manner forgotten or not used, although of great benefit in bigger boats.

To be equipped for hard fishing within the limitation of range, small boats should have:

• Radio and depth sounder, plus the mandatory safety equipment of flares, EPIRB, life jackets, safety sheet anchor and long anchor line, plus as much fuel as can be safely carried for the day's planned fishing and some in reserve.
• Drinking water.
• Spare propeller shear pin.
• Understanding of motor and regular service. The modern outboard is a dependable, sophisticated machine, but it needs regular service and checks. Many small boat skippers no longer carry small auxiliary motors. They prefer to maintain and be consciously dependent on the performance of their main power plant.
• Along with the necessary legal running and mooring light, small boats should have emergency lights and a powerful flashlight and battery lantern should fishing continue into the night.

▲ Practical and stable, smaller sized multi-hulls can be taken to fishing areas by trailer before heading out to sea, as at Moreton Island, Australia. *Photo: Jeff Webster.*

▲ Anglers at Baja California, Mexico, catch billfish as well as roosterfish. Yellowtail and dolphin fish in traditional Mexican pangas like this. *Photo: Peter Goadby*

- Gaffing and gaff rope attachment require thoughtfulness, or they can cause problems in small boat operations. Gaff ropes and gaff handles can be shorter than those used and needed on bigger boats. Cleats and other mooring line holders fixed in position have sufficient strength. However, care and thought must be given to the 'how' of handling big fish in small boats.
- Many small boats now have aluminum rocket launchers over the windshield to hold rigged rods. Others have rod storers at the rear of the helmsman's seat, fish or ice box.
- Small boats are practical for a center console configuration, which gives the benefit of full walk-around fishing and a forward area for fly, spin or bait rod casting.
- Short towers are often beneficial and useful on boats about 7 m (22 ft) in length.
- Carrying of live bait and necessary circulated or aerated seawater can be a problem. Some boats

have a live bait tank and fish box extending from the back of the hull or hulls, with the motor between these projections.
- Chum (berley) cans on small boats should be attached in such a way that if they are grabbed by

▲ Fully equiped small boats can carry all necessary equipment & tackle. *Photo: Peter Goadby.*

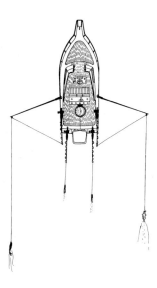

▲ Lures and baits can be fished together from small boats.

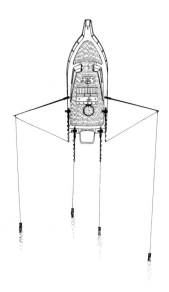

▲ Modern, small, open boats are practical for trolling as well as jigging and casting.

a big shark the shaking and rolling will not endanger the boat or crew (it is safer if they are able to be torn free).
• Plastic fish boxes are ideal for stowage of the necessary ropes, gaff heads, floats, tackle boxes, lures, baits and bait rigging equipment.
• Outriggers may be installed and are practical, but good fishing with angled rod holders is also possible.

Small boat fishing not only has benefits, particularly in light tackle fishing, but gives great enjoyment and, in common with big boats, yields many happy memories.

▲ A chum bucket can sit neatly on any size boat.

One of the benefits of small boats is that they can be towed, that is, moved by road from port to port, instead of the chore and expense of having to always travel by sea.

South African anglers, with their ski boats that are launched in the surf, have taken small boat fishing to an exciting and practical level.

Modern high-speed gamefishing boats are now as long as 24 m (78 ft) although 11 m to 16 m (36 ft to 53 ft) is still the most usual size range.

There are also important sportfishing areas where small boats are a must. The flats and shallow channels in Florida forced the evolution of a whole new generation of specialized fishing machines for bonefish and tarpon. Powerful outboard motors drive these shallow-draft stable boats at high speed through shallow water. Fishing needs and practicality have seen the integration of live bait tanks within hulls, obstruction-free casting areas, hulls that can be easily poled, poling-spotting platforms over the motor, plus holders to safely carry tackle.

The next-size generation of boats (from 6–8 m, or 20–25 ft) have also been well thought out, with equipment dictated by practical fishing needs, including center consoles, forward-mounted fishing chairs and a lightweight range of electronic equipment to pinpoint the sea bed. Fishing features are incorporated in fast, safe, sea-kindly hulls. The boats catch big fish as well as the light tackle species for which they were conceived.

Multihulls — twin catamaran hulls and the range of tri hulls — come into their own in small boats under 7 m (22 ft). These hulls can be driven hard into rough water, handle rough seas and bars safely and are stable fishing platforms trolling, drifting and at anchor. Another big advantage of multihulls is that they give great fishing area and load-carrying space.

Small boats can be maneuvered so the fish can be fought with the boat going forward, so 'backing up' is not the necessary consideration that it is on big boats. Small boats in their own way are often more practical and successful than the bigger boats, but one thing is certain: boats are part of the fishing team, and they and their designers, constructors and operators contribute much to the enjoyment and success of fishermen, whatever fish they seek.

BILLFISHING BOAT EQUIPMENT

The complete billfishing boat often has three outriggers instead of the traditional two. The third, middle outrigger is positioned on the tower or flying bridge and is the key to trolling a lure or bait well back in the center of the pattern. The lure or bait, sometimes called a shotgun, is often productive when billfish have looked at but not struck at the closer lures or baits.

OUTRIGGERS

In the beginning, when sportsmen first fished offshore, there were no outriggers, no drags on the reels, no harnesses and no chairs, yet many of the early fishermen won their struggles with the big fish. The organized sport of saltwater gamefishing began when Dr Holder and Colonel Morehouse first caught tuna in 1898. The Avalon Tuna Club,

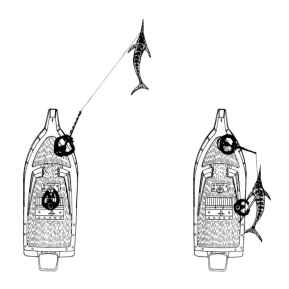

▲ Small boats can handle the big billfish as well as the juveniles.

the first in the world, was then formed. It remains a world leader in terms of rules and ethics.

About 15 years after this beginning, the silk kite was developed. It takes anglers' baits to a position in front of the fish and clear of the boat's wake. These California kites were later joined on the boats by bamboo outriggers. These early outriggers pulled teasers but did not pull the baits, which were kept rigged in the boats until the marlin or tuna attacked the teasers.

Harlan Major took the California kite to Florida and that great fisherman, thinker and innovator, Florida's Tommy Gifford, brought improved California outriggers back to Florida. In California, Tommy had skippered William Bonnel's boat *Tarpon*, which had California outriggers with teasers. Tommy not only devised strutting and braces so that his long outriggers on the small *Lady Grace* made boat and rig look like a grasshopper, but most importantly thought of the clothespin line release that allowed the line to come free when the bait was struck. Tommy's innovation and concept of the line release led to outriggers becoming a symbol of a gamefishing boat as well as a practical fishing tool. The objective and thought behind the outrigger and the line release on strike were similar to those that George Farnsworth of Catalina devised with his kite. The bait was lifted, trolled clear of the wake and looked as natural as possible.

Just a few years after those first Gifford outriggers sprouted on the Florida east coast, they had migrated to Hawaii, possibly propagated by Harlan Major's visit to Kona, where he finally landed a blue marlin after much experimenting with bait. In Hawaii, the bamboo poles of the outriggers were not as sophisticated as the developments on the east coast of the USA. In Hawaii, some outriggers, which had a different objective, were bound to the boat with cord and rope. They were used to pull the feathers, the wooden tarporinos, and the wooden and bath towel rail lures with their flexible rubber tails that became the first trolling lures for big fish. In the modern age of plastic and color, those lures spawned the kona head and knucklehead in the many shapes and weights now used around the world.

IGFA founder Michael Lerner, guided by Bill Hatch, the dean of Florida's fishing captains, used those bamboo-type outriggers in New Zealand and Australia in 1939 and immediately and positively showed their worth in trolling baits for billfish. Results speak louder than words and the use of

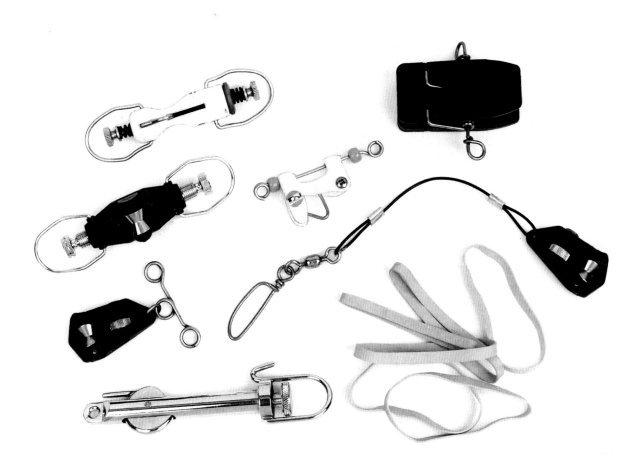

▲ Outrigger clips and line releases ranging from simple rubber bands to sophisticated light and heavy tackle models. *Photo: David Rogers.*

BILLFISHING

▲ Black marlin jumping into outrigger and outrigger halyard. *Photo: Paul B. Kidd.*

outriggers became an integral part of the mix that makes for successful offshore fishing. Outriggers spread like wings on offshore boats right around the world. Today, nearly 100 years after their introduction, outriggers are not only accepted but expected on gamefishing boats larger than 5 m (16 ft).

No one disputes that marlin and other pelagics can be and are caught on flat lines with bait and lures and that flat lines are an integral part of successful patterns. The benefits of the outriggers are there for all to see, whether fishing bait, lures or both.

Outriggers ensure that baits or lures can be trolled in the chosen position relative to the wake, ranging from right in the propeller wash to as wide as the outrigger spread and angles will allow. The riggers can be angled and set to give lift and position to skipping baits, and depth and natural action to swimming baits. They are used to position and angle lures of various designs to where each works best and most effectively. With natural baits, when generally only two or three are being trolled, they can carry the calculated drop

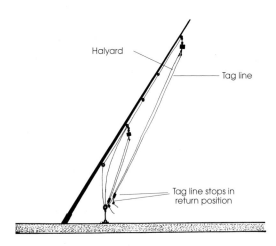

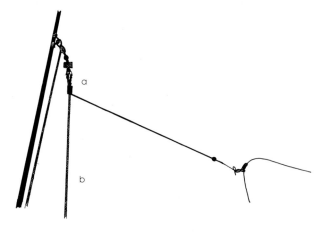

▲ Tag line stops drop the tag line to the bottom of the halyard for quick recovery after a strike.

▲ The tag line stop (A) that saves time after a strike (a plastic styrene or balsa ball prevents the halyards and tag lines jamming or pulling too far). (B) is the outrigger halyard.

back to assist the chance of a hook-up. With lures, they give the pattern a wider spread of water to allow tangle-free trolling of four or five lures. They are practical and necessary.

Outriggers may be at right angles (90 degrees) to the hull of the boat, but most are at around 60 to 80 degrees. Outriggers that are angled back so the tips are at less than a 60 degree angle to the hull defeat one of the objectives, which is to move bait or lure out from the hull wash and propeller wash.

Outrigger angle to hull varies with different bases and different positions on deck or cabin side. The angle of the outrigger when actually fishing is changed by the pull of baits or lures and by pulling the halyards tight.

Some of the early influential fishing writers and administrators of saltwater gamefishing decried their use and worried that outriggers gave gamefishermen unfair advantage over the fish. Some felt that outriggers, in giving an automatic drop back when combined with skillfully rigged baits, could give 100 per cent hook-ups, that the instinctive manual drop back and teasing by anglers

(who had learned from experience) would be unnecessary, and that there could be an increase in deliberately deep-hooked fish.

Experience over the next 50 years has shown that neither of these concerns is valid. It is unfortunately true that on some potentially superb boats, gamefishing outriggers have merely become extra flagpoles or status symbols on which to fly flags and pennants. These vary from the capture flags or tag-and-release pennants indicating a successful day, to the skunk or dead rat pennant that indicates what may diplomatically be called an unsuccessful day. For those boat owners who do fish but do not respond to the challenge of trolling for pelagic fish, the outriggers may be used only to place a drifting bait. Their use is not always understood, and for those boats that rarely go to sea their use may be simply for a pennant that says, 'Open bar — come and have one'.

In lure fishing, with or without outriggers, the consideration of 100 per cent hook-ups is not a problem, as many strikes are hit-and-miss on strike and very few lure-hooked fish are deep-hooked. This is a very sporting way to fish. The pioneering outrigger type in most fishing areas, including in the exploratory days at Cairns, New Zealand, Hawaii and many other ports, has been the humble bamboo pole.

They are most successful if allowed to dry — to minimize weight and maximize springiness. Bamboo poles, whether bound and wrapped between the nodules, painted or unpainted, are still ideal short-term outriggers, particularly on boats that are not completely equipped.

In this age of lightweight metals and plastics, the natural bamboo, spruce and Oregon pole outriggers have generally been replaced by aluminum and fiberglass poles. The simple outrigger bases that allowed only pivoting in and out, and the later sail track that allowed a great multiplicity of positions and angles, have been replaced by brass and stainless fittings and outrigger bases that are easy and positive in use. In positioning they are combined with either guyed or strutted aluminum or uncluttered fiberglass poles. Both these outrigger types are available in two or more sections, and different weights and stiffnesses, to give a range of choices to suit boats of all lengths and purposes. Fiberglass outriggers allow positive use of the maximum length of the outrigger, whereas the unstrutted top section of the guyed and strutted aluminum outriggers may be bent after the pull of a big bait or a hard strike. For this reason, on this type, many outrigger halyards are taken only to the furthest point of the guying and strutting.

Rough water, big baits and the hit of a striking fish put a heavy load on working outriggers, so they must be rugged and practical in design, construction and installation. Outriggers can be swung from the deck, from the side of the wheelhouse, the top of the wheelhouse or from the side of the flying bridge. The areas to which they are attached must be strong, and strengthened to take the load and shock without structural damage to the boat. A light cord from tip of outrigger to bow rail is a practical way to minimize whip and load. Baits need not be trolled from the full length of the outrigger.

Experience, skill and common sense are factors that help in getting the best results from the outrigger.

Outriggers are used in an almost diametrically opposed way when fishing with lures rather than baits. In bait fishing, the usual plan is to have one bait skip and splash, with another bait rigged to swim and wriggle below the surface as realistically as possible. In natural bait fishing, the outrigger clips are set just hard enough to hold the weight and pull of the bait, but light enough for the line to drop free once the bait is taken. The reel drag in natural bait fishing is set with just enough brake to prevent an overrun when the fish strikes the bait. If the angler prefers to control the drop back, the reel drag is set hard (around one-quarter to one-third the line class breaking strain) and the line drop back is trailed on the water — the length of drop back is, ideally, enough to allow the fish to turn and swallow the bait. With the long drop back and the drag set hard, skill, practice and a cool head are still required by the angler in backing off the drag while line is running out from a hooked fish, and transferring the rod and reel without overrun to chair gimbal or rod bucket. This can be a moment of truth, as an overrun can happen in a flash if the drag is eased too much — the rod and reel are difficult to take from the chair holder or coverboard if the drag is left too hard.

Outriggers are rigged with an outrigger clip or set of rubber bands to maximize hook setting and minimize drop back in lure fishing. The plan is for the fish to pull against the reel brake, as well as the weight of line and spring of the rod, as quickly as possible. The hope is for an immediate hook setting following the strike. The use of a tag line minimizes drop back, changing the angle at which the lures are trolled so that they are wider in the wake. The tag lines are rigged to assist in the controlled breaking of the rubber bands that may hold the line and provide the initial shock and impact to set the hook. Tag lines should reach no longer than from outrigger halyard pulley to the corner of the side and transom. If they are too long they may cause tangling of the tag line and fishing line.

In both lure and bait fishing, some crews rig their outriggers with halyards of heavy mono of 272 kg to 364 kg (600 to 800 lb) test. Others use braided cord, which could give the advantage of less stretch under load on the strike than monofilament. Monofilament has a longer life, as it wears less in use. Heavy glass or metal rings are bound to the outrigger pole to hold the halyard or halyards close in alongside the pole and minimize halyard sag. Cleats or other devices are now rarely used to tie off the halyard. The modern practice is for the halyard to be pulled down tight to the coverboard so that it may be freely positioned along the outrigger and held in place by the springiness of the outrigger pole or by the use of a heavy shock rubber to keep it taut. A twist at the bottom of the halyard is also useful to minimize slip. Two halyards are sometimes used: the main halyard runs the full length of the pole and another, shorter halyard runs about halfway up the pole. The second halyard gives the option of pulling a bait or lure that otherwise would be trolled from the rod tip or from some type of flat line, clip release or rubber band holder. The tag line or stinger should be long enough just to clear or reach the corner of the transom when it is hanging free. The tag line is often made of the same material as the outrigger halyard, and many tag lines are clipped on to the halyard in the usual position of the outrigger release if lures and tag lines are to be fished. The rubber bands are used to hold the trolling line. Many crews around the world follow the common Hawaiian use of braided 59 kg (130 lb) class line at the free end of the tag line, while others use a strong coast lock or other small-diameter wire snap that minimizes the area on which the rubber band is pulling to assist the breaking of the band on strike.

There is a growing world trend to use metal or other heavy rings or short tubes (about 5 cm or 2 in long) as an automatic tag line return. Light cork balls about the size of table tennis balls are sometimes used on the end of the tag line to ensure quick recovery and to minimize tangling. The tag line return allows the tag line to pull from the halyard top when the boat is under way and the lure is pulling. Not all lure-trolling fishermen use tag lines. Some experienced captains and crews prefer to use the usual roller-type outrigger clips, such as Aftco or Rupp, attached straight to the halyard, as for natural bait trolling. This outrigger release use is in line with the methods of successful lure fishermen, who believe that the fish hooks itself of its own impact and velocity as it takes the lure and closes its powerful lower jaw. In their opinion, very hard drags and gunning the boat to set the hook are unnecessary, and in fact the gunning of the boat may only have the benefit of running the hooked fish clear of the other lines and lures.

Fiberglass outriggers generally have more flexibility, whether built specifically as outriggers or from vaulting poles or windsurfer masts. Many boats have a short shotgun outrigger in the center line of the boat from the flying bridge, to run a shotgun lure way back in the center of the trolling pattern. Tangles not only cause frayed tempers but also frayed lines and leaders. For this reason it is important to always run the outside lines into position first, then the inner lines. When bringing lines back inboard, the reverse applies.

DEEP TROLLERS

Deep trollers are often successful as they take live or dead baits down to the depth at which billfish prefer to cruise. In essence, they are reverse outriggers which take the bait down deep, ready to come free on the strike. Baits trolled from deep trollers are productive over peaks and drop-offs in the ocean bottom. As for all other equipment on a billfishing boat, the deep trollers should be of high quality to ensure satisfactory fast operation at the chosen depth.

Points to remember for success with outriggers:

• Troll one bait skipping on the surface and the other bait swimming deeper. Other baits can be

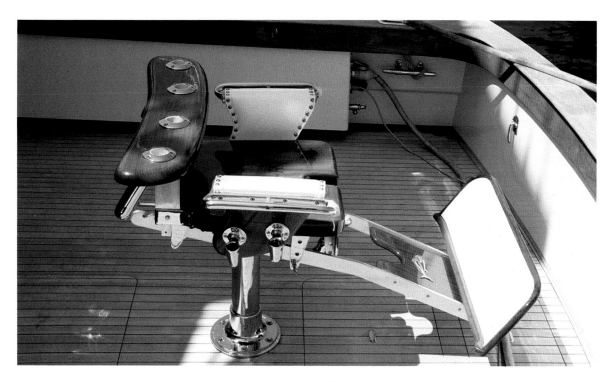

▲ The drop backrest on this Murray Brothers chair has been replaced by a rocket holder for light-tackle fishing. When used for heavy-tackle fishing a drop back rest is in place instead of the rocket holder. This modern chair also shows arm rest rod holders for straight and curved butts and the drop gimbal. *Photo: Peter Goadby.*

trolled on flat lines direct from rod tip to give a different action and provide the fish with a choice.

- Troll baits outside and alongside the boat's wake and propeller turbulence.
- Troll baits or lures so that they are well apart and don't tangle. It is easy with outriggers to troll four (or up to six) rods if common sense is used in positioning baits and lures. The 'V' or 'W' pattern has been described earlier.
- Provide some or all of the drop back necessary in fishing for marlin and sailfish, yet still allow the hook-up of wahoo and other fast strikers.
- Allow the trolling of big baits without a constant holding strain on the rod and the angler.
- Allow the trolling of baits with only a light brake on the reel, just enough to prevent overrun.
- Keep the leader out of the water so that the bait can troll naturally, without the creation of bubbles that may frighten a shy fish.

▲ Light, movable fishing chairs are helpful when multiple hook-ups are likely. They can be moved clear when a single big fish is being played from the fighting chair. *Photo: Peter Goadby*

▲ The rocket launcher developed by great angler Jo-Jo Del Guercio and the Staros Brothers brings light tackle to the heavy-tackle fighting chair. *Photo: Peter Goadby.*

- Keep a deep bait clear of the boat and other baits when fishing from anchor or on the drift.
- Improve the action of some lures, particularly of some of the big kona heads and vinyl squid replicas.
- When putting lures out, put outside lines out first. When bringing lures inboard, retrieve the center lines first to avoid tangles.

THE FIGHTING CHAIR: A HEAVY TACKLE NECESSITY

The modern gamefish fighting chair is visible proof of the power of big game fish. It helps the angler, yet gives the fish a fighting chance.

Way back when the first big gamefish were sought and caught, gentlemen anglers, dressed in plus fours, stood and fought them from small launches. In their capture photographs the gentlemen were dressed complete with ties, as if for a day at the office, although the plus fours worn in some photographs indicate this was a sporting occasion. The ladies wore dresses covering them from neck to ankle and wrist. Ladies and gentlemen both wore hats. The angler held the rod

and reel, the gaffer (captain, guide, wireman) held a fixed head gaff.

The giant tuna on the north-east coast of the USA were battled from dories rowed by a guide. The angler sat and fought the fish from a thwart.

In Florida, once again, it was a case of stand up and fight. Gradually the scene changed. Chairs gave the angler a chance to sit and pump the fish with the rod butt in a leather butt holder similar to that for surf or stand-up fishing, without grinding his groin away. Light tackle buffs used rod butt belts as they continued their stand-up fishing. Reflecting the dress of the anglers, those fixed chairs were office chairs with fixed backs. The need for removable backs to allow full pumping was soon recognized, and Harlan Major illustrated a plan for such a fishing chair with a gimbal. This was the basis of a model used around the world.

The need for footrests to help anglers battle it out with the giant tuna and black marlin was also recognized. The early fighting chairs had pipe footrests, which were crude but helpful. John Rybovich finally built the modern chair which,

▲ This fighting chair swings over the live bait tank to maximize available cockpit space. *Photo: Peter Goadby*

◀ The distinctive Rybovich sheerline and other features on the *Humdinger* are as much at home at Kona, Hawaii, as in the Atlantic and Caribbean. *Photo: Peter Goadby.*

with some slight changes, mainly by the Merritts and Murray Bros, has become the basic fighting chair for heavy tackle fishing wherever fish that warrant the use of heavy tackle are sought.

Bent butts that give the angler a further advantage led to simple gimbals becoming sophisticated drop gimbals, so the rod butt could pivot from low down to allow the angler a level pull on to the reel. The high tapered back, when dropped, gave the chair guide better directional control. The front of the chair seat was angled so that when pumping, the angler could come forward and slide with leg drive on a taper rather than a square cut seat. Footrests that had originally been narrow and pivoting became fixed, then curved at the ends to improve the grip and position of the angler's feet. This modern footrest is variable in angle and distance to meet variations in the build and height of users.

For maximum strength and safety, the fighting chair post goes through the cockpit sole down to the keel. The chair post is sometimes goose necked to compensate for the beam of big boats. The holes in the armrest of the original fishing chair have now become strong rod holders to suit curved and straight rod butts, so rods can be trolled from the chair as well

as in the coverboard. The height of the chair from the deck is determined by the depth of the cockpit coverboards and the transom. The seat should be about level with the top of the coverboard.

The fighting chair should be positioned to allow clear, safe movement between footrest and transom, and the chair post should be strong enough not only for the pivoting chair but for rod safety lines and gaff ropes. The chair is the focal point as well as one of the reasons for the fishing self-draining cockpit. Murray Bros have developed bait rigging boards and modified Jo Jo Del Guercio's multiple light-tackle rod, holding 'rocket launchers' to provide maximum benefit from a cockpit chair. The original rocket launcher was used on the chair post of the fighting chair, but it may be removed to give added cockpit space for stand-up, light-tackle fishing. In small boats, the chair is often positioned at the bow rather than the stern.

The complete modern cockpit, with fighting chair in white or natural teak finish and stainless steel and aluminum components and coverboards lit and highlighted by the harsh tropical sun, resembles a stark operating theatre ready for the operating crew — the fishermen.

Some cockpits have fixed or movable fishing

◀ Pieces fly from the mangled bait as a black marlin almost comes into the cockpit.
Photo: Peter Goadby.

chairs with simple gimbals as well as the powerful fighting chair. Other boats, seeking medium-sized rather than massive fish, have two fishing chairs in their cockpit. Anglers using these chairs obtain foot purchase from the deck or coverboard. This configuration does not allow the leg drive and power advantage that curved butts and seat harnesses guarantee.

Thousand-pound black marlin have been caught with straight butt rods, shoulder and kidney harnesses and fishing chairs, rather than the fighting chairs that are now almost standard wherever big fish are sought. Human ingenuity and the need for efficient performance to combat the power and activity of giant fish have triggered the development of modern fighting tackle.

This chair development is indirectly a tribute not only to the fish but to the pioneering fishermen who caught the fish with simple tackle and equipment.

SKIPPER AND CREW

Gamefishing is a true team sport. Consistent success comes to the angler, skipper and crew who understand this and always work as a team. Successful teams develop understanding, communication and prior planning to eliminate as many as possible of the 'unexpected' occurrences that cause loss of fish, damage to equipment and harm to fishermen. Angler, skipper, crew, boat and tackle are all ingredients in the mix for success. This applies to private boats skippered and crewed by a team and to professional skippers and crews.

The experience of professionals is one of the many reasons why anglers use charter boats, or employ skippers and crews on their own boats. All members of the fishing team must perform adequately if there is to be a consistent and safe result. Weaknesses, lack of experience and poor communication can cause not only loss of the fish but injury or accident to crew or angler, particularly when working with jumping billfish.

Experience, practice in working together and an understanding of what each person is doing or trying to do results not only in captures and safe fishing, but in enjoyment and team spirit. Communication, understanding and cool heads are the keys to success and pleasure for all involved. There is no need for nerve-grating, raised voices and shouting during the fight. This should be saved only for a real emergency. Unnecessarily raised voices are annoying and place added pressure on those who are already under pressure to perform.

It is important for all involved, even those who have great experience and who have fished together before, to talk to each other early on to gain an understanding of what each person is trying to do and what each expects of the others. Every facet of the day's fishing procedure in hooking and fighting fish must be understood. It is too late to establish complete rapport and understanding when the fish is right there. Communication must be established before the pressure builds. Differences in method, technique and experience make it imperative to quickly establish a plan and develop rapport, confidence and communication.

Without mutual understanding, fish and opportunity are wasted. Fish will be lost before being hooked on trolled baits and lures unless both the skipper and angler know what each is trying to do.

A typical example of problems right in the beginning of hoped-for action is when either the skipper or the angler is trying for drop back before trying to hook-up, and the other is expecting a try for an instant gunning of the boat to assist hook-up. Good communication can avoid such a situation.

Just as every team has a captain, so does every boat. The captain may be a professional skipper with a professional crew of one or two, or an amateur running his own boat crewed by family or friends. He is the decision-making member of the team; decisions affecting the boat and safety are his responsibility. Crew and experienced anglers sometimes have the opportunity to make suggestions, but often such fast action is required that there is no time to take advice — the responsibility rests with the captain.

On many boats with experienced crews, one of the crew will be doing the talking to both angler and skipper. On many private boats, the angler/owner skippers (such as Ted Naftzger of California, the world's top broadbill angler, with around fifty daylight fishing captures, and Australia's late Garrick Agnew with his many 452 kg, or 1000 lb, black marlin weighings) skipper their own boats to find the fish and get the strike. Someone else then takes over the controls for the hook-up, fight and boating of the fish. Naturally, anglers ask their skippers and crews what they think, what they want and what they need during the fight, and the skipper will try to meet the request. This is part of communication. In the same way, the skipper will make suggestions and tell the crew and angler what he is going to do — to back up, to run the fish, to circle — so that those in the cockpit are balanced and ready. The skipper has the advantage of maximum visibility from his flying bridge and can generally see what is happening more quickly than anyone else on the boat. The skipper will instinctively try to correct a problem or resolve a dangerous situation before it occurs.

◀ Captain Bart Miller maneuvers *Black Bart* to aid his crew and angler. *Photo: Peter Goadby.*

An active marlin jumping at boatside or a shark rolling or diving under the boat does not allow time for a debate or committee meeting to reach consensus on what is to be done. At this moment, the skipper is the one who can take action; he must make his decisions instantaneously, and yet advise those in the cockpit of what he and the boat are doing.

It is important not only to understand what each person is trying to achieve, but how best each can assist the other. Those involved must keep in their mind the power and potential for damage with each big fish, particularly when the leader is at or in hand. It is imperative as well as sensible for the captain always to maneuver the boat to give maximum assistance to those in the cockpit. Many of the top captains have graduated to the bridge after working the deck and dealing with cockpit problems first hand.

The hull sections of gamefishing boats are designed to facilitate fast and true backing up. With twin motor sportfishing boats, the skipper centers the wheel then basically doesn't use it while backing up. He stands with his back against the wheel and faces towards the transom, using the throttle/gear controls to direct and maneuver the boat.

In single motor boats, unless designed specifically for gamefishing and equipped with special mechanical steering (such as that made by Merritt), the skipper will use both steering wheel and motor. Single-propeller torque will cause the boat to back up and turn faster and more easily in one quarter than the other.

Experienced skippers familiar with single motor backup characteristics know ways to compensate, maneuver and control the boat for the benefit of angler and crew, as if the boat were equipped with twin motors and balanced rudders.

A successful skipper controls and uses his boat as if he and the boat are so well integrated that the boat is answering the skipper's thoughts rather than the direction of his hands.

It is interesting and instructive to sit and talk with experienced fishermen, to listen and learn. The conversation often drifts not only to great captures or great fish, but to accidents or potential accidents. There is an unofficial worldwide club, the Underwater Wireman's Club, with members who have actually gone overboard on the leader. As far as is recorded, there have not been any fatalities, but there have been real injuries as well as near misses and potential harm. Top captains Peter Wright of Florida and Bill Edwards of Queensland, Australia, are just two who have studied the problems of their leader men and would rather have them release leader on a fish jumping away from the boat than try to hang on. They would rather use leaders of strength around a maximum 210 kg (460 lb) and chance a lost fish with broken leader than have crew pull shoulders and damage ligaments or have a man go overboard. My own membership in this club goes back to a tussle with an estimated 425 kg (935 lb) mako in Australia.

Off Port Stephens we once lost a certain world record on 37 kg (80 lb) line and a possible all-tackle record for John Kellion of Sydney when a mako of around 450 kg (1000 lb) did not fight, and came in green after only a few minutes. We thought this big shark was a white pointer but when it was alongside, mouth open so that we could see the narrow teeth, we knew it was a mako. Everything went like clockwork, the shark was gaffed twice in the mouth, and it seemed a safe capture. But with makos nothing is certain, except the potential for trouble. This one went completely berserk when the tail was lifted with a small, sharp tuna gaff. Not only did that 'sure' record break free of the gaffs in its fury to escape, but the leader man (me) suddenly went overboard like a cork popping out of a champagne bottle. The brass rubbing-strips protecting the boat side planking and gunwale were torn and twisted like steel wool in that shark's frenzy to escape. The mako did not attack me, although I landed almost on top of it. I was able to scramble back aboard with the memory of a magnificent grey-blue shape, angry black eyes and long, white, powerful teeth.

There are different problems for different line and leader materials and billfish themselves. There is

▲ Angler Gus Fay has the wire almost in reach of Mick while Bill is ready with the gaff. *Photo: Peter Goadby.*

no doubt of the dangers created by big, active fish at the boat. Crews must understand and practice how they will take and hold the wire, do their wraps, pull leader, and how and when they will release if necessary. From the angler's viewpoint, there is nothing more disappointing and annoying than to realize that at crisis time the crew can't safely carry out their function of bringing the fish into range of gaff or tag pole. Good skippers and crews know what the angler is trying to achieve with the rod and reel without the need to continually yell instructions. They realize the benefit of quiet suggestions. Similarly, good anglers know and understand what skipper and crew are trying to do, and reciprocate by keeping cool.

The captain is fish finder, navigator, electronic whiz, boat handler, engineer, meteorologist, bait watcher, decision-maker and diplomat. The crew need to always work with their skipper and assist him in carrying out his responsibilities each day. Crew responsibility starts with having gear ready, the drags, lines and knots checked, and also includes bait catching, bait and lure rigging, hook sharpening, leader taking, gaffing, chair directing, drink carrying, diplomacy and communications, while remaining happy in the job. An ability to entertain and reminisce is also a real bonus.

Part of the pleasure of big gamefishing is to watch or be part of top crew work, when the skipper uses the boat like a quarterhorse, backing up, running the fish and making it easy for the angler, while the crew are ready and competent at all stages, particularly in their moment of truth on leader, gaff or tag pole, to complete the fight. Crews must be familiar with the tackle being used. The five types of leader material used have their characteristics and problems in being taken, wrapped and put back overboard as recovered.

Leader material is usually:

• Single-strand (piano-type) wire, or carbon or stainless steel

Patrick Bowen, wire man on Captain Bristow's ▶
Avalon, experienced first hand the dangers of
wiring when a 181 kg (400 lb) black marlin took
off as he wrapped the wire to bring it close for
tagging. In the second photograph Patrick knows
he is on his way overboard unless the line frees.
The third photo shows him in the water, still
holding the wire on the jumping marlin with his
left hand. He was assisted back onto the boat
and angler Alan Cordan brought the wire back
in reach so that Patrick could again wire the
marlin, which was tagged and released by Jay.
Photos: Captain Bill Harrison.

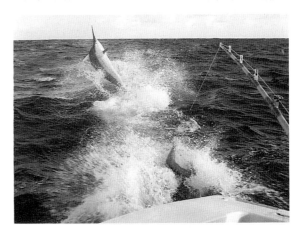

- Two twisted single-strand stainless steel wire to join a single carbon steel wire
- Multi-strand cable of stainless steel or galvanized wires
- Plastic-covered cable
- Monofilament plastic material such as nylon
- Fluoro carbon monofilament.

Chain of various types is also used in short lengths on some heavy and light tackle leaders down at the hook end.

The taking of the leader by an experienced leader man looks easy, but there are many potential problems to avoid. The wrapping of the leader around the gloved hands is the key to success in leader handling. Whoever is to take and pull leader should practice making the wraps, pulling leader and releasing, until completely familiar with the procedures.

The leader man should be ready to take the leader immediately it is within range. Once the leader is taken, the angler must ease the reel drag, put on the click or ratchet, wind the swivel to the rod tip, then lower the rod tip. The angler must be ready to move the rod clear of the wire man and be ready with the left hand to prevent an overrun or backlash if the leader man has to release the leader.

The reason for winding the swivel right to the rod tip, and the rod tip being lowered, is to minimize any possibility of the leader tangling around the neck, limbs or clothing of those in the cockpit, particularly the leader man as he moves and uses the cockpit space.

Some crew use the snap swivel to give a grip. Use of the swivel this way, however, allows the possibility that glove pressure may undo the snap.

If the snap is unclipped (and it does happen), the leader man is faced with hanging on and not releasing the leader, and often this is impossible. If it is recovered with snap undone, the snap can be closed or the wire held strongly. There is a chance of gloves touching the line, resulting in disqualification.

Of course it is possible for another person to do up the clip if time and leader distance allow. Great care must be taken to avoid a rule breach and disqualification (or line break) by touching line rather than leader. Under the IGFA fishing rules it is allowable for more than one person to pull leader, however the line must not be touched by anyone but the angler. If more than one person is pulling leader, each must be aware of what the other (or others) is (are) doing and work together. They must be extremely safety conscious and not let go without the knowledge and awareness of the others involved. The taking and pulling of leader is a time of ultimate team effort and responsibility.

The leader man, when taking the leader, should come up from under the leader with his hand positively, with the leader lying between his thumb and forefinger. (Some leader men come down from above with the right hand and from under with the left hand.) They turn their hand so the leader is wrapped around the palm of the hand. A single wrap will still slip under pressure, but even one wrap is better and more definite than any other way of pulling leader. A second wrap, the double wrap, is necessary to prevent slip. The wraps are repeated on each hand and a fish can be played by the leader man, keeping hands high and turning the body to assist as a shock absorber while recovering leader. The leader man moves about the cockpit — he is not immovable and flat footed. It is his stage and he performs with the leader and moves to allow the gaff or tag man into position for his shot and completion of the catch.

There are times when the leader must be released: to prevent breaking of the leader, or to prevent a man being pulled overboard. If a fish jumps away from the boat, or dives down like a rocket for the deep, skill, determination and cool confidence are required from the leader man. Top leader men know to maintain weight and pressure on the leader even when the gaff is in place. This continuing pull on the hook helps keep the fish under control at boatside.

This is particularly necessary when taking choked or stunned fish or quick captures. Release or easing of hook pressure can result in an explosion of power that can pull off balance those holding the fish and create danger with a fresh, green fish. A capture is usually completed with a second gaff or tail rope.

Many top gaff and tag men prefer to place the gaff or tag in the fish before its back breaks the surface of the water. It is less panicky then than when the back is above the water.

The same basic procedure is followed in tag and release. Whenever possible, the fish is brought right to boatside for safe removal of the hooks before release. If the fish is increasingly active and could be damaged by further pulling the leader, it should be cut to allow the fish to swim free even though the

▲ An Australian black marlin swims back to its cruising depth after tagging.
Photo: Greg Edwards.

hooks are still in place. The fish, if it appears to be stressed, exhausted or even dead, can be revived and resuscitated by being swum through the water for re-oxygenation until its glowing colors return. A length of heavy fishing line or light cord can be wrapped around the bill of a marlin or sailfish to allow safe towing and easy release of the fish when its color and activity show recovery. Scientific tracking has shown that fish recover from the trauma of a fight very quickly.

The leader is sometimes brought in by easy pulling, without the need for wraps. Sometimes boat and fish are already leading together for gaff or tagging. Sometimes there is a protracted tough battle; the minutes tick by in the hand-to-hand fight between leader man and super fish in a heart-stopping drama. The ability of a skilled leader man to battle a big jumping fish or a determined deep-swimming dogging fish is a critical — and dramatic — segment of the fight. Naturally, all involved hope the leader can and will be held the first time it comes into reach. Sometimes this is impossible, and the fight returns to the angler. It is for this reason that a second man must be ready for gaffing or tagging. Skipper and crew are then ready to resume the fight, particularly with big fish. On smaller fish,

either skipper or angler can safely perform the gaffing or tagging function at the moment of truth.

It is hard to be sure which performance grabs the watchers' or anglers' imagination more — the skipper on his quarterhorse in command on the flying bridge at one with the boat and the fish, or the leader man in the cockpit, face to face with his opponent.

All leader materials can be wrapped and pulled in the same way. Single-strand wire is easier than any of the other materials to free from gloves. The softer, more flexible materials tend to become embedded in the gloves and be more difficult to discard and free. For this reason, extra care must be taken with the wraps to prevent overlap and ensure that it is possible to get rid of the leader. Strong men can break most leader used, but just hanging on is not necessarily the best way of ensuring success. Top leader men resist the opportunity to bullock and may consciously choose to apply only the same weight or pressure as that previously exerted on the line by the angler. At other times they work to their maximum, their weight and strength.

Experienced skippers help the leader man by maneuvering the boat during this close-quarters

◄ A white marlin jumping on the leader. *Photo: Gil Keech.*

◀ Deborah Maddux
stands up fighting
a black marlin on
Hooker while Scott
Levin is ready for the
leader.
Photo: Jacquie Acheson

encounter. Fishing movies and videos sometimes show footage of the leader man standing, apparently casually, with one hand on the leader or in a wrap as the skipper backs the boat after a jumping fish — ready instantly for the opportunity to regain leader when the fish stops jumping and running.

In fights at close quarters, the skipper has the responsibility, the controls and the power to assist the crew and maintain safety. It is a time for quick thought, instant reflexes, and responsive boats, as well as understanding. Communication is always of top priority — with fish and boat close together.

The skipper's visibility from the bridge is much better than that of the crew at deck level. At this stage, many crew are working without their polarizing sunglasses, to minimize loss of vision from spray from flaying tails or wave tops. The removal of the glasses also eliminates another possible hazard — becoming entangled in the glasses or the holding cord. Some still wear them for protective reasons.

Crew should wear non-slip deck shoes while taking leader and gaffing; bare feet add to the possibility of slipping. On boats with twin motors, some skippers will have the motor closest to the fish idling in neutral and will maneuver with the other.

Some boats have covered foam padding around the cockpit edge, but my preference is for shaped teak that allows a firm surface for your body to work into. It is not slippery when wet, and is not cut by gaff points or other sharp implements.

Some leader men crouch to lock themselves against the coverboard, others stand upright balanced against it. They pull the wire high and swivel their shoulders and arms as shock absorbers against the active fish, ready to pull and wrap leader at every opportunity.

The leader should be held clear of the coverboard, gunwales and hull. The extra angle and pull over a hard surface could cause leader damage or a jam on high spots such as rod holders or other deck fittings.

Additional problems can be created by transom doors that are cut to open through the coverboard as well as the transom. These types of door give benefits when boarding and disembarking, when loading and unloading, but they can be a problem with big fish on the leader. If the leader slips or is pulled into the door opening, it can break or pull the wire man's hand down and off balance to jam against the immovable wood, fiberglass or aluminum of the transom. The trend for building transom doors that open in the transom coverboard as well as through

BILLFISHING

▲ Start fishing! Start fishing! Start fishing! The competing boats race to sea. *Photo: Peter Goadby*

the transom is increasing as longer and bigger boats are built. Skippers and crews are aware of this potential problem and try to maneuver the boat and position the leader man away from the problem area as much as possible, as they have to with the other problem projections created by trim tabs, outdrives, outboard motors, chum pots and even underwater propellers and rudders.

Other factors necessitate the leader being pulled and held as high and clear as possible. Hands and leader should be kept clear and above the level of the cockpit coverboard to minimize problems.

All on board should know early who is to gaff and wire or tag. This prior decision ensures minimal confusion at the critical end of the fight. Sometimes the skipper will gaff, sometimes the angler, if there is no second deckhand. Sometimes

◀ Darrell Jones brings us a new dimension and feeling on being there. *Photo: Darrell Jones.*

with a team of more than one angler, one of these will be considered of sufficient skill to gaff or tag.

Even if there is second crew, skippers are ready to leave their control station to assist and place a second gaff, meat hook or tail rope. Naturally, many skippers and crew prefer the angler and non-crew to keep clear of the cockpit at this stage. Once again, this decision must be made early and clearly understood well before crisis time. The decision is determined by safety and consideration, the experience and ability of the angler and the fishing team members or guests, and the acceptance of their competence by skipper and crew. Well-meaning but inexperienced or unskillful contributions can create rather than alleviate potentially dangerous situations and lead to the loss of fish.

The necessary clearing of the cockpit after the strike and hook-up can be assisted by others on board if this is accepted by skipper and crew. There is much to be done. The angler must get to the chair, the fish must be struck, set, harness clips attached to reel lugs either before or after the strike, and the fish fought. The other outfits must be quickly brought in, clear of the cockpit, and safety lines and leaders removed and placed so the leader cannot be washed back through the scuppers. Gaffs and tag pole and ropes must be readied, gaff points sharpened if necessary, gaff ropes cleated off securely and all potential obstructions removed from the cockpit working area. Crew should wear cutting pliers, and others should know where additional cutting pliers are placed for emergency use.

Camera persons must know and understand that they must keep clear of those working, as they can inhibit vision as well as create other possibly dangerous close-quarter encounters for themselves and others. Good photographs can be taken from up on the flying bridge with the photographer keeping clear of the captain. Video cameras can be taped in position on the safety rail, ready for action.

The skipper is responsible for:

- Safety of the boat and all on board.
- Maneuvering the boat for maximum benefit to angler and crew at all times during the fight and at boatside.
- Ensuring that the objective of gaffing and boating or tagging and releasing the fish in good condition is achieved.
- Maintaining communication with the angler to build confidence.

The crew is responsible for:

- Clearing the cockpit of rods and reels not involved in the fight, once the angler is in the chair.
- Assisting the angler into the harness ready for striking the fish or after striking the fish.
- Ensuring gaffs and ropes are ready and securely attached; blunt gaffs should be sharpened.
- Unclipping outrigger halyards clear of the coverboard and lifting them to bridge level in case of boatside jumps by the fish.

- Making sure that gloves are readied and non-slip deck shoes are worn.
- Checking pliers and cutters and making sure they are ready.
- Ensuring that tag and tag pole are ready.
- Ensuring that a meat hook, if it is to be used, is readied with a safety rope.
- Taking, wrapping and pulling leader when in reach and holding it until the fish is safely gaffed and tail roped, or tagged and leader cut.
- Deciding where and when to cut leader on release.
- Having tackle and baits or lures ready to quickly resume fishing.
- Clearing the cockpit of gaffs and ropes.

Points to remember for angler and crew:

- Talk quietly on the boat: avoid shouts or yells, particularly when fish are seen or are believed to be in the vicinity.
- Arms should not be moved around in violent gestures that can easily be seen by a shy fish. Pointing emphatically at a fish can cause it to turn away.
- The boat should be kept going ahead until the hook is properly set, then the forward way is eased off and the motors left in neutral, or the boat can be backed up to recover line. It is important for the angler to concentrate on setting the hook before he settles down to recover line. The two actions should be separate. After shortening up on line in the water, the boat should be backed up or maneuvered to one side of the fish to help the angler try to break any fighting pattern dictated by the fish.
- It is often safe to back up to initially recover line until the position of the fish can be judged. The big belly of line created by a long run and possible course of the boat may cause the hook to tear out or break off.
- If a billfish strikes slowly and shyly, the angler should allow the fish more time and line than he believes could possibly be needed for it to swallow the bait.

▲ To tag or to gaff? The crew hold a 200 kg (450 lb) blue marlin caught by Ralph Christansen Jnr on *Pescador* at St Thomas, Virgin Islands. *Photo: Captain Bill Harrison.*

- Anglers should, if possible, have previously checked reel drags against scales and thus know where to set the brake for a striking drag and then for the desired fighting strain. The pull against the scales must be made with the line running through all guides to give a true indication of the brake against the fish or the scale.
- One of the many benefits of lever quadrant reels is that the brake can be moved and reset to the desired position. The brake can be reapplied to any previous pressure. On reels with star wheels it is difficult to take advantage of pre-setting against

scales. In all cases, the angler should get the feel of the rod and desired brake to the greatest extent possible before a fish strikes.
- The striking drag should be about one-quarter to one-third the breaking strain of the line, and this may have to be eased back as the fish runs fast or jumps to the wide blue yonder. The maximum drag exerted is usually about half the breaking strain of the line until the double is on the reel, then the drag can be increased or thumb pressure can be used to take advantage of the doubled line. One-quarter strike is often chosen on light tackle and one-third on heavy tackle.

CHARTER BOATS

Charter boats and their operators make it possible for thousands of fishermen to seek billfish all over the world. The lessons learned overseas on charter boats can be applied by anglers when they return to their regular fishing areas at home. The skills and knowledge of charter boat captains and crews are invaluable, and in my experience they tend to be generous with their hard acquired knowledge.

There is a vast difference between fishing from a home port, where everything is available and familiar, and fishing far away. In addition to the problem of distance, there is the simple problem of limitations of what can be taken and carried. If charter boats are to be used, other factors need to be considered.

The following recommendations are made from long and sometimes uncomfortable experience. They are intended to reduce the stress and problems of fishing away from home. Billfishing should be a pleasurable challenge with no measures of disappointment, misunderstanding and, above all, no confrontation with anything but fish. Information, planning and elimination of possible problem areas are the key to a happy and successful trip with memories and a record of the trip.

Communication, confidence in all segments of the team and understanding of problems (ideally

◀ *Te Ariki Nui*, which has a special demountable tower, is a true long distance fishing wanderer, having taken multiple record holder Bill Hall of New Zealand twice to Australia and once to Tonga.

before they arise) are all important. Remember, too, that not all skippers and mates are familiar with your language, even if this is English — there is your English and English as it is spoken and understood by others.

In these days where many fish have high market values, the ownership of fish caught has to be established right in the beginning. There is often a chance of tension and argument when money in four or five figures suddenly becomes a factor.

A classic case of this is where a group of visiting friends and business associates charter a boat for a day's fun fishing. They have no knowledge of rules, records or the potential of the waters in which their charter boat's lures are innocently smoking and popping. Suddenly a lure disappears, the other outfits are brought in as a marlin's head wags from side to side, clear of the surface. All charterers take part in the action and pump with varying degrees of skill and results; finally the charter captain himself recovers the last few yards and gaffs the fish.

At boatside this is shown to be clearly a dream fish, huge. The marlin is too big for the regular scales and special arrangements are made to weigh it. The magnificent fish dominates its surroundings and an entrepreneur is quick to offer the charter captain a very high price for the fish if he can have it for mounting and exhibition.

The captain explains that his conditions of charter are that the fish belonged to his charterers. As the hubbub from the weighing and photographs dies away and the boat is cleaned up, the skipper asks for his charter fee. Payment is refused by the charter group because they say the captain should have known their fish might have been a record and, despite their decision to all enjoy the action on the rod, he should have made sure that only one of them did. The captain adds that if they will not pay the charter, what would they like him to do with the fish? The suggestions are uncomplimentary as well as impossible, but in essence are that it is his to dispose of. The captain smiles and accepts this, and a quick call to an entrepreneur ensures that the great fish is preserved as a reminder of what can be found from that port.

I learned a hard-won and lasting lesson in communication with charter crews. The story is worthy of retelling as it exemplifies the problems that can arise from lack of communication.

Our charter boat, skipper and crew were new to us but had a good reputation, although they were perhaps a little lacking in experience. The day started perfectly: we caught light tackle gamefish, mackerel, wahoo, some tuna — plenty for food and bait. Then we trolled for heavier tackle fish — we wanted billfish, particularly black marlin, striped marlin and sailfish. We had cobalt water, and baits and lures that worked perfectly across the warm water. The swells creamed and broke opal against the rocky headlands and golden beaches. It was a day when fins and tails could easily be seen and a bait trolled perfectly across in front of the cruising billfish's bill, a perfect day to fight. Yes, this was to be one of the days.

Trolling records turned into minutes, minutes into hours; Portuguese man-o'-war, vellella, violet snails, all confirmed what the thermometer told us — the water was right, yet still the only fins or tails were in our tiring imaginations.

Then there was a fin, blue, moving confidently, slicing the dark blue surface. Not a billfish but a mako, a big one, a certain world record on the lines we were trolling. It seemed no one else had seen it, but that didn't matter as mako course and boat course were coinciding perfectly. No need for drama of pointing, of shouted instructions; it was all going to happen without any yelling or pointing to claim what was going to be my record mako. Now the mako could be clearly seen, and the ripples and wavelets from his dorsal increased as he saw the bait crossing in front of his pointed nose as he sped up and water slicked faster off his white snaggle teeth. Now . . . but now never happened. A crash of explosions nearly lifted me off the deck as the mako submerged away from the bullets that peppered the surface near that muscular body. Gone, disappeared. The bait trolled on, untouched, its chance for fishing immortality gone. The crewman of the boat turned with a wisp of smoke still coiling lazily from the muzzle of a rifle we didn't even know was aboard. Now he yelled, 'Did you see that shark? He nearly got your bait!'

Our fault — my fault — not the deckhand's. We'd talked of billfish and gamefish to the skipper and mate, but hadn't mentioned sharks, hadn't even thought of them on a perfect trolling day in the warm current. Our crew did not know or care that it was a mako, that it would have been a record. To him it was vermin, a shark unwanted, a bait mutilator. He did what he thought was right, just what he did for other charterers, what he'd always done as a professional fisherman. When our tempers cooled down we realized it was our fault. From that day onwards we made someone fishing captain to make sure skipper and crew knew what the charterers wanted, to spend time building rapport to maximize concentration.

▲ Bill Hoey's lovingly maintained 12 m (37 ft) *Lady* is great for catching marlin at Kona, Hawaii. *Photo: Peter Goadby.*

Some points to consider:

- Cost of charter: Does the cost include food, drink, fuel and crew payment? Is payment to be made before or after the day's fishing?
- Length of fishing day, departure and return times.
- Ownership of fish caught. Anglers sometimes get upset when they find that captured fish are accepted as belonging to the crew who may sell the fish. Determine whether billfish are to be kept for mounting or tagged and released.
- Determine what weight of tackle is preferred.
- Make sure whose gear is to be used — boat's or angler's?
- Make sure that, in accordance with IGFA rules, the angler is given no illegal help in hooking his fish, even if it means that through inexperience he misses hooking up. Make sure that IGFA rules are followed at all times and that the crew understands the angler's wish to fish within the rules, including transfer of rod and reel from holder to chair gimbal, and the rules relating to live bait and cast baits.
- Be sure there is understanding that the object of the day is to release or capture one big fish or a bag of small fish.
- Everyone must understand the position of the photographer or photographic crew if there is to be one on board.
- Anglers should personally check the length of doubles and leaders, and the method of rigging on leaders, so they can't complain later. If these are not within the rules it is the angler who loses the record.
- Make sure gaffs and tail ropes are OK and within rules.
- Check on local superstitions so captain and crew are not unintentionally upset.
- Make sure that the boat and its facilities are suitable for everyone who will be going out on it.
- If tipping is customary, check to find out the standard percentage.
- Make sure that each angler will fit comfortably in the fighting chair and that the footrest or equivalent can be adjusted to suit each angler.

- Ascertain if skipper and crew traditionally tag and release all billfish, regardless of size. If you wish to keep a big fish for any reason, make sure this is understood.
- Make sure all anglers know how they are going to remove rod and reel from holders.
- Make sure the harness clips will fit the harness lugs of the reels in use.
- If anglers wish to use their own gear, it is advisable to make sure before leaving port that the rod butts will fit into rod holders and fighting chair gimbals.
- If there is difficulty in understanding between angler and crew because of language, try to find some way of overcoming this before going to sea. An interpreter may be necessary.
- Check local laws, closures and bag limits.

FIRST AID AND ACCIDENT PREVENTION

Many boats that fish offshore will carry first aid emergency kits and many skippers or crew have knowledge of emergency medical procedures. Despite this, experience has shown the benefits of the travelling fisherman carrying some simple and necessary personal medical supplies and equipment.

The sun is the old and continuing enemy of saltwater fishermen. Excessive exposure to the sun can cause headaches, heat exhaustion and the need for eye protection. Analgesics such as aspirin or other compatible medication with codeine can offset the effects of sun glare headaches; it is wise to carry your own. If heat exhaustion is likely to be a problem, salt tablets will assist in treatment and prevention.

Sunburn effects can be minimized by wearing a hat or cap with a brim, polarizing glasses, proven UV filter sunscreen or liquid, UV filter lip salve, light shirt, if necessary with long sleeves, and long trousers.

Exposure to the sun, despite these precautions, should be graduated from short spells, perhaps 20 to 30 minutes, to longer times. Of course fish will change all this with a hook-up, with fish heading into the sun on the very first day. The great number of UV water-resisting sunscreens and lip salves will save later pain and blistering. The SPF (sun protection factor) should be 15 or higher.

A liquid or cream antiseptic is beneficial for nightly application to hands or other damaged areas to minimize the possibility of infections, which can quickly arise from spines of fish or bait and line or knife cuts.

Fishermen should also carry in their kits Bandaids, sharp scissors, tweezers or a sharp knife and Lomotil. The last is useful for minimizing diarrhea caused by the changes in drinking water. A container of insect repellent is also worth having.

The fishermen's bête noire, seasickness, need no longer be a problem for most who wish to go to sea. Proven tablets such as Dramamine, Bonamine, Travacalm and Marzine are widely available, often without the need of a prescription. There is benefit in taking a tablet the night before heading to sea, then another or a half dose in the morning. The effects usually last through a day's fishing. It is worthwhile experimenting to see which brand and dose are most effective; some can cause extra drowsiness. Another product is the scopolamine patch, which lasts several days and is worn behind the ear. Some fishermen benefit from the use of wrist bands that exert pressure at key pressure locations on the wrist pulse.

The debilitating effects of seasickness and the efficiency lost because of it are unfortunate, so it is worth planning ahead to find out which is the most beneficial tablet or patch. It is too late when miles out to sea and concentration and performance are necessary for success.

Everyone going to sea should have some knowledge of mouth-to-mouth and cardio-pulmonary resuscitation (CPR). Brochures showing how to give mouth-to-mouth and CPR are readily available, so take the time to look over them. Ideally, skippers, guides or crew members should be skilled in this, just in case.

Travelling fishermen should also carry a supply of any medication they are taking for existing medical conditions.

◀ This jumping white marlin shows why marlin fishing is so exciting. *Photo: Gil Keech.*

BILLFISHING TACKLE

GENERAL SELECTION AND MAINTENANCE

A quick visual survey of airports in fishing areas shows the faith fishermen have in their own rod and reel selections, even if they are going fishing with proven professionals. Rod, reels and line are as personal in use, characteristics, dependability and familiarity as the equipment of other sportspeople.

The tackle industry is characterized by constant change and development, with manufacturers continuing to take advantage of new space-age materials.

Close examination of weigh-in photographs shows that only the fish have remained unchanged since the early days of saltwater gamefishing. Angler clothing has changed from suits and ties for men and neck to ankle length long-sleeved dresses for women to shorts and golf shirts, or even swimsuits. However, the most important difference is the tackle used. Early photographs show reels without brakes, rods with ring guides, and linen line. Later photographs show roller tips and star drags, then full rollers on the rods and lever drags on the reels. Many changes have been made in the name of progress. Some innovations have dwindled out after a short life, others have continued to evolve into the super tackle of today. Natural materials — wood, linen and simple metals — have been replaced by super-strong, lightweight, space-age materials.

◀ Fly rod entusiasists appreciate the fighting quality of sailfish. *Photo: Darrell Jones.*

It is perhaps ironic that the evolution of modern tackle has coincided with a powerful trend towards catching the saltwater gamefish on tackle other than the trolling tackle specifically developed for these big fish.

The willow wand of fly casting outfits, the short bait casting outfits and spinning outfits once expected to be seen and fished in freshwater streams and lakes are now familiar fishing tools in salt water.

Anglers used to this tackle in home fishing appreciate not only the attributes but the extra challenge and fun factor of fishing routinely with these light-tackle outfits. New space-age materials and engineering skills make this tackle tough, dependable and practical. The new materials are synonymous with strength, light weight, ease of maintenance, resistance to exposure, balance and power.

Today's anglers now have an unprecedented choice of manufacturers for whatever equipment they need. Competition in the marketplace has not only triggered the proliferation of improvements, modifications and new concepts but ensured that, in real terms, prices are lower than ever. There are still a few further developments in the flood of technological advances which seem to be nearing their peak, particularly in reels, that will benefit anglers.

Reel manufacturers now seem to understand that brake materials should allow the spool to roll smoothly under pressure of the brake material, that reels should weigh as little as possible yet be super strong, that reel spools must not burst or distort under line pressure and that the spool should have sufficient capacity. PENN use aluminium.

The perceived need for reels a size bigger than makers' recommendations or numbering varies in different fisheries, even in the same country. Skilled anglers who use a reel a size bigger than recommended are conscious of these benefits:

- Smoother drag with line pulling from high on the spool.
- Increased line capacity to cope with long run of fish and boat maneuvering.
- Adequate line length after line is shortened to remove abrasion, rubs or sun exposure.
- Cooler brake temperature from bigger brake area.
- Faster line recovery with bigger spool diameter.
- More comfortable fast winding.
- New rods have quality characteristics that benefit performance and dependability in excess of their price tag.

Those who balance the reel size and manufacturer's line recommendation believe they will not need a longer length of line. They appreciate the lighter weight and perceived maneuverability of the smaller and lighter reels. Stand-up fishermen may use the smaller reels for their chosen line classes. The extreme variability of chosen line classes for a particular reel size makes it difficult for manufacturers to produce reels with a brake range and capacity to suit all needs.

There is now an increasing range of reels with two or even three gear-speed selections. The multi-gear variable speed reels have positive gear changes that give the double benefit of a fast recovery ratio of 4.9 or higher, or low gear ratio of 1.1 to gradually lift and force the deep-swimming or tail-wrapped fish back towards the surface. Heavy tackle reels may have ratios of 2.2–1 and 1.1.

The benefit of new materials in brakes, spools and frames is evidenced in smooth casting and hard fishing. The new reinforced plastics and lightweight metals are featured in bait casting, trolling, spinning and fly reels.

Manufacturers of the fixed-spool spinning reel have turned this reel design, once chosen mainly for its convenience in non-line twisting and non-overrunning casting with lures of all weights, into a practical offshore fishing tool. The top-of-the-range spinning reels now meet the needs and demands of fishing for saltwater gamefish. Spinning reels that stand up to the rigors and perform well for line classes up to 10 kg (22 lb) are available in several brands with line rollers of non-grooving metal that roll readily as line is retrieved or stripped by the fish. Spinning reels are ideal and used extensively for casting live baits to sailfish and other lighter-weight billfish, PENN have one for 15 kg (30 lbs).

High-performance saltwater fly reels are essential. Saltwater gamefish are unrelenting opponents that quickly and frustratingly find any weakness in tackle. Once again several manufacturers offer dependable fly reels with sufficient line back-up capacity, balanced casting in light weight, with smooth braking capabilities and all necessary features to overcome saltwater species.

Rods for all fishing categories — fly, spinning, bait casting, jigging, high-speed spinning, live bait casting, stand-up trolling and conventional trolling — are built from modern materials to give the desired performance.

Rod blank design, handle and butt design all reflect the skill of rod blank designers and manufacturers who are aware that rods have to perform several functions. If used for casting they have to deliver the lures the required distance in addition to acting as springs against the power and jolts of the fish, and also be a lever to lift during line retrieval.

Trolling rods are the simplest in terms of performance functions, with saltwater fly rods the most diverse. Trolling rods are now finished with improved roller guides; other rods have efficient, cool, non-grooving ring guides, also used on some light trolling rods.

General points for tackle maintenance

- Rod should suit personal choice and be of top quality.
- Spinning reel rollers must roll freely and not be grooved.
- Check all line-bearing surfaces for nicks and grooves.
- Tackle should be within IGFA published specifications.
- Regular maintenance and inspection of rollers and ring guides is necessary in case of wear.
- With lever drag reels, pulling line from the tip with rod deflected and a spring scale will show the poundage at *Strike* and *Free spool*. The desired drag can be obtained with pre-set.
- Choose the best reels you can afford. Low-quality reels make the landing of record fish difficult.
- Perform regular maintenance and cleaning on all equipment.
- Use a reel a size larger than the maker's recommendation for line capacity.
- Drag must be smooth, not jerky.
- Handle should be lightly oiled to turn freely.
- Line should be laid on evenly.
- Check drag often while waiting for a strike in case the brake has increased with the heat of the day, has been accidentally altered while sitting in the rod holder or has been affected by flying spray or vibration.
- Make sure the reel is tight on the reel seat.
- Replace worn or aged sections of line, particularly near terminal tackle.
- Use double line if conditions allow, to gain maximum knot strength.
- Pull all knots and plaits tight and even after lubrication.
- Make sure knots and plaits will pass through guides.
- Use dental floss to over-bind and prevent slip.
- Make sure double line is even before and after swivel is attached.
- Test lines for breaking strain before using.

New materials, new shapes and the designers' recognition of how rods are used against fish power and deep sounding are evident in the straight and curved aluminum butts for trolling rods of all tip lengths. Slightly offset trigger grip bait casting rod handles, rather than the once mandatory pistol grips, are growing in availability and popularity. These longer, almost straight butts are comfortable and effective in casting, while giving tremendous benefit for fighting, with butt along and under the holding arm or with butt comfortably on the chest.

In every fighting category modern materials provide performance in all facets of use. Rods that are light in the tip to deliver the fly, the lure or the small live bait, but which have maximum lifting and holding power, are readily available.

Lines have always been critically important, and naturally the break point in saltwater gamefishing.

Again, manufacturers consider the characteristics they and the customers want in their product. Stretch and elasticity make the line more forgiving. Stiff lines may wear longer but not sit tightly on the reel spool. Soft, limp lines cast well, but some do not wear well. Some fishermen prefer thin-diameter lines that allow greater yardage on the spool, while others look for thicker-diameter lines because they believe this minimizes line wear. For offshore trolling fishermen seek hard-wearing lines which sit close and tight on reel spools.

Color of line is a factor that generates debate among fishermen. They want the line to be of minimum visibility up to the time the fish is hooked, then need maximum visibility for the skipper, guide and angler following the hooked fish. Some fishermen choose fluorescent colors, others prefer clear or very soft pink, blue-grey or

CHARACTERISTICS OF FISHING LINE MATERIALS

ADVANTAGES	DISADVANTAGES
Braided Dacron	
• Minimum stretch.	• Individual fine strands are easily cut or abraded to appreciably reduce breaking strain.
• Can be joined by proven splices or plaits.	
• Line readily visible to skipper and crew.	• Subject to wear in outrigger clips.
• Packs well on to reel spool under angler and fish pressure.	• Breaking strain reduces from exposure to sun.
	• More visible to fish.
	• Can be burnt if carelessly wound on too fast with a dry glove.
Spectra Material	
• Incredibly strong for minimal diameter.	• Knots are likely to slip, and care must be taken to slide knots together by wetting or wax.
• 60 kg (130 lb) lines of this material are of similar diameter to 15 kg (30 lb) test in older braided line.	• Slip can be minimized by completing knots with 60 second super glue or rubber adhesive.
• Stretch (a characteristic that helps in hook-up).	
• Sink in the water without heavy lead.	
Monofilament nylon	
• Minimum visibility to fish.	• More stretch than braided line.
• Can be joined with proven knots and plaits.	• Greater diameter than braided lines of equivalent nominal and starting breaking strain.
• Generally more resistant to abrasion, and high breaking strain maintained despite surface cuts.	
• Visibility can be improved with fluorescent color.	
• Choice of knots where Bimini twist or plaits are suitable in attaching leaders and hooks.	

green or white. Others prefer dark shades of these colors or even black.

Trolling lines are another area of divergent opinion. Advocates of braided line recognize the benefits of minimum stretch and lighter bags of line created by circling fish. Others, however, believe that the long wearing nature of mono-filament line and its ability to withstand abrasions and nicks outweigh the disadvantages of stretch and the resulting bags of line in the water. It is possible to combine the best characteristics of braided and monofilament lines by using the low stretch braided line with hard-wearing monofilament line for the last 50 meters (55 yards). The new Spectra super lines open up a whole new range of benefits and choice.

Discussions about the desirable characteristics of a line are logically influenced by rod characteristics. Rod blanks of exotic materials such as boron, graphite, kevlar and S-glass have inherent lifting power that offsets line stretch. All factors of use must be considered, as there are many line products on the market. It is a basic premise that good line does not cost, it saves. Fishermen in tropical areas in particular must consider the damaging effect of ultra-violet rays from the sun. Some line brands and colors are more quickly affected by the sun and salt than others.

Some brands of line consistently test higher or lower than the breaking strain shown on the labels. This can cause lost fish and lost records. Careful fishermen — those who seek and hope for records — use known and pre-tested line and re-test their purchase before filling reels.

Hook makers offer a wide choice of designs to give fishermen a product to suit their intended fishing. Hooks are available in different shapes, thicknesses and types of steel. Hooks that are not kirbed or offset are used with trolled soft or hard head lures and baits. Offset hooks are used to improve the odds of a firm hook-up in drifting baits. Short shank offset or non-offset hooks are used in live baiting sailfish or small marlin, where minimizing visibility is a major consideration.

Hook points must be sharp and strong, otherwise they will not penetrate. Hooks must be sharpened and re-sharpened before use, without removing so much metal that they bend or break. No hook is sharp enough straight out of the box. There is wide divergence of opinion of the advantages and disadvantages of hook designs and shapes, but when it comes to stainless or non-stainless some fishermen swear by one or the other. Others swear about them. Consideration is also given to which metal is best for the fish once released. The Norwegian hook maker Mustad has now released a hook that will corrode quickly in released fish. This company makes trolling hooks of various designs as well as hooks for drifted and live baits. The excellent trolling designs and other

hooks of the French company VMC are also popular, as are the live bait and other trolling hooks of American-made Wright McGill Eagle Claw hooks. Live bait hooks are made in a red finish.

The points of double and treble hooks used on lures must also be sharpened before and between use. Files, sharpening stones and electric hook sharpeners are all effective.

Visibility to the fish is always a factor to be considered. Black finish swivels minimize the chance of non-strike by the sought-after fish as well as the possibility of cutoff by unwanted razor-gang wahoo, mackerels and barracuda attracted by shine and movement. Ball-bearing swivels with coast lock snap are usually chosen for lure trolling, and crane swivels, again with coast lock snap, in other fishing where swivels are useful. Waterproof marking pens can be used on hook points and barbs to resist rusting after sharpening. Available in black or a variety of colors, this finish works well, lasts and can easily be applied and refinished.

Gaff hook points should also be kept sharp to ease penetration. The choice of gaff lies between fixed head gaffs and flying gaffs. Flying gaffs are used on marlin over 100 kg (220 lb). Fixed-head gaffs are successfully used on gamefish under these weights. Fixed-head gaffs are easier to use than flyers, as some people have problems holding both the rope and handle and retrieving the handle.

Heavy cane, as used in furniture, is ideal for gaff handles. It combines flexibility with sufficient rigidity. The fish-holding ability of fixed-head gaffs can be improved by attaching a light rope from around the gaff hook and along the handle. A loop on this rope assists crew holding on to an active fish. Release gaffs, fixed-head, short-handled and fixed-head gaffs are placed through the fish's lower jaw to hold it while the fly or lure is removed.

The increasing use of curved-butt trolling rods has polarized the choice of harness designs. Seat-

and kidney-type harnesses are needed to maximize the benefits of curved butts, while shoulder and combined shoulder and kidney harnesses are used with straight butts and in stand-up fishing.

Rod belts are a necessity for comfort and performance in stand-up fishing. Several designs take the length of rod butt and tip into consideration, as well as giving necessary protection and practicality while pumping and fighting the fish.

It is difficult for today's anglers to visualize the high degree of maintenance needed with past tackle: natural material lines that had to be wound off and dried after fishing and wet before use to provide maximum breaking strain; guides that could chip, fracture or groove; rods that could delaminate under pressure; reels that required almost daily stripping and service; brakes that became so hot that brake materials bonded and choked up; fly lines that required regular applications for desired performance; rod finishes that deteriorated in the sun and needed touch-ups on chips or fractures that allowed water into the cane or wood; wooden butts that also needed treatment to exclude damaging water; and wire leaders that had to be checked for corrosion or crystallization and discarded before fishing.

Even though today's tackle no longer requires the high rate of maintenance of the past, it does need regular attention as follows:

- Rods benefit from a daily wiping with fresh water.
- Roller guides should be checked and if necessary freed and lubricated to ensure that the rollers roll; older-type rollers should be checked for loose screws. If necessary, locking of screws can be ensured by application of nail polish.
- Reel brakes should be checked for smoothness, particularly after a fight or after heavy wetting from spray.
- Reels should be wiped with fresh water — not hosed or dunked — then wiped with an oiled cloth. Some anglers prefer to store reels with the drag fully on to inhibit moisture; others prefer the reels in free spool to ease tension on drags.
- Lines should be checked for wear and nicks, particularly where held in outrigger releases or rubber bands, and replaced if necessary.
- Lines should be run out for at least 90 meters (100 yards) behind the boat at speed to remove twist from the day's trolling. The top 45 meters (50 yards) should be taken from the line every day, depending on use, and the line redoubled.

◀ The gin pole on port side of the Hatteras' *Duchess* is another way of bringing fish inboard.
Photo: Peter Goadby.

HOOK TYPES

KIRBED OFFSET POINT HOOKS	STRAIGHT HOOKS	GENERAL POINTS TO REMEMBER FOR HOOKS:
• Whole drifting baits, where hook is embedded in the side of bait.	• Whole trolled fish baits where bait swims and hook is not embedded or is embedded in throat.	• Keep hooks sharp.
• Live baits trolled slowly for short distances.		• Do not file or grind hooks so far that the point is weakened, as it may break instead of driving home.
• Drifting strips.	• Trolled lures.	• Remove rust, but do not discard hooks just because the cadmium or zinc plating has worn off — brown hooks can be effective, particularly with shy fish.
• Bay of Islands rig.	• Whole fish bait in Panama Bimini live-bait style with hook on top of head.	
• All live baits and whole fish or fish cut for use when drifting or at anchor.	• Trolling baits on bridle.	• Check the eye of the hook where the leader wire will cause wear.
	• Live baits trolled for long distance.	• If fish are shy, use smaller, lighter hooks.
• Double rigs where only point and barbs are projecting.	• Trolling fish or squid baits with hook embedded.	• Paint or color live bait hooks so they are minimally visible.
	• Strip baits.	• Keep points free of baits or lures so that they do not choke back in the bait or tangle in the skirt.

- Monofilament leaders should be checked for wear, tooth marks and rubs.
- Lines should have a top shot regularly to replace worn line.
- Wire leaders, including the short length of wire in two hook rigs, should be checked for fracture and crystallization.
- Knots and plaits should be checked.
- Double lines and the top length of line should be checked and replaced regularly with a new line 'top shot' of monofilament or braided line.

Apart from line addition or replacement, or reel stripping to clean and smooth the reel brake, none of this routine maintenance is major or time consuming. The short time spent in common-sense maintenance each day helps to ensure a subsequent successful, enjoyable capture or tag and release. Preparation and maintenance allow for happy and successful fishermen with minimum worries and problems.

GAFFS

Gaffs should always be kept sharp. Points can be protected by a cork or a few centimeters (an inch or so) of hose or plastic tube. Heavy gaffs should be reinforced with a second welded rod to minimize the chance of straightening on big powerful fish. Gaffs in various sizes should be carried on board ready for instant use. The perfect gaff complement is: two flying gaffs from 30 cm (12 in) down to 20 cm (8 in); two fixed gaffs with 12.5–15 cm (5–6 in) bite; and two small, fixed gaffs, about 7.5–10 cm (3–4 in) bite. A large 60 cm (24 in) diameter landing net is a great help in landing small gamefish that are to be kept alive and undamaged. Strong spring clips are ideal for holding gaffs in position, ready for instant use, on cockpit sides or upright from cockpit deck to flying bridge. Large-size shark hooks, with or without barb, make satisfactory gaff hooks. The kirb or offset in the shark hook should be bent back so that point and shank are in line. These are for smaller gamefish.

HOOK AND GAFF MATERIALS

ADVANTAGES	DISADVANTAGES
STAINLESS	
Clean, corrosion resistant.	Can be bent, twisted and straightened more
Medium strength for diameter.	easily than carbon steel.
Can be sharpened to excellent points and	Point subject to bending.
cutting edges.	Rusts and corrodes.
CARBON STEEL	
Maximum strength for diameter.	Some carbon steel of high strength may break
Can be sharpened to excellent points and	rather than bend or flex.
cutting edges.	
Holds edges and points.	

FLY FISHING TACKLE

Fly-fishing is a fast-growing method of fishing, combining the thrill of hunting and sight fishing with the skill and technique of casting, hooking and fighting the fish on slender rod and fragile line class tippets. The shock tippet allowed by IGFA rules is 30.48 cm (12 in), and the tippet breaking strain classes are 1 kg (2 lb), 2 kg (4 lb), 4 kg (8 lb), 6 kg (12 lb), 8 kg (16 lb) and 10 kg (20 lb). Class tippets must be at least 38.10 cm (15 in) inside the knots.

Rods range from those that would be used for trout with No. 8 line to powerful fish tamers used with No. 12 line. The appropriate reel is a single-action carrying 275 meters (300 yards) of braided Dacron backing and 31 meters (100 ft) of monofilament backing. Saltwater fly fishing is a difficult challenge given the allowable length of shock tippet and the use of only fixed-head gaffs, as prescribed by the tackle regulations.

The fly fisherman needs to be completely familiar with a selection of knots that can be made quickly and safely. Various types of knots are used in leaders. The thinking fly fisherman carries spare leaders, ready for replacement, as well as a selection of flies. As with all fishing, the hooks must be needle sharp. It is always difficult to set hooks in the tough mouths of fish, but with the willow

wands of fly rods designed to cast flies the problem is increased. Those seeking billfish on fly know that the short length of shock or rub-resistant leader is often the vulnerable link in the chain between angler and fish. The drag and brakes and capacity of the modern saltwater fly reels give anglers a chance with heavy fish.

The design and materials of modern fly rods allow the angler to fight big fish aggressively. Master fly fisherman Lefty Kreh stresses the need for preparation, familiarity with knots, a tight loop to offset the effect of the wind, holding the rod high so the line will clear rough patches on the sea bottom, great care with jumping fish, bowing, and dropping the rod tip with jumping fish or those changing direction fast on the surface. He stresses the need for practice in casting and fishing to gain instinctive and complete familiarity with the tackle once the fish are found.

Buck fever is a natural problem for all fishermen; however, with fly fishing the margins for mistake are minimal even with wire or heavy monofilament shock leaders. Nylon-covered wire is popular for shock leaders.

SPINNING TACKLE

It is doubtful whether the innovative thinkers and engineers who invented today's spinning reel ever thought that it would be used for billfish. It has become a versatile and practical piece of fishing equipment used by novices and master anglers alike.

Spinning tackle, based on the egg beater, ranges from ultra-lightweight, balanced outfits for small and lightweight species right through to the heavy outfits designed to cast lures and live baits and to battle billfish. They are also used in jigging.

A double line and leader combination meeting IGFA saltwater or freshwater tackle regulations, combined with a wide range of lure types and weights, ensures the popularity of these multi-purpose outfits. As with other tackle, fish teeth dictate use of wire, with practiced use of monofilament in other species. Double line is of benefit in knots, and in saltwater species may be wound on the reel spool. In some fisheries powerful, high-capacity spinning reels have replaced overhead casting reels for casting live baits to billfish.

Reels are now made in tough, long-lasting construction to withstand the needs of rugged fishing. Naturally, as with other reel types, the more practical long-life, tough fishing tools are more expensive than those of lower cost and often similar in appearance.

Rods used for live bait rock fishing for billfish are a compromise between a surf or spinning rod and a trolling rod. The reels used are top-quality, big-fish lever drag trolling reels that have to give the same standard of performance, or even better, on land as they do on boats. The roller guide rods have the same basic characteristics of length action and tip as overlength trolling rods of around 2.4 m (8 ft). The extra length, although giving the fish extra mechanical advantage, is helpful in keeping line clear of the rocks. Live baits are cast out by hand or by the rod to a position where wash and current will take bait and float out in deeper water. Small, sliding breakaway floats or sometimes a balloon are practical floats for the live baits.

High-speed overhead casting or in some locations spinning reels give active fishermen a chance at pelagic species as the gamefish move close to rocky shores, sometimes singly or in small schools, sometimes in big active schools. Conventional surf rods are satisfactory in combination with the high-speed retrieval reels. This fishing gives a new dimension to action. Long gaffs and great care and watchfulness are

◀ John Donnell, ready for a flurry of jumping from this Costa Rican sailfish, applies maximum pressure. *Photo: Darrell Jones.*

also necessary for the capture of pelagic gamefish from the immovable rocks.

The first star drag offshore reels were made for W. Boschen of California after he landed the first broadbill on rod and reel in 1913. The star drag quickly became the standard brake against fish of all species and size.

In the early 1930s fishermen and engineers acknowledged that there must be a better drag or brake. New concepts appeared in Mitchell Henry, on Fin Nor and on Kovlosky reels. After World War II the concept of lever drag reels with brakes that could be preset was accepted. Penn Reels, who had produced the star drag work horses since the 1930s, were active in meeting the demand for lever drag and two speed reels.

The power and dogged fight of saltwater gamefish have forced constant improvements in saltwater trolling reels. A few years ago only Fin Nor in their 12/0 size manufactured a gear-changing trolling reel, although manufacturers had experimented in the 1930s. The gear-changing feature gives anglers the benefit of 2:1 ratio for fighting fish near the surface as well as for fast line recovery, and 1:1 for turning and lifting and changing direction of deep stubborn fish. Fin Nor now have gear-changing reels to suit light as well as heavy tackle, plus a special model 12/0 with three gear options.

Penn Reels and Shimano also have a range of two-speed gear-changing trolling reels. Lever drag reels with large, smooth brake areas are available in these three brands plus those of Daiwa, Abu, Mitchell, Everol, Gladiator, Olympic, Hardy, Duel, Policansky and other makes.

Penn were the first with wide spools to meet the need in some fishing situations for extra line capacity. Anglers also meet the need for increased line length by using a reel a size bigger than that designed by the maker.

The pre-set feature on the lever drag trolling reels gives anglers the chance to set the drag or brake to the desired poundages before starting fishing by pulling against a spring scale either straight from the spool or through the rod. Adjustment by the pre-set allows the necessary brake or strike and full drag positions. The lever brake design allows the angler to return the brake to a previously selected position after being backed off or increased as necessary.

With fly and spin fishing, practice is necessary to improve casting accuracy and lure presentation as well as in line recovery. On trolling reels, practice will help you become familiar with pre-set brake, winding and pumping action. If fishing charter boats have unfamiliar reels, then a familiarization session with the tackle is a top priority. Practice at home on the patio, with line attached to a heavy chair, is beneficial.

LURES

Trolling lure fishing for billfish often adds to the feeling of challenge. There is extra satisfaction in successfully fishing for the peak ocean predators on manmade lures. Lure making is itself an achievement; attracting and catching billfish on them is doubly difficult. The quest for saltwater gamefish on lures instead of natural or live baits is as old as fishing itself.

The development of space-age synthetic materials in the last 50 years, plus the knowledge of the where, how and why of successful lure fishing, has brought it to its peak of universal acceptance. Today's and tomorrow's world of plastics, colors and non-corrosive metals has opened a Pandora's box for those who fish with lures.

Modern, adequately stocked tackle stores, as well as specialist stores, offer the angler an apparently bewildering collection of lures, some of which are designed to attract fishermen as well as fish. Fishermen are attracted to lures like iron filings to a magnet. We keep on acquiring, making and buying lures hoping that maybe, just maybe, here at last is the lure that is *the* one, the lure that is irresistible to fish.

The ingredients for success with lures are mostly the same as for success with natural baits. Simply fishing with proven lures is no substitute for research, preparation and knowledge. Success with lures comes from fishing where the fish should be, knowing which species to seek, how big they should be and when action is most likely.

Lures are fished in all levels of the water column from surface to bottom. Lure fishing can consist of trolling, casting, jigging, sight fishing, or raising fish unseen from the deep. Lures range from those presented on slender fly tackle to the stump pullers on 60 kg (130 lb) class trolling tackle. The tackle range and type meets the size and power of fish of most species and weight. In fact, a bigger spectrum, a wider potential of species and habitat is possible than exists in bait fishing.

Saltwater lure fishing on all tackle gives the additional satisfaction that the great gamefish are responding to manmade rather than natural creations. To this must be added the satisfaction that comes in fishing with lures which give the fish every chance, not only because of a possible reduced hook-up rate but because the fish may throw the lure, beating man once again. The growth and refinements of all tackle have been part of the lure fishing explosion. On fly, bait casting, spinning, jigging and trolling tackle, lures have accompanied the move for anglers to use much of the same types of tackle they are familiar with in their freshwater fishing.

Florida and Hawaii have long been the universities and trendsetters of successful lure fishing. Each is a leader in certain techniques. Florida leads the way in light tackle of all kinds, particularly fly, jigging, bait casting and spinning, the basic tackle designed and evolved for freshwater use. The rigors and demands of saltwater fishing have forced the evolution of beefed-up tackle so fishermen have a chance with the fish. These developments give more fishermen the chance to enjoy the challenge of saltwater fishing and the pleasure that comes from skillful use of lures, tackle and line that by their lightness and lack of bulk give action and activity for anglers, even those with disabilities. Satisfaction is derived from finding the fish and getting action not only where the angler or the captain figured the fish would be, but in seeing the fish and getting a strike and hook-up.

Judicious use of natural and artificial teasing is part of modern lure fishing, particularly in saltwater fly and bait casting and spinning. The challenge of billfish and other big saltwater species has brought much of the world together in the quest for big fish on all tackle types.

Hawaii is to offshore lure trolling what Florida, the Caribbean and Central America are to casting lures. The development of lures as a deliberate first choice rather than a poor cousin to baits for the oceanic pelagics has been centered in Hawaii. From these jewels of the ocean, lure trolling has spread into the skilled live-bait areas of the world — the Caribbean hot spots of Bimini, Walker's Cay, Puerto Rico, St Thomas and Venezuela. It is popular from California and Baja California and other Mexican areas to Australia, New Zealand, Tahiti and Fiji in the Pacific, and Mauritius in the Indian Ocean. The offshore world is now a world of lures.

The names associated with saltwater lures are often those of the captains who developed and used them. Zane Grey, a master angler in all waters, was a skilled fly caster; he recognized the value of flashy action and teasing in salt water. He combined some of the benefits of lures in his teasers, which were lures without hooks; he placed his hooks in carefully rigged natural baits. The availability of modern plastics might have finally ensured Zane Grey's transition from hookless teaser to lures with hooks.

The casting and trolling lures used for light gamefish and with bait casting and spinning tackle are metal spoons and minnows that travel below the surface, usually at low speeds, or surface poppers and chuggers. Some spoons, such as Drone 3½, can be trolled fast for small billfish around reefs and in open water.

LURES

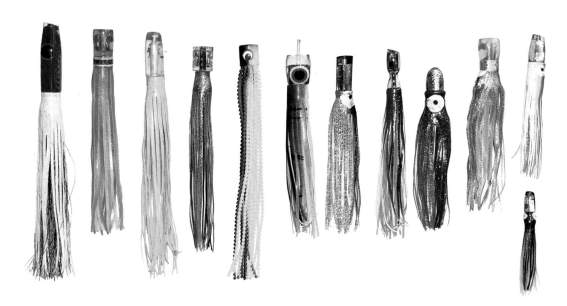

▲ Smaller plastic trolling lures work well on sailfish and marlin. The Sadu Frehm lure on the left uses stranded material with a molded outside skirt in a successful marlin lure. The others by Pakula, Sevenstrand, C&H, Moldcraft, R&S, Marlin Magic, Doornob, Gary Eoff, Top Gun and other makers around the world are ideal for sailfish. *Photo: David Rogers*.

▲ Hard plastic trolling lure heads have either parallel or almost parallel sides to which skirts may be glued or, as in the popular Hawaiian makes, two tapered ridges to which the skirts may be slipped inside out and tied in position. Both types of cast heads allow for skirt replacement after mangling by toothy critters. *Photo: David Rogers*.

The Australian-designed lures and some of the big Rapala bibless, high-speed lures can be trolled at up to 18 knots. Both types of minnow are available in a range of sizes.

Lures are also integral to the capture of small tunas, mackerel and similar species for use as bait for trolling, either dead or alive.

Both trolling and casting lures come in a big range of colors, so local advice should be sought for best results.

The blue water churns opal and white as the boat hull creates a propeller wash that gradually disappears back into the rest of the ocean. The propeller wash and turbulence are flanked by four or five white lines of bubbles. The boat seems to be just travelling because of its speed of 8 to 10 knots, but this boat is fishing, marlin fishing, not travelling. Those bubble trails stream from flashing lures, lures that attract and trigger action in marlin and tuna.

The locality of this scene, once synonymous primarily with Hawaii, could now be at any of the world's proven marlin fishing grounds. The boat and lures could be found off southern Queensland and New South Wales in Australia, New Zealand, Tahiti, Cabo San Lucas, Mexico, Mauritius or anywhere in the Indian and Pacific Oceans' warm waters. The same scene is repeated day after day at Walker's Cay and Bimini in the Bahamas and on the east coast of the US from Florida to New York, in the Azores, the Ivory Coast of Africa and to Madeira.

The 1980s saw the spread of artificial trolling lures from Hawaii to fishing grounds wherever anglers seek marlin. There have been surprising benefits from the change from natural baits to artificial lures, the 'fantastic plastics'. The benefits of lure fishing have become evident as anglers and crews change from natural to artificial baits. The benefits show in the number and size of the marlin tagged and released, or verified on the weigh station.

Advantages of trolling with lures for billfish:

- Increase in fishing time, as no time is wasted catching and rigging baits. Just run out pre-rigged lures when water temperature and sea bed configuration indicate worthwhile fishing. Prior to this the boat can travel as fast as practical until natural indications say 'fish'. Even at high speed, two or three high-speed, bullet-shaped lures can be run to give hook-ups at 20 knots or more.

- Increase in length of season. Results from lure fishing boats have proved that good fishing is available for longer periods than before, and have indicated that the chance to take marlin, particularly striped and big blues, is there on a year-long basis.

- Easier rigging. It has been shown that more people can adequately and competently choose and rig proven lures than could skillfully rig baits. Lures last longer and do not fall to pieces while trolling (although of course lures as well as baits are vulnerable to the cutting choppers of the marine razor gang).

- Lures add variety in speed, color and action. Enjoy the excitement and visual action of marlin following, to strike and strike again.

- Lure fishing gives an immediate chance for repeat action, as the successful lure pattern can be quickly formed again.

- From the beginning, teasers were an integral ingredient in raising marlin to the baits. Lures retain those benefits — they are teasers with hooks. The challenge of teasing a fish into striking, of being part of the hook-up, is just as intense as bait fishing.

- There is every probability that a marlin hooked on a lure will be in better condition for release than one that has swallowed natural bait.

- Tag and release can be carried out as effectively on lure-hooked marlin as on those of natural bait hook-ups.

- Lure fishing in many areas produces heavier fish than those taken on bait. Cairns is of course an exception at this stage but here, too, marlin up to 455 kg (1000 lb) are taken or released on lures each year with some boats operating spectacularly with lures.

- The greater speed at which lures are trolled allows more territory to be covered, more potential attractants trolled and presented to more marlin.

Offshore fishermen are fortunate that they have the ready opportunity of acquiring and using proven lures either made locally or imported from successful lure makers to give the very best action and color combinations available. Many tackle store staff are knowledgeable and experienced in recommending what is working and suitable for various boats and in rigging.

Theoretically, skilled lure makers could reproduce the same lure to give the same results in endless repetition. Unfortunately this is not the case as, despite every care in the manufacturing process of heads and skirts, there is slight variation in the combination. The changes could come in the curing rate that affects the final shape of the lure, in the position of the tube insert, and in the thickness and length of the skirts. Then, of course, there is the possible difference in the rigging of hooks. For all these reasons successful fishermen zealously guard their 'hot' lures — those that attract fish and action.

IGFA Vice President Dudley Lewis long recognized these factors with decades of successful lure fishing in his home waters of Hawaii. Once he found a lure that worked in a particular position on his boat *Leimalia*, that lure was used on the same rod and reel and went back to that proven position day after day.

History shows that this paid off as that one lure was successful each day on the same rod and old Penn Senator reel to win the prestigious Hawaiian International Billfish Tournament for his team. That lure, a Joe Yee salt and pepper (ground shell on black) straight runner, took all their tournament fish. The lure was lost eventually to a monster marlin and, despite trying other lure heads that

appeared identical in every way, Dudley did not find another that was as dependable and hot.

Many fishermen have recorded similar experiences. They go through the sickening trauma of their special lure being lost through a mistake, carelessness, or to fish that were too big or broke away for some reason.

Some fishermen run a variety of colors and head shapes every day. They fish darker-colored lures on dark, cloudy days and lighter colors on bright, sunny days. Some change their colors in changing light or, if not getting action, hoping for a jackpot. Others stick to their proven positions and colors.

Brookes Morris, the fighter pilot who became a thinking fisherman and lure maker with his radically shaped Doornob lures, fished both the KHBT and the HIBT in 1987. His team were defending HIBT champions from 1986 and they realized that it was all or nothing on the last day if they were to retain their HIBT crown. Fishing from big fish captain Freddy Rice's *Ihu Nui*, they gambled on the color combination that had produced most fish for them in these tournaments. To win or get a place they needed several average marlin on those lures or one really big lunker that with the bonus points for heaviest of the day, heaviest of the tournament, plus bonus points for a 24 kg (50 lb) test, would top the 337 kg (742 lb) fish already landed by the great Hawaiian lure maker, Joe Yee, on 24 kg (50 lb) tackle.

It all happened for the team on *Ihu Nui* when a giant blue grabbed one of those five identical lures and took off into the air like a loaded jet airliner. This marlin was big enough, but perhaps too big for the 24 kg (50 lb) tackle. Angler Gil Kraemer, skipper, crew and team worked in copybook fashion for the capture. The spontaneous applause from the spectators at the weigh station told the story that here was a really big fish. It weighed in at 481.94 kg (1062½ lb), the heaviest of the tournament, and scored not only the necessary tournament points but a still-standing world record — who says the great ocean marauders do not eat plastic? Here again was a marlin that for whatever reason found the color, the action, the sound, the vibration, the fizzing bubbles irresistible.

Bubbles — the smoke trail — are one of the features of lure action that billfish fishermen look for. Many choose lures that pop the surface about every thirty seconds, that run fairly straight and produce the smoke trail. Many shapes and color combinations regularly produce. Some heads are scooped (to create dart and dive), some are angled (straight runners), some are straight cut (pushers), some have jet holes, some have bullet noses, some are weighted, some are unweighted. Success comes from using well-rigged lures and running them in a pattern to suit the boat. Eyes in the lure head or on the skirt are regarded as worthwhile. Some riggers even skirt their lures with skirts that have eyes, even though the lure head already has eyes on the insert or the insert is all eyes.

It is interesting that generally in the Atlantic the lure riggers and successful lure fishermen use the heavier, stiffer-type skirts similar to those made by Moldcraft and Newell, whereas in the Pacific and Indian Ocean fisheries the softer Sevenstrand and Japanese Yamashita and Yozuri skirts are most popular. There is of course much mixing of preference for lure skirts, and some mix both types and upholstery materials. The length of the skirt once on the lure also varies with personal preference and the action sought. Tangling of the skirt on the barb of the second hook can be avoided by cutting the tails so that they clear the point of the second hook. Characteristically long-wearing plastic upholstery material has maintained its popularity over the years. It is a popular skirt material, particularly for the outer skirt in Hawaii and Madeira.

Australians are fortunate to have several proven and skilled lure makers scattered around the coast to provide top fish takers. Pakula, Top Gun and Pacific brands as well as many copyists of these successful local and overseas designs give plenty of choice. The Australian-made lures as well as the Joe Yee, Guzman, Sadu, Black Bart, C&H, R&S, Schneider, Moldcraft, Lock Nut, Gary Eoff, Marlin Magic, Doornob, Sevenstrand and Braid give an almost bewildering selection of quality products from which fishermen can choose.

Successful color combinations vary, depending on light conditions and sea conditions, the boat wave pattern and position of the windows (the smooth unbroken surface in the boat wave pattern and propeller suds). It may not be productive to run a white or basically light-colored lure where the propeller surface wash is dominant, while a dark lure may be effective.

Color combinations are in some ways like the fashion business, with changes each season. Some of the established fish-taking combinations resemble basic fish colors, green over yellow (dolphinfish), blue over white, light blue over pink, blue or lime green over silver (many bait fish), brown over blue or pink fleck (squid). There are, however, productive skirt colors that do not seem to relate to nature: black over green, purple, orange, red or pink, red over yellow, blue-silver over green-gold, or yellow orange and green in combination. Silver or gold fleck seems to improve attraction, certainly for the fisherman, as do skirts that are darker on one half than the other. Head colors range all the way from black to pearl white. Black seems to be successful with other dark colors in heads and skirts, as they are readily silhouetted against the light. Light colors, particularly blue and green with reflective inserts, add flash and excitement, the panic action of bait fish. Despite the results with natural look-alike lures, many believe lures work in both hard plastic and soft heads because they attract the fish who attack something 'strange'. Whatever the reason for their working successfully, the tournament competition results and record books tell the story of lures. The age of plastic is here and now.

THE HOOK-UP IN LURE FISHING

Action of Fish	Action of Fisherman
• Attracted to boat and lures.	• Reel alarm click ratchet is 'on'. • Strike drags are set as hard as possible within line breaking strain around (¼) of the line class to (⅓) on heavy tackle.
• May look at and just follow lures.	• The fish may be teased into striking.
• May strike at lure.	• Boat can be sped up or lures jigged to increase attraction and help set hooks.
• Pulls stretch/spring resistance out of line and rod and hooks up against drag of reel.	• Angler should be careful to avoid overruns or excess drag.
• Runs away because of hooking, line drag and forward way of boat.	• Once a big fish is hooked all other outfits must be brought in; if a small fish is hooked the other lures may be worked to try to hook others from the school, so rod can be taken to chair gimbal.
• Jumps, runs away hard or sounds.	• Drag can be eased a little. Boat can be backed up or, when the fish slows down, it can be chased or run to recover line.

RODS

Bait casting tackle and spinning tackle can be used for trolling but most effective trolling is carried out on tackle purpose built for trolling lures and baits from a boat. This tackle is equally effective on trolling live or dead baits, or when used on the drift or at anchor.

Trolling tackle comes in all tackle classes with roller guides used from 3 kg (6 lb) class up to 60 kg (130 lb) class. Some anglers prefer the short rods with short tips of around 122 cm (48 in), while others prefer standard-length rods with rod tips of around 165 cm (65 in).

Butts also come in a range of lengths, both straight and curved. A few heavy-tackle rods with long tips to clear wide transom corners have been built with straight butts, the length of which can be varied to suit angler or chair gimbal; the angle of the rod tip can be adjusted with a locked curve above the reel. With this rod a handle is fixed to the reel to assist balance and lift.

Under IGFA rules the rod tip must be a minimum 101.6 cm (40 in), while the butt cannot exceed a maximum 68.58 cm (27 in). These measurements are both taken from a point directly below the center of the reel. These limitations do not apply to surf rods. The minimum tip length covers all rods, not just trolling rods. Short trolling rods have been around for many years and have both advantages and disadvantages. Some believe they are of benefit basically for lighter lines up to and including the 15 kg (30 lb) category. Others believe they are of benefit from 15 kg and heavier, that is, 15 kg (30 lb), 24 kg (50 lb) and 37 kg (80 lb). The short stand-up rods are used with straight or curved butts. Short stand-up rods around 185 cm (62 in) overall with tip length close to the minimum allowed under IGFA rules (101.6 cm, or 40 in) with a butt length sometimes close to the maximum allowed 68.58 cm (27 in) are popular in some fisheries. At present the world trend is towards stand-up and fight, even with really big fish.

Lift and power are important design characteristics in trolling rods, while the features of rods used for casting as well as fighting are not necessary. Trolling rods walk the fine line between the need for lift and power (using 25 to 33.3 per cent of line class during the fight, more if the double is to be of benefit) and the need for flexibility in the tip section to act as a spring shock absorber.

The tips of some of the custom-built modern 24 kg (50 lb), 37 kg (80 lb) and 60 kg (130 lb) line class rods are deliberately made longer to assist in clearing the transom and side coverboards on the bigger boats.

Trolling rods are the most specialized of all rods, as they are there primarily to do one job — catch the fish. Good anglers take advantage of the design characteristics by varying their pumping action, depending on circumstances, during the fight. The value of short pumping, of recovering even a few centimeters (an inch or so) at a time, of attacking the fish, of keeping line tight at every opportunity, is now widely understood and practiced. Modern trolling rod blanks are now available in a variety of exotic materials — graphite, boron, kevlar, S-glass as well as other types of fiberglass. Most are built on hollow blanks but some economical and adequate rods are built on solid glass.

All members of the fishing team seeking billfish have specific responsibilities and areas of operation. Crew men can make or break a day through insufficient skill and enthusiasm for bait preparation and keeping the rods backed up, rigged and ready to go.

◄ Skip Smith backs *Hooker* hard as his angler, Jerry Dunaway, fights on light tackle.
Photo: Jacquie Acheson.

RIGS AND RIGGING

The big fish, the fish the angler had been seeking, praying for, was close to the boat. The leader was almost in reach, the great head again cleared the surface, throwing water and spray. This fish was easily a potential record, a 'dream fish'. Now the fish was leading, heading tiredly towards the slowly moving boat. The leader man nervously tugged at his shorts, the gaff men were ready, tense. They knew what they had to do to complete the catch. The skipper watched from his bridge, ready to keep the fish clear of propellers and rudders, working to keep that tired fish coming to the boat, helping his angler.

The leader man reached for the wire, took his first wraps, then suddenly cursed: 'She's gone'. The gaff men replaced their gaffs. The leader was pulled in board so all could see what happened; strangely, the full length of leader seemed to be there. All on board were quiet as the last length was pulled aboard. All the wire was there, only the hook was gone, gone with that huge fish. Inspection of that leader end mutely told the story. It had been rigged without enough twists in the haywire and had pulled free. A record lost irretrievably for the sake of just a few minutes at most in rigging — a few more necessary wraps to ensure the leader could not unroll.

Sleeves and knots can also cause problems that result in lost fish, fish that would have been records, the culmination of anglers' dreams.

Careful rigging is one of the keys that open the door to success in fishing. It is no coincidence that those who know and understand and are skilled in how to rig, whether for fishing with baits or lures, consistently bring in the fish and the tag and release cards. It is satisfying for everybody on board to know that everything possible that could be done to bring about a successful conclusion has been done.

It is easy to make mistakes in this most critical section of every day's fishing. Crimps, sleeves and knots that have not been completed properly can and will slip on the fish that matters.

Ties in wire that are loose or have been done short with insufficient twists will let go on big fish with hard pulls. It is much better to use more twists than the believed maximum, to rig again properly, than to take a chance. Always make sure, particularly with swimming baits, that the leader has in fact gone through the eye of the hook.

Conscientious crews will discard single-strand wires, whether of stainless or pre-straightened galvanized type, once the bait is chopped, swum out or no longer usable, or has taken a fish, even a small fish. They know it is safer to replace the leader than to have it break through a kink or flexing crystallization just when it matters. They have learned from bitter experience that discarding used wire will help ensure the capture of the fish, the big ones they seek. They also take great care to ensure that with swimming baits and those where the hook eye and leader loop are not visible, the leader wire has actually passed through the eye of the hook, not just alongside it. One of the most embarrassing and frustrating moments in fishing comes when that carefully rigged bait is taken by a big fish or any fish, then the line becomes tight but there is no hook, no action, and inspection reveals a perfect complete loop. This disappointment has happened with many top bait riggers; after that they check carefully that the hook eye and leader loop are safely connected.

Riggers need to think and decide just what is needed for each type of leader material. It is better to over-rig and be on the safe side than to take chances. Many top crews who use heavy gauge .035, .040 and .045 single-strand wire use as many as 20 to 22 haywire twists before the barrel wraps. They know from bitter experience that fewer wraps may hold but that this number will hold on heavy wire, even though 15 wraps may be sufficient on medium-weight wire and eight to 10 on light-gauge wire. Crews who choose monofilaments for their leader quickly learn the need, whether using one or two sleeves, to crimp

▲ IGFA vice-president Jack Anderson fights above the chair on a deep-fighting grander black marlin on the Great Barrier Reef, Australia. *Photo: Peter Goadby.*

them evenly and tight. They learn not to crimp the outer edges into the mono, and to turn the leader back through the sleeve and to burn the end of the mono to create a blob that will minimize the chance of slip. It is beneficial to crimp with press or pliers that suit the sleeves used. Sevenstrand, Hi Seas, Nico Press and Jinkai crimpers give dependable results with the sleeves made for them.

Care must always be exercised with knots.

Speed in replacing baits or lures is part of the success pattern of top crews. They coil each leader the same way, from hook end to loop for attachment to snap. Leaders should be coiled right to left, and the coils should be even — about 30 cm (12 in) in circumference. The leader loop end should be left free about 45 cm to 60 cm (18–24 in) and then looped three times around the coils. This coiling is used by most professional crews as well as on angler-crewed boats for speed and uniformity. Use of the plastic-covered wire twists manufactured for garden or kitchen bag use provide a satisfactory holding material, even for leaders pre-rigged with lures.

It is important to use leader materials matched to the maximum size fish expected. Heavier-than-necessary leader adds a safety factor but has the real disadvantage of restricting the desired action of baits and lures and adding to the problem of visibility.

The choice of hooks is important. Baits and lures for trolling should be rigged with straight, that is not offset or kirbed, hooks. Trolling offset, kirbed hooks increases the probability of bait or lure spinning. Apart from the problems created for line and leader by twisting, this action is not wanted on the baits and lures, as it is not generally attractive or strike inducing to fish.

Hooks used for bait trolling are not kirbed or offset. Hooks used for live, dead and cut bait, fishing at anchor or on the drift are kirbed or offset. Short shank are popular live-bait hooks. These have point and shank in line. Some anglers choose hooks that are kirbed or bend the hook to give this effect. Long-line and Polynesian-style full circle hooks are also popular with live bait. Hooks are available in a variety of finishes. Mustad are usually cadmium plated, while VMC have another non-corrosive finish. Mustad also makes a range of stainless steel hooks.

The use of non-corrosive stainless steel hooks raises a question in the minds of some fishermen and conservation organizations who feel hooks that will corrode away after release or break away have greater benefits.

To be effective, hooks must be made sharp and kept sharp — the sharper the better. Some prefer the hook points to be round needles, others prefer triangulation and others four edges from the point. Some conservationally minded anglers depress or remove the barbs on their hooks, as they intend not only to give the fish more than an even chance in the fight but also to release most of their fish.

The choice of leader material is also important. All types of leader have benefits and disadvantages. The weight and diameter of the leader is governed by the benefits and need for minimum visibility, strength, abrasion resistance, flexibility and resistance to crystallization fracture. Australian shark fishermen in some areas are convinced of the benefits of plastic-covered wire even though the necessary wire strength, plus the plastic coating, makes for a thick leader. These heavy-looking leaders would seem to be highly visible. Experience has shown that even the blue, clear or green plastic over the multi-strand wire increases diameter but improves fish taking.

Bait and hooks rigged on the plastic-covered wire have a higher strike rate than on smaller diameter uncoated wires. Plastic-covered wires can be pulled and wrapped by the leader man in the same way as other leader, despite its bulk and tendency to slightly adhere to gloves. One disadvantage of coated wire is that the wires, whether stainless or galvanized, can corrode under the plastic coating once subjected to salt water.

Leaders to be used for drifting or at anchor are usually rigged with a single hook. A two-hook rig is rated by many to be of benefit in lure fishing for billfish. Some lure fishermen believe there is benefit for their billfish lures in rigging so the hooks are rigid or as stiff as possible to maximize the odds on hook-ups with both single and two-hook rigs.

Rigging for trolling lure fishing has created added awareness of the benefits and problems associated with hooks and leaders overall. The knowledge can be applied to other fishing techniques. Lure fishing is the fastest growing recreational fishing style right around the world, so it is beneficial to review lure trolling in great detail.

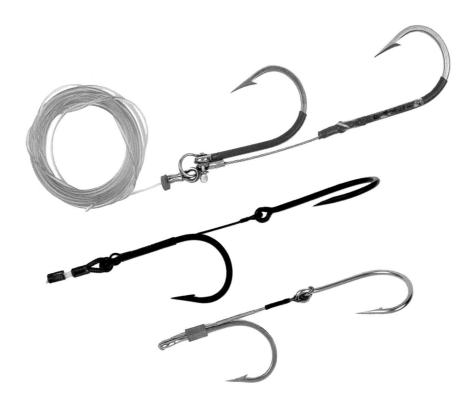

▲ Two-hook rigs used in billfish trolling have the hooks at angles ranging from 0–180 degrees. From top to bottom, the hooks shown here are: Pakula with red shrink plastic to add rigidity, Doornob Lip-Latch with black teflon coating, and Comstock. Murray Bros, Moldcraft and C&H also offer rigged hooks. Pakula and some other riggers use a small stainless shackle to join hooks to an eye on the leader.
Photo: David Rogers.

Most offshore lure fishermen rig for billfish with two hooks, usually of the same size and type, although some do mix designs and sizes. Hook types are usually Mustad 7731, 7691, 7754 or similar designs in VMC. Some riggers choose similar Mustad shapes in stainless Nos 7732 and 76915. When rigging with two hooks, care must be taken to make sure that the minimum length between the eyes of the hooks is the shank's length of the longer of the two hooks. Some part of both hooks must be within the lure skirt; the eyes of the hooks must be not more than 30 cm (12 in) apart.

Supple 49-strand wire is the best compromise for trolling action lures such as minnow-type, high-speed bibless and spoons. This wire is made in various breaking strains from 60 kg (130 lb) to 370 kg (815 lb). The lighter breaking strains are ideal for high-speed action trolling. Single-strand wires in either stainless or galvanized wires of seven strands and plastic-covered wires of seven or other low numbers of strands, are less supple than 49 wires. The penalty fishermen pay for the advantage of suppleness on the 49-strand wire is that each wire strand is very fine and thus easily cut, and so weakens the wire overall. This wire is also ideal for the leader on the second or rear hook.

Single-strand wire also has inherent problems, particularly crystallization associated with flexing. Each leader material has its benefits and its disadvantages. It is up to the lure or bait rigger to know and understand the characteristics and benefits of each material.

The following basics cover rigging for successful offshore trolling for marlin.

LEADERS

Monofilament leaders are used, except where and when toothy critters regularly cause problems. Supple stainless wire leader made from 49-strand wire is then used instead of monofilament to

Line class up to and including 10 kg	Leader maximum: 4.57 m (15 ft) Double maximum: 4.57 m (15 ft) Combined leader and double: 6.1 m (20 ft)
Line class 15 kg and above	Leader maximum: 9.14 m (30 ft) Double maximum: 9.14 m (30 ft) Combined leader and double: 12.19 m (40 ft)

Fly fishing class tippet must be at least 38.1 cm (15 in) long measured inside the connecting knots. With knotless leaders the last 38.1 cm (15 in) will be the class tippet

minimize or prevent cutoffs. To prevent monofilament leader wear at snaps and hooks, plastic tube or coiled plastic-coated stainless steel coils are used. Riggers often prefer to use plastic tube to minimize bubbles at the snap and the plastic stainless coil at the hooks. One or two sleeves can be crimped to form the loops at each extremity of the leader. For extra non-slip security, before crimping, the end of the leader can be heated with a lit match or other flame to create a bulb (keep the flame and melted mono well clear of the other leader material). When this bulb or knob cools, the leader is pulled against the sleeve or top sleeve and the sleeves crimped tightly and evenly.

Experienced riggers, mindful of stretch and elasticity, keep well within the maximum allowable lengths of leader and double and the combined length. These are:

A big fish and an active fight apply forces to the leader and double that not only cause stretch, but can change the shape of loops in mono and wire so as to affect compliance with the rules and tackle regulations when submitted after a capture. Rig well inside the limits.

Wind-on leaders, which simplify crew work when the fish is close, are growing in popularity across all line classifications. The effort involved in the creation of a wind-on leader is worthwhile given the benefits it brings for both tag and release and capture.

<u>CHOICE OF LEADER MATERIALS:</u>

Monofilament of a hard type in 100 kg (220 lb) to 275 kg (605 lb) test is ideal for the main length of trolling leader. The heavier leader material is chosen where big marlin are expected.

Wire, that is 49-strand or two or more twisted strands of heavy single-strand wire (around .040) or other cable wire, should be used for the leader linking first and second hooks. Wire from coat hangers is sometimes used by those who strive for extreme rigidity in their two-hook rigging. Some two-hook rigs use monofilament nylon, but most use a wire of some type on the second hook for protection from abrasion and cutting. To give the desired action and 'smoke' trail, it is important that the lure swims on a supple leader. Two-piece leaders are sometimes used. These are 1–1.5 m (3–5 ft) of 49-strand wire used at the lure, joined by a snap to a longer trace of monofilament or nylon-covered wire to bring it to the desired overall length allowed by the rules. The coastlock or Hawaiian corkscrew type and the McMahon snaps are all satisfactory for this purpose. Two-part leaders also give the benefit of the lure not sliding right up near the monofilament line. Space-age fluorocarbon leaders are the latest development and give some interesting benefits that influence wider use and experimentation despite its present pricing. It is believed to be invisible in the water, particularly from below the surface.

HOOKS

Cadmium plated and stainless steel hook types are successful and practical. They should be made very sharp and checked often and resharpened if blunted or bent by a strike or after coming into contact with hard hull or deck. Hook points should not be sharpened to the stage that they are too thin and thus subject to bending or breaking. Most riggers in their sharpening leave plenty of metal for strength, even though the point down to the barb is in fact very sharp in a round, triangular or even four-sided configuration. When sharpening hooks with a file, most use the file so it is stroked from barb to point not from point to barb. Final smooth honing can be obtained by the use of sharpening or oil stones of various types. Razor-sharp hooks are a key factor in hook-ups and fish at boat. Hooks must be sharpened and checked for sharpness each time they are brought in, particularly after a strike.

CARE OF LURES

Care must be exercised when bringing lures inboard or readying them for trolling. It must be remembered that the polyester plastic used in kona heads and indeed the finish on most lures can be easily damaged and chipped by careless handling against the boat or cockpit. Once inboard, the leader should be coiled and the lure placed where it is safe from going overboard and available when needed. Do not leave lures and hooks on the cockpit deck. Rusting of hooks occurs after the cadmium plating or galvanizing has worn away as a result of electrolytic action between the aluminum or brass sleeves, stainless wire, hook plating and metal of hook or hooks.

Use of trolling or other beads is helpful in ensuring that the hooks are pulled evenly against the rear of the lure head. Several beads can be used to regulate the positioning of a single hook in the skirt, or in high-speed lures to give body.

SWIVELS

Most correctly balanced and rigged lures do not spin. Despite this, it is beneficial to use top-quality, ball bearing Sampo snap swivels with snaps of

The Characteristics of Leader Materials

Advantages	Disadvantages
Single strand stainless steel	
• Thin diameter.	• Stiffness.
• Moderately high strength for diameter.	• Breakage and lowering of breaking strain by flexing and vibration of active lures.
• Low visibility, particularly in brown color.	• Electrolysis.
• Minimum trolling bubbles.	• Wire will coil after strike.
• Maximum resistance to tooth-cutting gamefish and sharks.	

Advantages	Disadvantages
Single strand galvanized carbon steel	
• Thin diameter.	• Lowering of breaking strain if kinked.
• High strength for diameter.	• Rust.
• Initial medium visibility then loses shine.	• Breakage and lowering of breaking strain by flexing and vibration on active lures.
• Minimum trolling bubbles.	• Wire will coil after strike.
• High resistance to tooth cutting from gamefish and sharks.	

Advantages	Disadvantages
Single strand rigged by Haywire twist, sometimes with Flemish Eye	
	• Low breaking strain if kinked.

Advantages	Disadvantages
Low number of multiple strand galvanized wires	
• Medium diameter.	• Stiff for breaking strain.
• Visibility reduces as wires oxidize.	• Breakage and lowering of breaking strain from flexing and vibration.
• High strength for diameter.	• More bubbles and interference than single strand wires.
• Medium visibility until oxidized.	• Rust.
• High resistance to tooth cutting from gamefish and sharks.	
• Less subject to kinking.	
• Rigged by crimping sleeves.	

Advantages	Disadvantages
High number of multiple strand stainless e.g., 49-strand	
• Medium diameter.	
• Medium strength for diameter.	• Breakage and lowering of breaking strain from flexing and vibration.
• Medium visibility in brown color.	• Can be cut and broken by big sharks rolling.
• Medium resistance to tooth cutting and fish rolling.	• More bubbles and interference than single strand wires.
• Resistance to kinking.	• Electrolysis.
• Suppleness and flexibility allow maximum lure performance.	
• Rigged by crimping sleeve.	

THE CHARACTERISTICS OF LEADER MATERIALS

ADVANTAGES	DISADVANTAGES
MULTIPLE-STRAND MEDIUM-DIAMETER GALVANIZED CARBON STEEL	
• Medium visibility once strands oxidize. • Resistant to kinking. • Highly resistant to tooth cutting and body rolling. • Rigged by crimping sleeves or wire and solder.	• Those with fibre centre more liable to corrosion from inside than those with wire core. • Not supple or flexible, liable to crystallization from flexing and vibration. • Rust.
PLASTIC-COVERED WIRES IN STAINLESS OR GALVANIZED	
• Apparently medium visibility even in big diameters. • Resistant to kinking. • Medium breaking strain. • Reflects diameter and type of wire insert. • Minimum electrolysis or electrical field for reception by sharks' ampullae of Lorenzini.	• Will corrode or rust under plastic covering, so should be discarded if discoloration is present. • Large diameter makes slightly more difficult to pull leader, but wraps can be taken. • Plastic coating makes a more slippery surface when recovering leader.
MONOFILAMENT NYLON OR SIMILAR MATERIAL	
• Maximum flexibility. • Minimum visibility. • Resistant to kinking. • No electrolysis or rusting. • Rigged by crimping sleeves.	• Bigger diameter than wires of equivalent breaking strain. • Can be easily cut and abraded by teeth or rough skin or by touching or rubbing on boat. • Stretches under weight of fish and recovering leader.

Coastlock, McMahon or Hawaiian corkscrew types. If ball bearing swivels are not used, a top-quality crane swivel and snap is often satisfactory. Swivels must always be of dependable quality.

Some fishermen minimize the number of hook rigs needed for their lure stocks by using a stainless thimble at the lure end of the leaders in combination with a small shackle. Hooks can thus be easily transferred from one leader and lure rig to another by undoing the shackle and attaching it to another leader-rigged lure.

Bill marks and unavoidable rubbing, chafing and wear or possible leader nicks and cuts on monofilament leader or expected crystallizing of wire by action at the lure head dictate the necessity for regular leader inspection, particularly where it goes through the lure tube. If mono leader is used, wear can be minimized by the use of plastic tube over the leader and down into the lure head. Some fishermen prevent their lure sliding up the leader by using a crimped sleeve or wedging a match, toothpick or skewer in the tube or by binding the leader above the tube with dental tape. Many believe that a lure that has slipped up to the swivel gives the increased possibility of a chop off from wahoo or other fish when it is travelling at high speed through the water behind a hooked fish. Others prefer to take this chance and feel that if the

▲ Molded squid type skirts come in a wide range of colors and sizes from Yamashita, Sevenstrand and Yozuri. The heavier sheet-type molded skirts from Newell and Moldcraft come in a triangular and beaded finish. This material is tough and slightly stiffer than the molded squid types. The squid type skirts should be cut so they are shorter than the eye of the second hook to avoid tangling. *Photo: David Rogers.*

lure is free to slide up the leader it helps keep the hooks in an active fish. Lures that do not slide up the leader slightly increase the difficulty of lure recovery in tagging and release.

EXPERIMENTATION

Because of variations in boats, lures and sea conditions, it sometimes takes time to put together the right combination for a particular boat. Continue experimenting, even once knowledge is gained, and when lures are lost. The keeping of a log is most helpful for this.

Most success falls to skippers, crews and anglers who maintain concentration and a constant watch on lures and what is happening in and on the sea. The factors that aid success in bait fishing are equally important with lures.

To avoid tangling when putting lures out or bringing them in, follow this suggested procedure.

When putting them out, the outside and far back lures are placed in position first, then the short or inside lures. When bringing them in, reverse this procedure: bring in the inside and short-positioned lures first. The one rule in lure fishing technique, as in all fishing, is that there isn't just one way of doing something. Each fisherman may have a personal preference, but there are lots of different ways and even more opinions and interesting alternatives. You pay your money, make your choice and take your chances.

Here is a small sample of frequently heard opinions on the best techniques:

Skirts

• Stiff skirts
• Soft flexible skirts
• The old red rubber sheet and upholstery material combination (particularly with silver or blue)
• A mixture of soft and stiff materials
• Skirt ends cut evenly

- Skirt ends tapered
- Glued skirts (to lure head)
- Tied skirts (to lure head)

Tag lines

- Great — they minimize drop back and improve hook-up from rod tip
- Never use them; it is preferable to use roller releases

Hooks

- Use only galvanized or cadmium-plated steel, never use stainless
- Only use stainless

Hook position in trolling

- Both in line
- At 180 degrees to one another
- At 90 degrees to one another
- At 60 degrees to one another
- At any angle
- Place them so hook points out towards boat wake
- Place them so hook points in from boat wake

Hooks

- Use two hooks
- Use one hook

Second hook rigging

- Mono
- Flexible wire
- Very stiff wire
- Hooks free swinging
- Hook made as rigid as possible by binding with dental tape, plastic insulating tape or rubber band, or with sliding surgical rubber tube or shrink tube

First hook position

- As close as possible to flush at rear of lure
- Lure recessed so hook is partly inside head

Second hook position

- As close to first hook as rules allow
- As far from first hook as rules allow

Hook size

- As big as lure will carry and work
- As small as pull from line class dictates

Hook points

- Round
- Triangular
- Rectangular, with top and cutting edge

Hook colors

- Shiny silver
- Black tape or paint
- Red
- Yellow
- Orange with tape or paint
- Green

Hook shapes

- 7731 type point out, hopefully for more hook-ups (perhaps easier for fish to throw)
- 7690 type point turn in (so hook harder to throw, but perhaps fewer hook-ups)

Lure eyes

- In or on lure head only towards rear
- In or on lure head towards front (particularly with fish shape inserts)
- In head and on skirt
- Only in head
- Only on skirt

Angle of lure head

- Scooped and angled
- Bullet
- At 90 degrees hollow on pusher
- Cut at other angles, such as 150 degrees
- Sharp edges on cut
- Rounded edges on cut

Body taper on lure

- Even
- Even to a ridge, then a slight reduction in diameter

- Even to a ridge, then parallel
- Bubble bulge in center or rear third of head
- Barrel shaped, tapering from front to rear

Tube in lure

- Brass
- Aluminum
- Teflon
- No tube
- Positioned in center
- Positioned in top or bottom third

Lure head colors

- Clear
- Light blue
- Light green
- Purple
- Dark blue
- Red
- Yellow
- Color stripes top or bottom
- Swirl mixture of colors
- Colored mother-of-pearl effect

Lure material

- Hard, to give clarity and flash
- Soft, to encourage return strikes

Inserts

- To look like fish or squid
- Rectangular reflective
- Thick reflective or color
- Thin reflective or color

Action

- To smoke without breaking surface more often than every 60 seconds
- To dive and wriggle before resurfacing
- To stay on top and splash
- To revolve around an axis
- To pop about every 60 seconds — or more often — then dive
- To run straight

Weight

- Weighted inside lure with around 75–100 g (2½–3½ oz)
- No weight

Lures and bait

- Run lures when trolling live or dead baits
- Lures only with lures; bait only with bait

Acceptance

- Some swear by their lures
- Others swear at and about the thought of them

Trolling speed

- 7 to 10 knots — most shapes including soft fish replicas and squid
- 4 to 7 knots — knuckleheads and minnow types
- 12 to 20 knots — high-speed metal head and jet lures

Bird teaser and other flashing teaser

- Some like to use them
- Others prefer interest and action to be only on the lures with hooks in them

Changing lures if no action

- Change often as light changes — a new one might work to bring a strike
- Don't change once successful pattern and colors are established

TEASERS

The use of teasers in successful billfishing goes back to the start of fishing for marlin. The world's first rod and reel marlin, a striped of 92 kg (203 lb), was taken by E. Llewellyn of Santa Catalina in 1903.

The pioneering Catalina method was to troll flying fish rigged without hooks until the marlin were sighted and following, then to replace the hookless flyers with those complete with hooks. Some of these southern Californian boats trolled their teasers from poles. These no doubt gave Atlantic captain Tommy Gifford the idea for the outriggers he built and developed on his return to Florida after a season skippering in southern California.

After using Tarporenos for king mackerel, barracuda, cobia and amberjack in the Florida Keys, Zane Grey realized that the darting, diving action and flashing colors were attractive to billfish as well as to toothy reef dwellers. The big wooden or hollow metal teasers he used in his exploratory fishing were oversized Tarporenos trolled without hooks in conjunction with rigged natural baits. Zane Grey and anglers of that period experienced the thrill and satisfaction of seeing billfish raised by the teasers and transferred the killing strikes from unnatural hookless teaser to hooked natural bait.

Coincidentally the scooped head and towing angle of the Tarporeno and the teaser were adapted with the addition of feathers and other early skirt materials to the first trolling plugs that became kona heads in Hawaii. These early trolling lures, with heads of brightly painted scooped or angled wood, were developed with heads made from chromed towel rail with wooden inserts. The skirts were made of feathers, rubber sheeting in red and black and other simple materials. Later, plastic upholstery material and silver-coated plastic and clear plastic cast heads opened up a whole new world of teasers — teasers with hooks, ready for a hook-up.

The use of outriggers and the benefit of combining outriggers and flat lines with natural baits led to a reduction in interest in teasers. The development of soft rubber and then plastic fish and squid replicas opened up a resurgence in teasers. Skilled fishermen in Florida trolled these replica combination teasers in conjunction with natural baits or lures. Later developments combined soft head pusher and straight cut heads in combination as teaser or daisy chain, with hooked lure behind the hookless teaser rigged on the leader or on a coathanger rig. The teasers were beneficial, particularly on sailfish and white marlin in the Atlantic and Caribbean.

The teaser rebirth with soft plastic squid and fish replicas and soft and hard plastic-headed lures, sometimes with final hooked lure, has spread worldwide. Teasers, with or without the final hooked lure, have been taken to optimum development by Captain Skip Smith and his crew on the *Hooker*. The multiple world-record angler-owner captures by Jerry Dunaway and fellow record-breaking angler Debra Maddux have given teasers a new boost. The pattern of teasers trolled on *Hooker* raises the billfish then, after a skilled assessment of size, weight and potential record, a bait or lure complete with hook is presented to the billfish raised by the teaser.

The bird, so called because of its wings, had its origin in commercial fishing. Anglers and captains who use them in billfishing believe they attract more strikes and raise billfish.

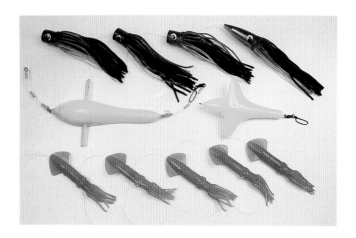

◄ Birds (yellow) of various shapes work as teasers when trolled ahead of a lure. Molded plastic squid (red) can be rigged as a teaser in a daisy chain or coat hanger spreader rig. Captain Skip Smith of *Hooker* combined Moldcraft pusher lures (black) with a final lure in a bullet shape for a most successful combination. *Photo: David Rogers.*

◀ Silvery queenfish rigged as swimming bait on the Great Barrier Reef. The herringbone stitching on the belly cavity allows maximum flexibility as the bait swims.
Photo: Peter Goadby.

One of the techniques used on *Hooker* in their string of record breaking is to research what records are possible in the area, particularly billfish, and to have outfits in the possible line classes ready to use. The sighted and estimated fish is offered a bait on a line class that could turn the fish from another unknown opponent to be tagged and released into a record claim fight balanced to the tackle.

Teasers, with their unbroken links to the start of modern sportfishing, will continue to be part of the fishermen's armory in their quest for the big fish; so, too, will teasing with natural bait species.

In all fishing methods, trolling and fishing at anchor or drifting, it is important for the angler to know how and when to tease, to excite a shadowy, unexcited predator into explosive action. Often this is done by experienced crews before the angler is aware of the need. There is, however, a special exhilaration and satisfaction for anglers when they trigger a following fish to action on the baits or lures.

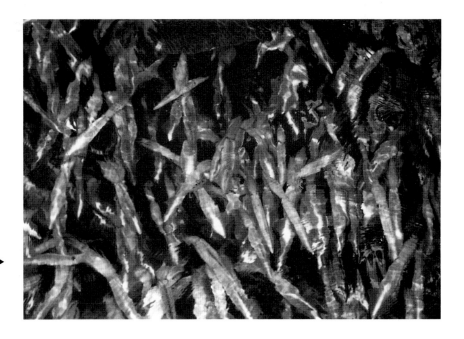

Countless arrow squid ▶ school for mating each year off Santa Catalina, California.
Photo: Peter Goadby.

Teasing with lures or baits or part of baits is effective after an initial strike as well as with shadowing, casually interested predator species. Sometimes it is necessary to work and tease the big fish several times before obtaining the hoped-for strike. Changing to a live or more lively bait will also often trigger a strike from a sighted but non-feeding, non-killing fish. This form of teasing, which may entail the extra activity of two or three released, unrigged live fish, or removal of part of a tail or other fins to give the bait an unusual or wounded action, may be beneficial. Spare rigged baits, lures and live baits should be ready just in case.

Water jets and sprays are integral to the successful pole fishery for tuna. It could also be of benefit trolling for marlin with both bait and lures, despite the possible annoyance of wind-blown spray to anglers on the deck.

RIGGING BAITS FOR TROLLING, DRIFTING AND CASTING

Successful offshore trolling is now often regarded as fishing with lures or live bait. Despite the popularity and success rate with those two methods, there are times and places where fishing with dead natural baits is still, and always will be, important and productive. Modern fishermen should be competent in all methods. Success goes hand in hand with learning and using the methods of today.

The number of skilled riggers of natural baits that made the difference between fishing and a boat ride prior to the development of lure and bait fishing has regrettably decreased. However, crews on the Great Barrier Reef show that the skill and tradition is not lost. This is also the situation in a few other billfishing areas. The best of these riggers are sought for their skill and knowledge. Many of the best show no inclination to take the step to captain.

FISHING WITH NATURAL BAITS

Natural baits are effective, particularly in established fisheries where local bait schools, sea bed configuration, currents and usual hunting areas are well known.

It is a pity that the number of skilled bait riggers has declined with the increase in lure and live bait fishing. There is still, and there always will be, a need for natural baits rigged to troll, in association with live baits, for small marlin and sailfish and to troll in proven areas for giants of the species. There is pleasure in watching and learning as skilled bait riggers practice their art and skills in making a dead fish act naturally to entice the peak predator fish of the ocean. Knowledge of how to rig baits is still important in this plastic age. Knowledge of when and where to use bait and how to rig baits well can determine whether a fishing trip is a monument or merely a milestone.

The benefits and results from trolling at least one dead bait in conjunction with live bait are well proven. So, too, is the strike and capture rate associated in trolling for big or light game species. Knowledge gained from professional crews can be successfully applied in angler-skippered and crewed boats of all sizes.

Natural baits rigged for anchor or drift are usually rigged to hang head down, although some rig whole fish tail down so they are pulled headfirst in the current and drift. Neatness is an integral factor in successful bait rigging. Billfish swallow baits headfirst so trolling baits must be rigged so they can be turned to swallow. The baits must troll head first as in the New Zealand rig and have light ties that will break when the marlin strikes so it will be turned to be swallowed headfirst.

The other trolling rigs must turn either about the hook or loop in the leader wire at the hook. Ties on drifting and anchor baits must be strong so the hook is firmly held.

◀ Plastic skirts and a small lure are added to some small natural fish baits to aid attraction, change the action and prolong the trolling life of the bait. *Photo: Peter Goadby.*

The point of the hook must be kept clear of the bait so that when the fish is struck the point will be driven into the fish, not back into the bait.

Bait must be fresh or preserved by lightly brining or salting body cavities or applying formalin formaldehyde to the bait in storage.

Trolling baits should not be stiff. Stiff fish will spin when trolled, so the backbone should be removed for part or the whole of its length or broken and stretched by 'working' (flexing) the bait.

Baits should be of a size to suit the fish sought, even if this means missing out on larger or smaller species for which the baits and hook sizes are unsuitable. The size of fish used for baits to attract even one species of fish can vary widely, but even if the bait is small the hook still needs to be of

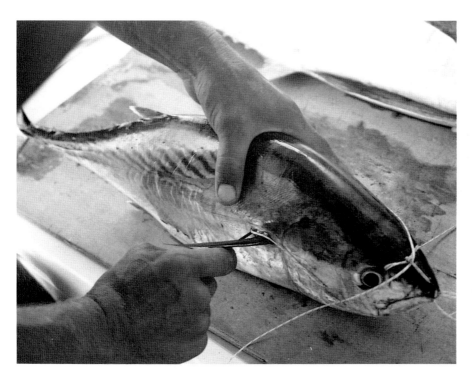

◀ Kawa kawa and other heavy baits are rigged to ensure the bait holds together. *Photo: Peter Goadby.*

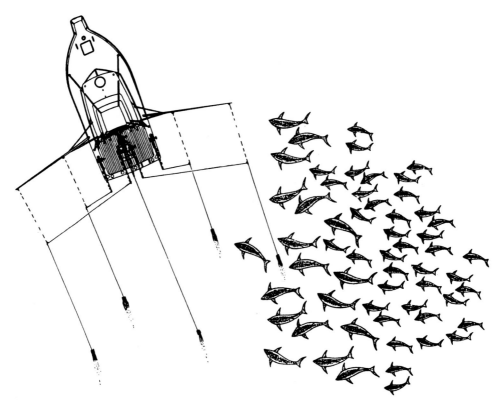

▲ When trolling for bait tuna position the lures in front of the school.

sensibly large size. Long, easily trolled barred mackerel and wahoo up to and over 10 kg (22 lb) may be used for the jumbo black marlin at Cairns, where these big baits take 68–90 kg (150–200 lb) specimens; but small 120 to 240 g (4–8 oz) chub mackerel, goggle eye, mullet and ballyhoo (garfish) are used for small marlin and sailfish.

It is important to ascertain where natural bait can be obtained, whether caught or bought and whether it is to be used alive or dead.

When using whole or cut baits it is of prime importance to tie the fish or the cut bait firmly to the hook to prevent any slip with the consequent bunching and choking of the point of the hook. Drifting baits should be attached firmly, particularly at the eye of the hook.

Variations in rigging methods and types of baits give the gamefish a choice. One bait rig may interest and attract while others are ignored. A range of baits rigged in different ways gives more chances. As with lure trolling, the pattern — that is, the positioning — of the baits is important. Each rig works best in a given position on outriggers or flat lines.

Baits for big marlin are usually trolled from outriggers so there is one skipping, surface-splashing bait, sometimes trolled from only halfway up the outrigger. The other, a swimming bait, is trolled from the full length of the rigger. The skip bait is usually a tuna or bonito or some species of toothy mackerel, queenfish or rainbow runner; kahawai are popular in New Zealand, as are flying fish in California and Mexico. The swimming baits are rigged from smaller toothed mackerels, scad (double-lined mackerel), small queenfish, mullet, kahawai (Australian salmon) and bonefish. Mahi mahi (dolphin fish) and barracuda are sometimes used.

▲ Deck hoses and a plastic fish box make a successful and practical live bait tank. *Photo: Peter Goadby.*

CATCHING THE BAIT

Billfishermen have sometimes shown their dedication to their chosen offshore fishing by wearing T-shirts inscribed: 'There are two kinds of fish — Billfish and Baitfish'. Despite this enthusiasm for the peak predators, the catching of the humble bait species remains an integral part of billfish success in some areas.

Charter boat captains and crews are often intrigued by the simple pleasure and excitement shown by their charterers when they take part in the daily bait catching. Some of the baits are bigger than their previous captures, particularly if previous fishing had been freshwater oriented.

It is no coincidence that the top captains in most ports are those who are successful in bait catching and thus in their quest for the long-nosed opponents.

Bait catchers and riggers in Florida specialize not only in bait for sailfish and blue and white marlin in home and nearby Caribbean waters, but in bait species exported to other world hot spots.

The demand for the professionally caught and prepared bait species such as ballyhoo (garfish), mullet and squid of various sizes and mackerels of necessary sizes created an industry which is now slowing down. The use of live bait and lures has restricted this demand. The skills of bait riggers and crews who are experts in their profession, such as 'Split-tail' Charley Hayden and Charley Perry, Mutt Cable and others, made them familiar names on the top boats.

The Japanese Skibuti known by many names in various parts has revolutionized the catching of various small chub mackerels, yellowtail scad (yakkas), goggle eyes and other bait species. The taking of these live baits and ballyhoo (garfish) in cast nets offshore has revolutionized the use of live bait for billfish. Live bait cast to sighted billfish has replaced the bait trolling of the past.

The catching of these small live-bait species and their storage in live bait tanks in good condition acknowledges the importance of live bait in today's billfisheries.

Similar importance and expertize is also evident in live-bait catching of bigger species. In Hawaii once the decision is made to 'go with livies', many skippers and crews pull in their trolled big plastic lures so that the bait species sought — small yellowfin, kawa kawa and little tunny and skipjack (striped tuna) — will not be spooked by the big lures.

In other parts of the world, rainbow runners and small yellowtail and kahawai (Australian salmon) are sought.

Live baits of all sizes must be handled carefully. Small bait species taken on small hooks should be shaken free over the bait tank without handling, or with minimum handling. The bigger live bait such as the small tunas can now be kept alive in plastic cylinders called tuna tubes. The small tunas used for live baits should be grasped in a wet towel or cloth and held firmly upside-down for hook removal and bait rigging. The upside down holding stops panic and has a tranquilizing effect on the tuna brought to boat.

Very small plastic squid, feather or fish hair lures representative of the size of fish that are the prey of the small tunas are successful bait-fish catchers.

TROLLING TACTICS

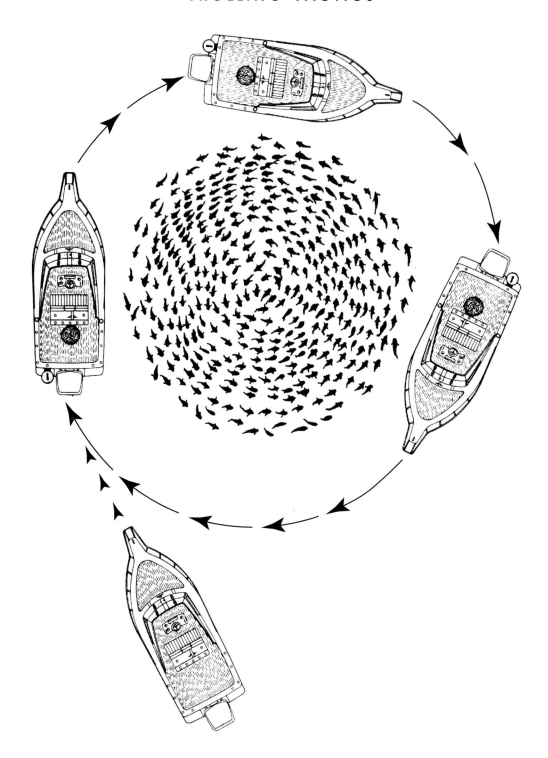

▲ The safe way for several boats to troll a bait patch and for additional boats to enter the trolling sequence.

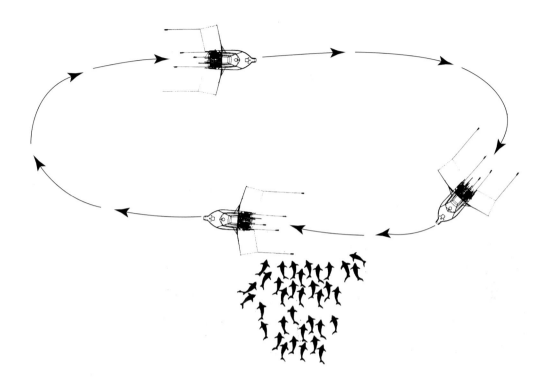

▲ A practical, all-round pattern for one boat to work a school for best presentation and minimum frightening of fish.

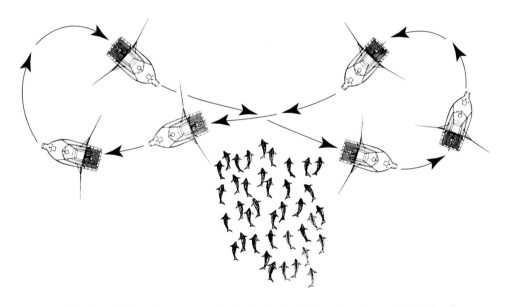

▲ A safe and productive pattern for more than one boat to work a school.

Green, pink and silvery white are successful colors. These small lures are called kin kin in Hawaii — a word spreading around the world to accompany the name mahi mahi for dolphin fish and kawa kawa for little tunny types.

IGFA rules specify that only single hooks be used in these lures to be eligible for a record claim. Many skippers choose to use double (two prong hooks) in the small lures run for tuna bait species. If a potential record in a species is landed the capture would not be eligible for a record claim. Treble (three prong hooks) are not as popular as the double hook in this use. Single hooks are more likely to tear out. Double hooks, in addition to other benefits, allow the bait fish to be lifted in board on the leader. The use of gaffs and landing nets can be counter-productive in creating stress damage and loss of time.

Remember, fish for bait fish where bait species should be. Use small lures of the size of the fish on

▲ Captain Bill Edwards, working with angler Ted Naftzger on a giant black marlin, backs up *Tainui*. Photo: Peter Goadby.

which they are feeding. Look for hovering birds fluttering at the surface or way up high. Pull in the big lures and baits if the decision is to really go for bait. Be careful in the preparation and preservation of bait. Availability and care of bait can change a day's fishing from hours of boredom into seconds and minutes of welcome pandemonium.

Baits for smaller billfish are rigged from small mullet, ballyhoo (garfish), chub mackerel, goggle eye (yellowtail scad), blue runner and squid. Small eels are attractive to Atlantic white marlin. These species can be rigged for both outriggers and flat-line trolling.

Strip baits cut from side fillets and belly strips make productive trolling baits. Whole fish and strip baits for small billfish are often run in combination with plastic skirts, plastic squid, feather lures or hexheads.

Drifting bait species include tuna, bonito, mullet, toothy mackerels, yellowtail, amberjack, trevally, jacks and squid. Pilchards, sardines and anchovies are top light-tackle, small-hook baits. Squid are the best bait for swordfish, both in daylight fishing and drifting at night.

Excitement in the action of the bait often means success, as does apparent competition; if bait fish appear to be chased or escaping from another fish, all the baits seem to be chased and struck.

Successful baits are easy for a hunting fish to find by sight, scent, vibrations, or the combination of all three. The success of the Cuban deep-drifting combination of a cluster of big and small fish, lifting, moving and catching all available light takes full advantage of these requirements — sight, smell and vibration.

Any pelagic or fish caught from the sea bed, surface or in between can be used for live bait. Tuna, bonito, yellowtail, amberjack, trevally and rainbow runner are popular big fish live baits and chub mackerel, goggle eye (yellowtail scad), mullet, ballyhoo (garfish), blue runner, sardines, anchovies and fresh-caught reef fish are prime baits for smaller billfish and tuna.

Those listed above are established baits. To these can be added caught-on-the-spot species for both live and dead baits. The peak predator species are opportunistic feeders that take a great variety of fish and other marine life.

The effectiveness of dead whole fish drifting baits can be increased by partly filleting the bait fish to allow free escape of blood and oils, while still retaining some of the silvery skin to contrast with dark red flesh.

Dead bait fish or the tail portions of big fish rigged as baits for use at anchor or on the drift will often spin like tops in tide or current, twisting and damaging the line. The best way to prevent this is to cut the tail lobes right in short so that there is no natural propeller to catch the moving water.

The edges of strip baits should be trimmed and bevelled off so that the strip trolls flat. The edge of the Panama strip can be left at the natural belly thickness or bevelled before it is sewn up, as the bait rigger wishes.

It is often helpful with strip baits to sew the eye of the hook to the strip and the front of the strip to the leader to give extra support for long trolling periods.

The hole through which the hook sits in strip baits should be long enough to allow the bait to flap and flash on the surface. The hook is anchored by the leader through the eye of the hook in the swimming mullet rig — the mullet 'swims' freely around the slit in the belly where entrails and backbone were removed. This slit is not sewn up the full length, if at all; one or two stitches behind the shank of the hook will suffice.

LIVE BAIT FISHING

The attractiveness of the baits to billfish depends on the care taken when handling the baits so they stay lively and active.

Chub mackerel, green mackerels, goggle eye and yellowtail scad can be caught on light line and then transferred to live bait tanks without being

TYPICAL BAIT SPECIES FOR BILLFISH

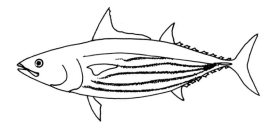

Skipjack tuna

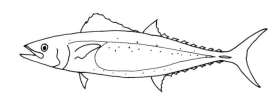

Scaly mackerel

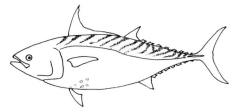

Kawa Kawa- little tunny

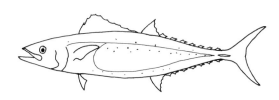

Scad

Pilchard

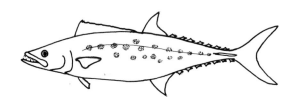

Spanish and other small mackerel

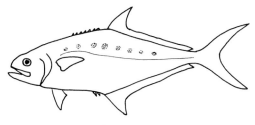

Queenfish

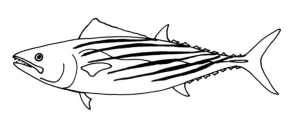

Bonito

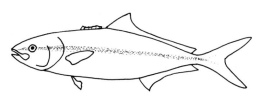

Yellowtail kingfish

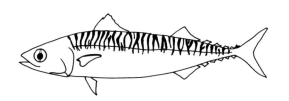

Green (chub) mackerel

Rainbow runner

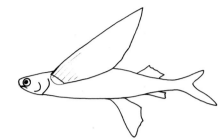

Flying fish

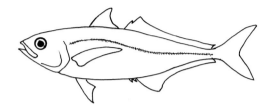

Yellowtail scad goggle eye

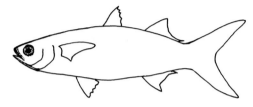

Mullet

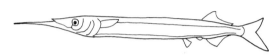

Ballyhoo - garfish

TYPICAL BAIT SPECIES FOR BILLFISH

Fish	Usual catch method	Use		
Skipjack tuna	Trolling small lures	Live bait	Dead bait	Strips
Kawa Kawa- little tunny	Trolling small lures	Live bait	Dead bait	Strips
Pilchard	Net	Live bait	Dead bait	—
Queenfish	Trolling small lures	Live bait	Dead bait	Strips
Yellowtail kingfish	Trolling lures	Live bait	Dead bait	Strips
Scaly mackerel	Trolling lures		Dead bait	Strips
Scad	Trolling small lures on a daisy chain with paravanes		Dead bait	Strips
Spanish and other small mackerel	Trolling lures		Dead bait	Strips
Bonito	Trolling lures		Dead bait	Strips
Green (chub) mackerel	Bait and shibuki	Live bait	Dead bait	Strips
Yellowtail scad goggle eye	Bait and shibuki	Live bait	Dead bait	Strips
Mullet	Net (cast net)	Live bait	Dead bait	Strips
Ballyhoo - garfish	Net (cast net)	Live bait	Dead bait	Strips
Flying fish	Lights at night	Live bait	Dead bait	Strips
Squid	Squid jigs	Live bait	Dead bait	Strips

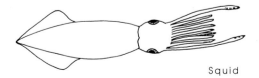

Squid

handled. The schools can be chummed up then caught on bait on small hooks or Joes. The bait fish will drop clear of the hook into the bait tank if the hook is turned upside down, or the wriggling fish touched against the side of the tank. Skipjack tuna, other small tunas, amberjack and yellowtail often benefit from being lifted inboard with a landing net. The bait fish should be held upside down while the hook on which it is caught is removed and the big fish hook put in place. They can be held with a wet towel to protect their body slime.

Small bait fish can be kept alive and active for long periods at sea in tanks filled with circulating, aerated water. They can be released if not wanted at the end of the fishing day or kept in holding traps. Skipjack and the other live bait species can be kept alive for a short time by running a deck hose into the mouth of the ram ventilators. Tuna tubes, with their water flow, assist in keeping most baits alive.

One of the keys to successful fishing with live bait is to have the leaders ready for instant use. Leaders for skipjack and other big bait species should have hooks sharpened, the dacron or other

bridle fixed on the shank of the hook and the rigging needle in place. The needle passes the loop of the towing thread through the opening sinus above the bait's eyes. The loop which held the needle is quickly passed over the point and barb of the hook two or three times before the bait is slid overboard to swim at its chosen depth. It is sensible to have the live bait and leader already attached to the line to be fished before the bait is rigged and the bait and leader placed overboard. Care must also be taken to ensure the snap is safely done up.

The positioning of the short, sharp hooks varies with both the current and whether the bait will be trolled or fished on drift or at anchor. Baits to be trolled and fished in a fast current have the hook placed through the nose, those fished at anchor or drift are rigged in one of several locations on the back. If kirbed (offset) hooks are used they should be positioned from one side or the other so that the point will pull clear not back into the bait. It is important to remember the importance of the lateral line and back bone and take care to ensure that the hook is clear of these important areas.

BAIT RIGGING

The tools needed for bait rigging are: one large and one small diameter deboner; rigging pliers in a sheath; a stiff, short-bladed knife; a long, thin-bladed filleting knife; an ice pick for making holes in the heads of bait; light, medium and heavy cotton or linen rigging thread; light and heavy waxed nylon thread; leader materials; lead sinkers, preferably egg-shaped or oval for swimming baits; short and long bait needles (at least one with a slotted eye); hooks; crimping sleeves; crimping pliers; files; sharpening stones or a sharpening tool; and wire cutters.

'Split-tail' Charley Hayden, who can rig mullet and other baits so they call up gamefish, recommends several methods of trolling mullet. These are wedge and debone; deboned swimming mullet; split tail; split back and cut back.

▲ A small black marlin almost jumps into the boat and shows the tuna bait swallowed headfirst. *Photo: Peter Goadby.*

The cockpit space on ▶ the *Blowout* is used practically. The live bait tank has a viewing port and is of a height that allows storage and quick availability of fishing tackle. *Photo: Peter Goadby.*

TO WEDGE AND DEBONE

Cut out and remove a diamond shaped wedge from the red spot on the head to first dorsal. Debone through wedge. Make a short slit in the belly to insert the hook. Use ice pick through the head red spot to make a clean hole for the leader wire. Slide leader wire through head and hook. Twist the leader wire together with haywire twist to give a wide loop so the bait can be turned by the marlin. Use a needle to take thread from one side of the head to the other above the hook. Tie around the head two or three times. Sew the mouth closed.

DEBONED MULLET

Bend mullet at throat. Debone through the throat, cut at anus and cut another short slit near pelvic fins for hook insertion. Use an ice pick through the head red spot to make a clean hole for leader wire. Slide leader through head and hook. Twist leader together with haywire twist to give a wide loop. Sew the mouth closed.

SPLIT BACK MULLET

Remove the backbone from top of back after cutting along both sides of backbone and breaking near tail. Use an ice pick through the head red spot

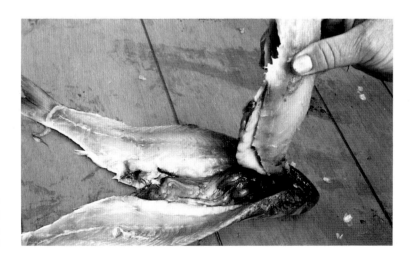

Charlie Hayden has cut his split ▶ tail bait so the backbone can be removed in one piece. *Photo: Peter Goadby.*

to make a clean hole for leader wire. Twist wire tight on lips.

SPLIT TAIL MULLET

Start diamond wedge closer to nose than red spot. With a short, stiff knife, cut a wedge almost back to dorsal. With longer fillet knife, cut along body and split the tail from anus back. Use head cut to free backbone. Turn over and make a similar cut on other side. Backbone and gut can then be lifted clear. Gills are also removed without damaging the throat latch. This bait works well with a weight under the chin. Place sinker on leader wire and slide leader through hook that can face upwards in wedge cut. Make haywire twist tight against lead (about 13 twists). Tie thread two or three times around wedge area.

CUT BACK MULLET

Cut along top of back, including dorsal fins. Cut down both sides of back bone so it can be removed with gut. Use an ice pick to make a clean hole for leader wire. Thread wire with sinker through head and hook in place on underside of body. Twist the wire tightly against lead.

BALLYHOO (GARFISH)

Prepare leader wire. Haywire twist leader onto hook and make an upright pin of about 1.25 cm (½ in). Twist 15 cm (6 in) of soft copper wire around head of bait. Flex the body of ballyhoo. Break bill about halfway and use it to pull skin from under rest of bill. Measure where hook will be positioned, bend body of bait and slide hook into place. Push pin through head and wrap copper wire around mouth and down bill so that the leader wire sits in the groove made by the skin removal. Pull leader and if necessary enlarge slit around hook. This rig can also be used with two hooks, the second of which has point up, the first point down.

BIG SKIP AND SWIMMING BAITS

Gills and gut should have been previously removed from bait fish.

BIG SKIP BAITS

Sew mouth shut. Sew belly slit closed with herringbone stitch. Tie strong thread or cord five or six times around the shank of the hook so it cannot move. Leave two lengths of about 60 cm (2 ft). Pull each of these threads or cords on a needle one at a time through head and throat and tie off firmly. Then pull the threads through belly sides and shoulder to make a strong towing halter, using the strength of the head and shoulders. Check to make sure that the point of the hook will not dig into the shoulder of the bait when the bait is turned by the marlin for swallowing head first. If using a piano wire or galvanized wire leader, it should be attached to the eye of the hook with 20 to 22 twists and five to six barrel rolls.

BIG SWIMMING BAITS

Sew mouth shut. Use an ice pick to make clean hole for leader. Slide leader through hole in head and through the eye of hook. The hook should be in the body cavity behind the pelvic fins. A loop of leader about 5–7.5 cm (2–3 in) should then be made so the leader wire can be twisted and barrel rolled. This loop will ensure that the bait can be turned for swallowing by a marlin. As with the big skipping baits, the wire should be twisted evenly 20 to 22 times with five to six barrel rolls. Care must be taken to ensure that the wire twists are tight and even and twisting and wrapping does not heat the wire. The fish's belly should then be sewn with herringbone stitches about 2.5–5 cm (1–2 in) apart. Some riggers take this stitching over the backbone for extra strength.

These brief descriptions refer to single-strand piano or galvanized wire. Other leader materials, such as monofilament nylon, plastic-covered cable, or two strands twisted of stainless single-strand wire either singly or in conjunction with others can be used e.g., short, single-strand wire is joined with a snap swivel to monofilament leader.

▲ A fixed loop from the hook eye to where the hook shank is tied to the head of the tanguigue prevents slippage while trolling and at the strike. The thread harness through head and shoulder keeps bait intact when attacked by a marlin. *Photo: Peter Goadby.*

Points to remember

- Do not break the throat latch of any baits.
- Keep the hook and wire in the center of the body and head width.
- For light tackle, single-strand wire should be twisted evenly and tightly with six to eight twists and finished with three to four wraps, then broken flush by bending the wire into a right-angled crank.
- On heavy tackle, single-strand wire should be twisted evenly and tightly with 20–22 twists and finished with five to six wraps before breaking the wire flush with a right-angled crank.
- When making knots, make an extra overlap in a surgeon's knot so the thread will hold as the knot is completed.
- Rig baits neatly.
- Leader material should be chosen carefully; all have some advantages and disadvantages.
- If hooks cannot be removed in a tag and release, cut the leader behind the wire man when he requests. He knows when he wants it cut, when it is safe to do so and then when to release.
- Examine all leaders after use and discard if there is the slightest doubt. Many crews discard single-strand galvanized wire after one use so they are working with maximum-length leaders in the best possible starting condition.
- Store baits and leaders in a refrigerator or icebox so they will not tangle.

KNOTS, PLAITS AND JOINS

Human error is usually the reason for frustrating fish loss. Hours of work and effort may be negated by a few seconds of carelessness in the preparation of critical knots, plaits or other joins in single and double line.

Double line, even though the allowable length has been reduced in IGFA regulations, is still important in rigging, though it is less useful at the final stages of the fight. The maximum allowable length of double line and double line/leader combination if maximum length leaders are required means that double lines are short or in many cases are not used at all, even on heavy tackle. One of the great benefits of double line under the present regulations is increased knot strength in all lines.

It is important to know how to make the Bimini roll, the plait or braid, or spider hitch to create a double line. It is important to know how to safely join and replace the top length of line, and worn line, without replacing the full length. Practical knowledge of knots is integral to success for fly fishing and light tackle. Fly fishermen use more knots in number and variety than in any other kind of fishing.

Faulty ties are often associated with trying to work quickly or while unbalanced by the motion of the boat. Knots should be checked regularly; even if they have not come undone they may have moved and be ready to finally come apart.

Knots and joins reduce the breaking strain of line to varying degrees. It is therefore important to know which knots are strongest, most dependable and easiest to tie. Anglers who fish from charter boats often depend on guide, captain or crew to tie the necessary knots. Despite this, every angler should be proficient in the necessary knots and carry in his kit the few necessary tools: pliers, knife, dental tape, dental thread, 60-second glue or rubber glue.

One of the reasons fishermen carry pliers on their belts is to assist in holding the loose end and pulling tight. Monofilament weakens quickly as it is pulled over itself, so lubrication with saliva, water or beeswax on the line before the knot is made and pulled down tight keeps the monofilament cool and able to move smoothly.

Knots used in joining lines particularly benefit from application of a few drops of 60-second glue or rubber type contact cement to give added security, as well as smoothing the passage of line and knots through the guides. If dissatisfied with the knot or not sure if the standing and loose ends are in correct positions, cut the knot and do it again. Some fishermen find a combination of the knots they need in Vic Dunaway's Uniknot system. Others choose to use an improved clinch, an Albright or Uniknot joining knot plus the Buffer or Homer Rhode Loop.

Dependable knots come with practice, familiarity and repeated use. It is important to know the loss in breaking strain in the various knots. Knot strength can be checked against line testers or scales. It is important to know the advantages and disadvantages of the various knots.

Some knots are ideal on light lines, but not on heavy. The Spider hitch is satisfactory on light line classes if carefully and evenly tied. Many fishermen have reservations regarding its use on line classes above the 15 kg (30 lb) class.

Crimps and sleeves are now commonly used on heavier breaking strain monofilament leaders in place of knots. The sleeve loops are dependable as well as being smaller in bubble-producing bulk.

RIGGING TIPS

Knots

- Make all plaits, joins and hitches longer than absolutely necessary. For example, plait for 5 cm (2 in) instead of the 2.5 cm (1 in) that satisfactorily holds on double line.
- Tie off with two tight half-hitches instead of one at the finish of the plaits, roll knots or any other knots finishing with hitches.
- Burn the end of the free line into a knob by melting the end of the line with a match or cigarette lighter.
- Plait in one or more strands of dental floss, dental tape or waxed thread on line joins and doubles to minimize slip in plait or braid.
- On heavy lines, bind over the loose ends as an extra precaution.

This 37ft Merritt has numerous world records for ▶ its owners at Kona. *Photo: Peter Goadby*

- Make sure all knots and plaits are pulled tight at all stages and that the strands are running straight; make sure there are no weakening half-hitches or loose lengths in the main line.
- Splice braided line. Splice hollow braided line with the special splicing needle supplied or fine piano wire through the hollow center of the braid. Some ease it once or twice through the outside line. Bind both ends.
- Join monofilament to braid by tapering the monofilament and sliding up the center of the braid. Bind the ends.

Leaders

- Slide one or two sleeves or crimps over the leader.
- When attaching the hook, make an overhand loop in the leader after sliding on plastic anti-rub tubing or coil spring tube, as made for long lines.
- Continue with a second overhand loop to form the Flemish Eye at the swivel end if not using anti-rub sleeves.
- A single loop with plastic anti-rub is neat and effective for the ure leader loop at the swivel end.
- Bring short end of loop down through the sleeves and pull in tight.
- Crimp sleeves with crimping pliers; select sleeves for a neat and tight fit.
- Cut off any protruding length of wire so it is flush with sleeve.
- If only one sleeve is used, the free end of the wire or monofilament can be tucked back under the sleeve before it is crimped. In this instance, sleeves should be big enough to take the third strand. Always crimp sleeves tightly and burn the ends of

the monofilament or nylon-covered wires into a globule to guard against possible slipping.
- Use 2.4–3 m (8–10 ft) light-tackle leaders in stand-up fishing so that the fish can be gaffed without the leader being handled. On heavy tackle with a chair, use the maximum length allowed by the rules and common sense for stretch.
- Continually check leaders for wear and kinks.
- Fine leaders and monofilament garner more strikes than heavy, more visible leaders.
- Make sure no corrosion or crystallization shows beneath used, nylon-covered wire. If corroded, discard it.
- Make sure the wire is twisted, trimmed or cut to eliminate cutting edges.
- Keep leaders coiled, neatly bound with Scotch tape or plastic-covered copper wire or garden twist, or in plastic bags or zip-lock bags ready for instant action.

Swivels

- Use swivels as small as the line breaking strain dictates. If strength is unknown, check against scales.
- Black swivels and snaps are less visible.
- Inspect swivels to make sure they are not damaged by wear.
- Make sure swivels will turn.
- In areas where striking fish cause cutoffs, rig with the swivel into the middle of the leader and join double to leader with a neat knot.
- Use snaps of a proven, dependable type.
- Bind over knots of line to swivel to minimize bubbles.

RIGGING MATERIALS

Braided line pulled tight with bound ends

Monofilament line slipped inside opened braided line

Opened braided line

Braided line

Tapered monofilament

The top shot: it is possible to join monofilament to braided line by opening out the end of the braided line and tapering and roughing up the monofilament The braided line overlaps the monofilament by the longest possible margin (30 cm, 12 in or more) as it pulls tight over the mono. The ends are bound with dental tape or waxed nylon to further strengthen the join. Super Glue (60 second glue) or rubber glue can further minimize the chance of slip at each end.

Single strand wire

Monofilament leader

Monofilament can be combined with single strand wire for light tackle billfish trolling — 37 kg (80 lb) mono and No 8 wire is a good combination. On heavy tackle for medium billfish (150–300 kg, 300–600 lb) 180 kg (400 lb) mono and 180 kg (400 lb) multistrand wire can be combined.

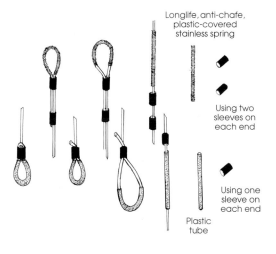

Longlife, anti-chafe, plastic-covered stainless spring

Using two sleeves on each end

Using one sleeve on each end

Plastic tube

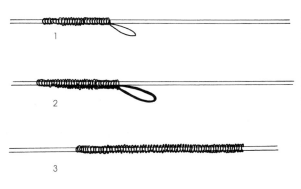

Single or double sleeve leader eyes: on monofilament leader, slip can be prevented by burning the end of the monofilament leader or by using a bigger size sleeve so the leader can be passed back. Wear on monofilament leaders can be minimized by a sleeve of plastic or a section of longline abrasion-resistant, plastic-covered stainless wire spring. Always crimp tightly and evenly.

For rigging:

1. Dental tape, dental floss and other waxed threads can be looped or bound in tightly around the fishing line with half hitches to give loop for outrigger slip with pin or clothes peg type.

2. Heavy dacron or monofilament can be bound on and locked on to fishing line so it does not rub on outrigger clip.

3. The main fishing line can be whipped with waxed thread for protection when trolling.

KNOTS

Improved Clinch Knot
To attach hook to leader. Wet knot as it is pulled up tight.

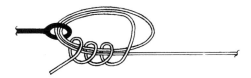

Jansik Knot
A strong, quick way to attach hook to leader.

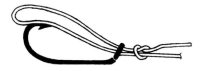

Bait Hook Knot
To attach hook to leader.

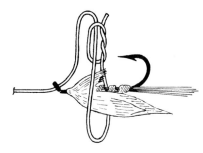

Turtle Knot
To attach hook to leader.

Roll Knot
Similar to roll for double. A popular knot to attach by single or double line to swivel or ring.

Return Knot
To attach leader to hook.

Double Clinch Knot
Wet the knots as they are pulled up tight.

Piano Wire Twist with Safety Clip
For strip bait.

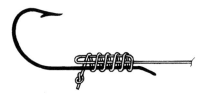

Australian Clinch Knot
To attach hook with or without eye to leader.

Fisherman's Knot or Double O Knot
Used for tying line to swivel.

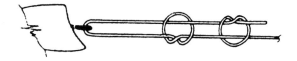

Drop Loop
To attach lure to leader.

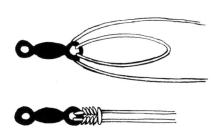

Buffer Loop
To attach lure to leader to give loop for lure to work.

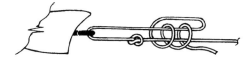

Bimini Hitch
Turn swivel inside loop of line four to six times, then slide up tight.

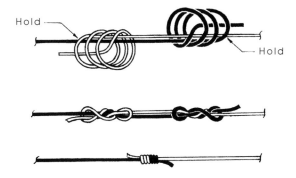

Leader Knot
To join leader.

1

2

'3

4

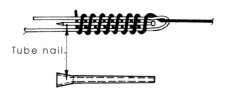

Tube nail

Nail Knot
1. Nail knot. 2. Offset nail knot. 3. Double nail knot. 4. Nail knot with tube.

To Join Sevalon to Monofilament without Swivel or Ring

Blood Knot

Stu Apte Improved Blood Knot
For joining leader to line. The improved knot uses the double strand of the lighter line in tapered leaders or tippets. Used to join shock leader to nylon.

KNOTS

Hook

Half Barrel Knot
To join to hook and for joining lines of similar diameter.

Albright Knot
To attach long leaders to fly line.

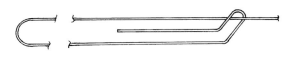

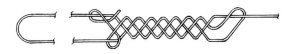

Double Line Plait
A strong, safe way for knotting double line. Plait must be tight and even. Also used to join two lines of equal size.

George Parker's Plait Join
Solid line indicates extra line to act as a buffer and to form the third line for the plait.

(w) Bimini Twist (Double Line)
To form a double line finished with a half hitch on each strand A similar knot can be used to attach double line to swivel.

1   2

3   4

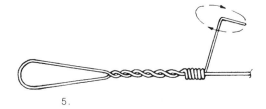

5.

1. Round Eye Single Loop. 2. Round Eye With Flemish Eye. 3. Piano Twist Single Loop. 4. Piano Twist With Flemish Eye. 5. Haywire Twist With Single Loop.

Always finish single strand wire with wire twist. The 'crank' finishes the twist without a cutting edge. Pliers and other cutting tools leave a sharp edge to damage hand or line. Single loops are often used rather than eyes to reduce bubble.

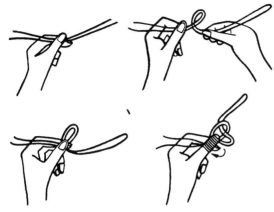

Surgeon's Knot

To join line to monofilament leader or lines of different diameters. Always wet knot as it is pulled up tight.

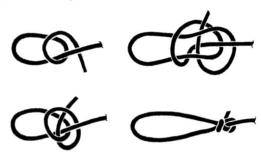

Perfection Knot

To make a strong loop.

Spider Hitch

To make a quick double line for lines up to 10 kg (20 lb) class.

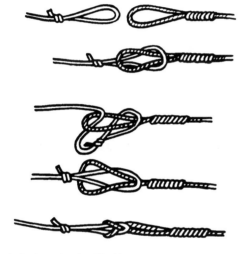

To Join Leader to Fly Line

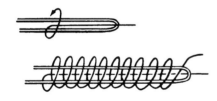

Improved Albright Knot

Jam Knot

To join leader to line without swivel or ring.

Vic Dunaway Uniknot

The basic Vic Dunaway uniknot with six turns can be used for many joins. A uniknot must be pulled evenly and tightly. A uniknot tied with each line can be used to join lines.

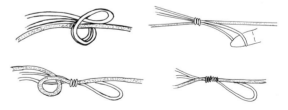

Joining Leader to Double Line

1. The uniknot can be used to join leader of up to four times the breaking strain of leader to line.
2. The uniknot is tied three times with double line around the leader.
3. The leader with uniknot three times around double line.
4. Wet knots and pull together hard and evenly.

COMPETITIVE BILLFISHING

TOURNAMENTS

For some fishermen, a tournament is just another day's fishing, but for others it is a highly competitive sport that requires even more effort, more planning, more thought, more of everything than usual, including, ideally, more fish. The worldwide trend towards tag and release has affected tournament tactics to some extent, as many tag and release competitions award the same points for each fish of the target species irrespective of estimated weight.

Tag and release tournaments therefore often direct team thought and effort to where they should find the most billfish or other point-scoring species, whereas in take tournaments the effort is directed to where the biggest fish should be. The world's number one billfish tournament, the Hawaiian International Billfish Tournament (HIBT), is a blend of tag and release and take. Bonuses for marlin over 220 kg (500 lb), the heaviest of the day and the heaviest of the tournament ensure that those who catch the big fish, as well as those who tag and release a number of marlin irrespective of weight or recover a tagged billfish, have a chance of winning the distinctive wooden billfish trophies.

One of the most important tactical decisions that must be made in a tournament is whether to

◄ A sight to gladden HIBT tournament chairman Peter Fithian's heart: a world record (which has since been broken by Ray Hawkes) 483 kg (1062 lb) blue marlin on 24 kg (50 lb) line.

use your own experience and choose your own area in which to fish or to follow the lead of other contenders by fishing where they are — if it's good for them it might be good for you too.

In tournaments involving multiple line classes, a critical question that affects each day's fishing, particularly as the days go on, is whether to fish light or heavy classes. It is important for success to evaluate what is needed to win. Early in the tournament it is logical to fish the lighter line classes for maximum points for each capture, then if the fish are running big or the leading points are low, to go for quick, certain points on smaller fish, plus the maximum chance of holding on to a big fish if one strikes and hooks up on the heavier classes.

Another consideration that affects choice or change of tackle category on the last day is that because trophies will be awarded that evening, fish or tag cards must be presented for point awards by a certain time cutoff. In tournaments without this cutoff this is not a consideration.

Successful tournament anglers confer and take advantage of the knowledge and experience of skipper and crew. Teams using charter boats must make every effort to build co-operation and confidence among the team. Recognition of charter effort at the end of each day's fishing also helps in co-operation with other boats in the draw if boats are changed each day. It is important for the team and professional crew to decide beforehand whether the team is to take part in the gaffing or tagging activity.

Regular radio reporting schedules are used by hard-working teams not only for information on the other teams in contention, but to dissect information on strikes, size, type of fish and areas of activity. It is important to have assessed by prior research what is most productive and when most strikes are likely to occur, for instance, whether at the top or bottom of the tide.

Once a fish is hooked, concentration and alertness are vital. By this point, most teams would already have drawn straws or made a team decision on who is to take the strike. Those who are to take the strike are usually ready in the cockpit while the other team members rest in the shade. Strikes are often rotated on an hour-on, hour-off basis, often combined with 30 minutes ready for strikes on rods on one side of the boat, changing to move and readiness for strikes on the other side when trolling. Drifting or at anchor strikes may be taken strictly on the time basis or rods on the left or right side of the boat in the interest of fairness and equality in the team. Of course some teams may decide that because of experience or tournament pressure, one particular angler will take all the strikes.

WORLD RECORDS

World record holders basically fall into two categories — those who fish specifically for records and those who, during routine fishing, are lucky enough to get the right combination of size, line class, weight and species to make a world record. The latter are perhaps the most fun records. There is, however, a great satisfaction in planning, looking for and catching a record.

It must be remembered that while only the angler's name appears in the record chart, record fish catching, like most fishing, is a team effort.

In planning for records, it is important to see which record categories are in reach. Some anglers and crews who seek records do not put bait in the water until the fish is seen and its weight estimated so that balanced tackle for the line class can be chosen.

Many other anglers work on the philosophy that to gain the maximum experience from their fishing, they should choose the tackle class for the size of fish they hope to catch. They know that a fish of a certain weight may be a record in one of the light line classes, but fish a line class in the hope of handling a really big fish if it takes a bait or lure. The smaller fish of lesser weight are released in any case, so the plan is for these fish to be brought to the boat with minimum trauma and tagged and released, or just released. This also allows maximum time for fishing and seeking a really big fish.

One of fishing's great satisfactions is when a fish of unexpected size takes a lure or bait on a line class traditionally considered too light for that particular species and size, and is brought to the boat by teamwork and a bit of luck. Fish caught under difficult circumstances, even when they are not records, are sometimes longer remembered than those that made records.

If anglers, skippers and crews hope to make record captures, the best chance of success will come from even greater research, planning, preparation, dedication and concentration than are standard for any successful fishing trip. For many anglers, skippers and crews it is vastly satisfying to help others gain a record.

The planning and preparation for record chasing starts long before a bait, lure or teaser is put in the water. It is important to research and decide what fish can be expected at that time of the year in the current conditions.

Those seeking records need to ascertain:

- What records are potentially available.
- Where the fish of the record size are to be found in the greatest numbers.
- Whether equipped boats with experienced crews are available. (Is it practical to take a boat with a skipper and crew to the area if satisfactory craft and experience are not available?)

- Expected weather conditions (rough seas add to the difficulty of breaking a record, particularly on light line).
- Who can provide personal data and share previous experiences.

It is also important to make the following preparations:

- Check the IGFA fishing rules and tackle regulations for what they will disqualify (check lengths of gaffs, ropes, leaders and terminal tackle).
- Tackle must be serviced; new, tested lines of the chosen category with plenty of spare lines wound on; leaders must be prepared and ready for action.
- Cameras must be checked and in working order.
- Availability of scales and weighing facilities should be checked and if necessary, planned and provided for.
- The captain and crew should not only to be competent and capable of giving the angler every chance of success, but should also understand the objective of the day or trip so everyone is striving for the same goal.
- Preparation of line and the replacement of worn line or the lengths exposed to the ultra-violet rays of sunshine is necessary each day or after each fish.
- Once the fish is found and hooked every effort, all experience and all concentration must go into capturing the fish.

Points to remember for record breaking

- Every potential for loss must be eliminated and minimized: a cleared cockpit, sharp gaffs, gaffs tied off, understanding of procedure and agreement about who is to do what are all critical.
- Communication between the members of the team is crucial, not only for success in capture or release but for the safety of those in the firing line working in the cockpit.
- In the event of a capture, the decision must be made whether to return to port and weighing scales to maximize the weight of the fish or to continue the day's fishing to try for more action.
- The fish must be kept wet, under sacks or other material, to retain maximum weight.
- The line sample, terminal tackle and all necessary photographs, test certificates, measurements and paperwork must be completed to establish the claim.

GAMEFISHING RECORDS

The first marlin, a striped of 125 lb (56.8 kg), was caught on rod and reel in 1903 in California.

The first marlin over 300 lb, a striped marlin of 339 lb (154 kg), was caught in 1909.

The first black marlin on rod and reel was landed in 1910 in Australia.

The first broadbill swordfish was landed in 1913. It weighed in at 358 lb (162.7 kg) in California.

The first gamefish marlin over 400 lb (181.8 kg) was weighed in in 1916.

The first gamefish over 900 lb (409 kg), a black marlin, was weighed in in 1926 in New Zealand.

The first blue marlin in the Bahamas was weighed in in 1933.

The first gamefish over 1000 lb (454.5 kg), a black marlin, was caught in 1952 in Peru.

The first gamefish over 1500 lb (681.8 kg), a black marlin, was caught in 1953 in Peru.

The first gamefish on 80 lb (36.3 kg) line over 1000 lb (454.5 kg), a black marlin, was caught in 1966 in Australia.

The IGFA rules must be observed continually during each day's fishing, as record fish can strike at any time. Familiarise yourself with existing records to save a record claim being eaten.

SCIENCE AND THE FISHERMAN

TAG AND RELEASE — THE MODERN WAY TO FISH

One of the most dramatic and reassuring trends in modern billfishing is the almost universal recreational acceptance of tag and release, or just release. Between the commencement of tag and release on the Great Barrier Reef in 1968 and the end of the 1994 season, more than 22,000 black marlin had been tagged and released in Australian waters. Some of the marlin were in excess of 350 kg (770 lb) while some were heavier than 455 kg (1000 lb).

More than 93 per cent of the billfish brought to boat in Australian waters are tagged and released. This increases to 97 per cent for black marlin on the Great Barrier Reef.

Some captains and anglers prefer to release instead of tag and release because with big marlin they are reluctant for those extra pounds to be applied on the leader, particularly if the fish becomes violent as it might harm itself.

The survival rate of tagged and released billfish is quite amazing. Some of the fish that the records show as having travelled the furthest or been free the longest are those that at the time had been exhausted and seemed unlikely to survive. Some billfish shed their tags before recovery. Some tags from recaptured marlin are not returned by

◀ Perfect teamwork between Captain Col Earl, crew and angler made for the successful tag and release of this grander black marlin on *Reef Hunter*. Photo: Paul B. Kidd.

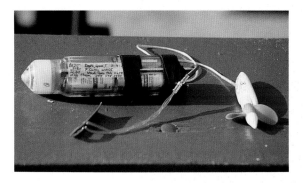

▲ One of the types of sonic tag used by Doctors Carey and Block, and Doctors Holland and Brill in telemetric experiments on Hawaiian marlin. *Photo: Peter Goadby.*

longliners. A high proportion of the tag returns come from native and recreational fishermen. Return by longliners would be most beneficial for the continued gathering of knowledge.

Marlin have been reported to have been re-hooked only 45 minutes after release.

Our thirst for knowledge means that tags are designed to give as much data as possible. The silicon chip tag successfully used on tuna would give similar useful data from billfish. Satellite tags that transmit wherever their aerial breaks the surface will help in the long-time tracking of marlin as they have with Atlantic blue sharks.

Some tags that transmit signals and are tracked by boat have already provided valuable information on swimming depth and direction. Four satellite

▲ The *Pescador* crew with a tagged Atlantic blue marlin for Ralph Christiansen Jnr at St Thomas. *Photo: Captain Bill Harrison*

tags were placed in blue marlin at Kona, Hawaii during the tournaments of the Hawaiian International Billfish Association for Dr Barbara Block and her Pacific Ocean Research team. A tag from this program was recovered north at Kaui after two months.

Resuscitation of the fish is an important factor in tag and release programs. It is a wonderful experience to hand hold a billfish by its bill and swim it behind the boat until the color and activity of the fish show that it is regaining strength and balance. Big marlin are towed by a line around the bill until recovery. Sometimes towing to achieve the desired result may take 15 minutes or longer. This activity is, however, worthwhile in every way.

The trend to tag and release is the result of co-operation between fishermen and scientists. The species released include fish that are popular as food, but are tagged and released to assist the survival of the fish and to gain knowledge of their wanderings and growth. This overrides the taking of fish for weighing and food. It is better for many reasons to tag and release instead of capture and kill.

There are many major tag and release programs around the world. Many of these are international, with fish tagged and released and then recaptured in different countries and high seas. Some anglers choose to simply release rather than to tag and release in the belief that information gained can work against their interests by providing information that benefits those who are already putting pressure on the gamefish and shark stocks. Similarly some domestic and international commercial fishermen do not return the tags they recover from caught fish because they believe knowledge gained can be used against them or benefit the country or area of origin. This is unfortunate. It is now imperative that all fishermen and scientists co-operate in gaining factual data to assist sound management and survival of the fish for future generations. In the USA the tagging programs located at Woods Hole, La Jolla and Narragansett are world leaders in the gathering of knowledge of ocean gamefish through tagging and release and tag recovery.

Some tag and release programs involve tag and release by commercial and recreational fishermen and scientists, as well as tag return from these groups. In others the tag and release and recoveries are mainly undertaken by the sportfishermen and scientists. It is

◄ A black marlin at Cabo San Lucas about to be tagged with the new nylon tag of the Billfish Foundation for angler Jorge Redondo. *Photo: Captain Bill Harrison.*

◄ Black marlin are held after tagging and hook removal, or leader cutting by hand or with a line, until their colors light up, indicating resuscitation. *Photo: Peter Goadby.*

generally true that the greater the number of fish tagged and released, the better the information and potential of the program. Where sportfishermen participate in commercial programs such as that on southern bluefin tuna, some of the information and important recoveries have come as a result of releases by sportfishermen, further proof that fish survive the trauma of capture and release very successfully.

Tagging programs are based on all coasts of the US and in Hawaii, Canada, England, Ireland, Japan, Korea, Spain, Senegal, South Africa, New Caledonia, New Zealand and Australia. Tags and data from the programs, particularly from the USA and Australia, are used in other countries that do not have domestic tagging programs. Much of the tagging effort and important data for management is directed at the pelagic species that are important both commercially and recreationally.

These and other saltwater co-operative tag and release programs give sportfishermen (whatever their preferred fish and wherever they fish) the chance to help science, the fish, their future fishing and that of future generations.

Scientists and fish managers do not have the practical opportunities of active fishermen who can observe and monitor the living marine world, so observation and reporting by fishermen helps fill in the gaps in knowledge. Occurrences that are commonplace to fishermen are sometimes important

and helpful to scientists, and yet are only now being reported. Thankfully more and more anglers are using their cameras to record and pass on what they see to scientists.

Fishermen in all parts of the world proudly display tag and release and tag recovery certificates in their offices and homes. These fishermen are rightly proud of their contribution to the gathering of knowledge.

There have been many examples of how tag and release information has been helpful to recreational fishermen and to the fish. It was scientist–fisherman and tagging leader Frank Mather of Woods Hole laboratory who noted the frightening decline of the Atlantic bluefin stocks as well as proving their trans-Atlantic crossings and possible populations.

▲ Big rays often work with sailfish schools. Cobia in Florida often work with rays feeding on the seabed as they disturb the crabs and other food. *Photo: Greg Edwards.*

▲ Blue marlin at Kona, Hawaii on the wire, ready for tag and release. *Photo: Peter Goadby.*

Tag recoveries in black marlin released with tags supplied and co-ordinated by NOAA's La Jolla, California laboratory and New South Wales Fisheries of Sydney, Australia have provided valuable information on this once mysterious marlin. Information from tagging in the Great Barrier Reef fishery and other parts of the Australian coast was of assistance in the decision to close a large section of the waters off the northern Great Barrier Reef to local and international longlining. Data from the programs showed the importance and movements of this stock not only from Australia's east coast, but generally through the western and into the central Pacific.

The published papers from tag and release programs co-ordinated by NOAA's Jim Squire (which coincided with the start of the Great Barrier Reef giant black marlin fishery in 1968)

and Dr Julian Pepperell of New South Wales Fisheries, Australia cover 9008 black marlin tagged in the Cairns/Lizard Island area plus a further

▲ The leader is cut down short on the hook. *Photo: Peter Goadby.*

2505 from other east coast ports from 1968 to 1986. Recovery of some of these black marlin showed that the fish were in the area near where they were tagged one, two and three years later, while others were recovered as far as 7000 km (4200 miles) from release well north of Tahiti.

Other important recaptures have been made north of the Equator around Papua New Guinea, off New Zealand and at many points on the east coast of Australia. So far there have not been any tag returns through the Torres Strait or in the Indian Ocean.

There have been two black marlin recoveries that show the tremendous distances travelled by this species. One was recovered between New Zealand and Australia, 5700 km (3420 miles) after release off Baja, California; the fish had travelled an average of 9.4 km (6 miles) per day. Another, tagged at Christmas Island south of Hawaii, was recovered off the coast of New South Wales, Australia after 137 days; it had averaged 24.9 km (15 miles) per day for the 3411 km (2000 miles).

The speed of travel is difficult to define accurately. Black marlin have been recovered near where they were tagged after as long as 36 days. One was recovered only 14 km (9 miles) north-

west from its release point after 725 days. It would indeed be interesting to know its wanderings in those 725 days. It may have travelled 3872 km (2322 miles) north in 172 days, or 4200 km (2520 miles) north-east in 210 days or 1415 km (850 miles) south in 75 days, as have other black marlin, before returning to the release point.

Fish movements to the south are important for thousands of anglers off Australia and New Zealand. Two Great Barrier Reef black marlin have been recovered off New Zealand. The tag recoveries south of their northern Great Barrier Reef release area shows a heavy movement in that direction in various age groups. The recovery of New South Wales tagged marlin on course and back to the northern Great Barrier Reef area shows the two-way movement.

It is intriguing to think of the wanderings and activity of the tagged marlin between release and recapture: the time spent hunting, in fleeing from predators, the periods of stay where bait schools and other food are prolific. Dr Pepperell's paper shows regular recoveries back near the place of tagging after 330 to 410 days. This time period is repeated after two, three and four years in the Cairns–Lizard Island area.

◀ Black marlin is released on Dr Ruben Jaens' 400 kg (880 lbs) *Duyfken* on the Great Barrier Reef, Australia. *Photo: Peter Goadby.*

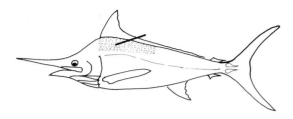

▲ All billfish should be tagged high along the body in the shoulder muscle, above the lateral line.

Dr Pepperell's New South Wales Fisheries data and report on tag returns on Australia's east coast sailfish from Dunk Isle and Cape Bowling Green on the Great Barrier Reef and Moreton Bay in southern Queensland indicate a completely differing pattern from that of the wandering black marlin or the Atlantic sailfish. So far there is no indication of south/north or north/south or distance at all. The tag recoveries have been back at their area of release after varying times.

Tag returns on striped marlin in New South Wales showed they stayed in the same canyon area for at least two months before continuing their wandering. A tagged New Zealand marlin of this species headed north-east towards the Cook Islands

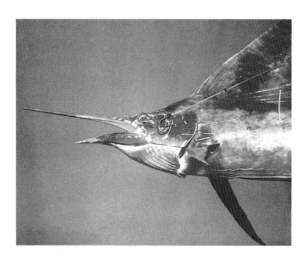

▲ A tagged sailfish shows its dorsal fin as it recovers and swims to freedom.
Photo: Tim Simpson.

after a long-distance recovery. Most of the striped marlin tagging has been carried out off California and Baja, California, in the NOAA/NMFS tagging program co-ordinated by Jim Squire at La Jolla. Returns show that the striped marlin move south from California off Baja and other Mexican ports, while those tagged off Baja have continued to swim south and south-west with recoveries of 5500 km (3450 miles) and 3700 km (2300 miles) being two of the many.

The 1990 NOAA Billfish Program listed striped marlin tag recovery No. 490, released on 26 October 1986 and recovered off Cabo San Lucas in March 1989. Another tagged off Lanai, Hawaii was recaught off Wainae, Oahu 35 days later, while another tagged off Kona, Hawaii was recaptured 92 days later north of Hawaii.

Captain Bobby Brown is the pioneering tag and release captain in Hawaii, with many tags and several recoveries of all three Pacific marlin in Hawaiian waters. The prestigious Hawaiian International Billfish Tournaments also moved to tag and release with recognition and acknowledgment of the tagging angler and team at the weighing station in the tournaments.

Blue marlin recoveries are important, as fewer have been tagged by sportfishermen than other species. At 30 minutes between release then hook-up and recapture, a Kona Hawaiian blue marlin probably holds the marlin record for the shortest time free. Tag returns already show that Pacific blue marlin tagged off Kona, Hawaii were recovered one and two years later in the same area. As in other parts of the world, Hawaiian recreational fishermen are responsible for a high percentage of tag returns. It is disappointing that many local and international commercial fishermen, those who kill the majority of billfish, tuna and other gamefish, do not return all the tags they recover.

Atlantic blue marlin have been revealed to travel from the Virgin Islands in the Caribbean across to Africa's west coast. Atlantic big eye tuna tagged off central Africa have been recovered north to the Canary Islands and across the Atlantic to Brazil.

Tag recoveries of Atlantic sailfish have provided information not only on their journeying off Florida to Venezuela, but have shown they live far beyond the generally accepted seven- to eight-year term previously known in tag recoveries. An adult-sized sailfish estimated at the then life expectancy of seven years, tagged off Florida, was recovered 10 years later off Venezuela, giving a new and positive idea of life spans, while others have been free for five years. White marlin have been proved to wander from the east coast of the USA to the Gulf of Mexico and further south to Venezuela and Brazil, while others have moved eastward out into the Atlantic to be recovered after 10 and 12 years.

Anglers, skippers and crews can be truly proud of their release records and assistance to science. Tag and release is not only a major contribution in time, expenditure and experience, but often entails the possibility of human injury, particularly when fish are close to the boat for tagging or release with hook removal or leader cutting. There is sometimes a chance of physical harm when billfish jump at the boat.

At the 1988 and 1989 Hawaiian International Billfish Tournaments, co-operation between anglers, skippers, crews and scientists was experienced far beyond that established in the previous 28 years of

▲ Black marlin sometimes have deformed bills, lost fins or lobes of tails. *Photo: Greg Finney.*

the tournament. Scientists Kim Holland and Richard Brill were conducting tracking experiments in 1985 on billfish and tuna with electronic tags. They had experienced success with yellowfin tuna, but billfish hook-ups from just one boat were more difficult. The scientists wondered if the tournament committee and the competitors, skippers and crews could help with marlin, even with the pressure of the tournament. Tournament boats were successful in bringing blue

◀ Numbered plastic and stainless headed tags with related information cards and applicators in tag poles are now an important part of the equipment carried on most offshore sportfishing boats. The certificates shown here are from New South Wales Fisheries in Australia. *Photo: Peter Goadby.*

▲ Kawa kawa and skipjack live baits are often speared by marlin before being swallowed. *Photo: Peter Goadby.*

marlin to the boat so they could be tagged with the electronic tags by the scientists, who then tracked the marlin. In 1989, the experiments and need for participation were doubled, when Dr Frank Carey and Dr Barbara Block engaged in telemetry electronic tagging and marlin-following experiments using even more sophisticated electronic tags. Again, competing boats were successful in contributing live blue marlin for electronic tagging for both project teams.

Preliminary general information from the telemetry programs showed the value of this angler/crew/scientist co-operation. The initial information

showed that marlin not only survive but quickly recover from the trauma of struggle and being brought to boat to resume their daytime 51–91 meter (28–50 fathom) and shallower (0–10 meter, or 0–5 fathom) night-time cruising and hunting along the ledges with the tuna schools, with depth relative to the upper layer of the thermocline.

Some of the releases moved north, some south, while others stayed near the fish aggregating device (FAD) or ledge where first hooked, rising in the water levels with the tuna school.

As well as conducting tag and release programs, scientists at the HIBT have for over 30 years examined and recorded the stomach contents of the weighed fish. Those contents show that the marlin feed on bottom-dwelling fish species as well as pelagic species and squid. One of the surprises has been the presence of juvenile billfish in the marlins' stomachs. Baby marlin and broadbill appear in the stomach sacs along with the remains of bills and swords. One blue marlin had the sword of another marlin right through its gills.

The size and weight of tuna removed from marlin stomachs and throats have also been surprising. A 340 kg (748 lb) blue marlin taken on a lure right where boats had been slow trolling live

◀ Striped marlin at Baja California ready for tag and release. *Photo: Peter Goadby.*

baits all day had a 30 kg (62 lb) big eye tuna in its stomach. The contents of the big eye's stomach were not recorded, but here was a clear example of the predator/prey life cycle. That marlin was taken by Dick Davis while fishing with Captain Bart Miller, a master bait fisherman who had baits positioned perfectly to give his angling team every chance, yet these and other baits were apparently ignored in favor of man's plastic creation. An 820 kg (1805 lb) blue marlin, also taken on a lure, had a 63 kg (140 lb) yellowfin in its stomach.

Scientists and fishermen from around the world come together for the HIBT and the summer congregation of blue marlin in this year-round marlin fishery. Scientists have provided fishermen with much useful data, including information about the spring structure of marlin backbones and the two different types of marlin muscle tissue: narrow, red muscle tissue and wide, white muscle tissue. Marlin use the narrow band of red muscle when cruising and the white muscle when explosive power is needed to avoid being killed, to chase and hunt, or to jump and escape. Fishermen now more clearly understand the benefits of using attacking techniques during fishing to trigger and burn out the power of that white muscle. The marlin can cruise comfortably for hour after hour on their red muscle, so angler tactics must ensure that the fish is provoked to use its white muscle instead.

A wag remarked after a presentation on billfish physiology at a billfish symposium that billfish are truly 'hot-headed' fish in the way they strike and jump, run and sound, charge and jump at boats and strike at lures and baits time after time, particularly after teasing. The remark came after a presentation of a paper on 'brain heaters'. Scientists have established that marlin do have heaters in the brain and in the eye muscle that keep the brain and eyes warmer than the surrounding water. According to Dr Barbara Block and Dr Frank Carey marlin eyes and brains are 4°C (7°F) warmer than the rest of the marlin's body. Another scientist, C. C. Lindsay, has written

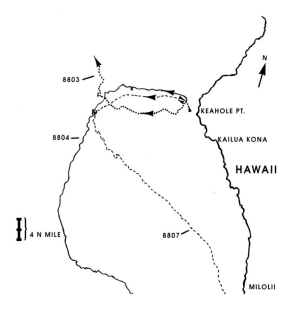

▲ Migration of Doctors Holland and Brill's sonic tagged marlin.

that marlin muscle tissue is 2.5°C (4.5°F) warmer. A broadbill's brain is 1.4°C (2.5°F) above the temperature of the rest of its body. New Zealand's Dr Peter Davie, a regular visiting scientist at the PORF laboratory at Kona, lists 142 papers relating to billfish anatomy and physiology in his book *Pacific Marlin Anatomy and Physiology*.

These papers and others on migration, stock and fishing pressure and billfish-related subjects show that billfish are indeed VIF (Very Important Fish) to the scientists as well as to recreational fishermen. It is a pity that as much interest in their survival is not often shown by commercial fishermen and fisheries managers. Broadbill swordfish and marlin are shown in Japanese and other papers to be target species of the efficient longline industry, yet are repeatedly referred to by fisheries managers as incidental take in the tuna fisheries. This is yet another reason why sportfishermen should not only know more about the fish, but about the industries that are dramatically reducing stock. The published papers from Billfish Symposiums I and II, held at Kona, Hawaii in 1972 and 1989, contain much of the world knowledge about billfish and fishing pressure.

◀ Even black and white film shows the glowing striped marlin with its lights turned on. *Photo: IGFA — Lerner Expedition.*

The age of the fish and rate of growth are regular points of discussion wherever fishermen and scientists meet. Research on marlin has shown that both males and females live to about the same age, although the males do not grow much beyond 190 kg (420 lb) whereas females of the same age weigh over 450 kg (1000 lb). It seems logical that males do not grow to the massive weights and size of the females, as several males are needed to fertilize the millions of eggs produced by the female.

Marlin, unlike many other fish, have only tiny otolith ear stones, yet under a powerful microscope they display similar qualities to the larger ear stones of other species such as rings resembling those that occur in trees or on the scales of some fish. In some programs, tag and release has now been combined with injections of tetracycline. This compound stains the otoliths and bones in the fins, so study of the time between injection, tag and release and recapture, combined with the number of rings beyond the stained bone, will confirm whether the rings are annually laid down.

Learning from scientists and thus improving one's knowledge of the fish and marine environment is one of the great pleasures as well as necessities and benefits of fishing for the great gamefish. Fishermen and scientists both have much to learn. Contribution to scientific knowledge, conservation and management of the resources will ensure not only the survival of fish species but that of future generations of fishermen.

National marine fisheries service catch and release quick reference card

Why release fish?

1. A fish is too valuable a resource to be caught only once.

2. A personal commitment to conservation adds fun to fishing.

3. Size, season, and bag regulations make release mandatory.

4. Stressed fish populations need your help to recover.

5. The future of sportfishing is in your hands. Pass it on!

How to begin

1. Decide to release a fish as soon as it is hooked.

2. Land your quarry quickly, don't play it to exhaustion.

3. Set the hook immediately. Try to prevent a fish from swallowing the bait.

4. Work a fish out of deep water slowly, so it can adjust to the pressure change.

5. Use hooks that are barbless and made from metals that rust quickly.

6. Always keep release tools handy.

Handling your catch

1. Leave the fish in the water (if possible) and don't handle it. Use a tool to remove the hook or cut the leader.

2. Keep the fish from thrashing.

3. Net your catch only if you cannot control it any other way.

4. When you must handle a fish:

- Use a wet glove or rag to hold it.
- Turn a fish on its back or cover its eyes with a wet towel to calm it.
- Don't put your fingers in the eyes or gills of your catch.
- Larger fish can be kept in the water by holding the leader with a glove or by slipping a release gaff through the lower jaw.
- Avoid removing mucus or scales.
- Get the fish back in the water as quickly as possible.

5. Protect against personal injury by handling each species carefully and correctly.

Removing the hook

1. Cut the leader close to the mouth if a fish has been hooked deeply or if the hook can't be removed quickly.

2. Back the hook out the opposite way it went in.

3. Use needle-nose pliers, hemostats, or a hookout to work the hook and protect your hands.

4. For a larger fish in the water, slip a gaff around the leader and slide it down to the hook. Lift the gaff upward as the angler pulls downward on the leader.

5. Do not jerk or pop a leader to break it. This damages vital organs and kills the fish.

The final moments

1. Place the fish in the water gently, supporting its mid-section and tail until it swims away.

2. Resuscitate an exhausted fish by moving it back and forth or tow it alongside the boat to force water through its gills.

3. Use an ice pick, needle, or hook point to puncture the expanded air bladder on a fish taken from deep water.

4. Watch your quarry to make sure it swims away. If it doesn't, recover the fish and try again.

5. REMEMBER, A RELEASED FISH HAS AN EXCELLENT CHANCE OF SURVIVAL WHEN HANDLED CAREFULLY AND CORRECTLY.

Prepared and distributed by the US Department of Commerce National Oceanic and Atmospheric Administration, National Marine Fisheries Service, 9450 Koger Boulevard, St Petersburg, Florida 33702, Ph: (813) 893 3141.

FADS

The word 'fads' has several meanings for fishermen. For some, 'fads' describe the current trend of the month — the lure, the bait, the technique, the color, the secret that produces action. There are fads that do produce gamefish of all species. These fads are spelt FAD — Fish Aggregating Devices. Some fishermen think the initials stand for Fish Attracting Devices. The attractant as part of FADs comes from the shelter that these manmade devices with their underwater structures give to the tiny forms of marine life, the fish crustacea and squid that are ceaselessly hunted by bigger predators that in turn are hunted and eaten by bigger predators right up to the peak predators, the sharks, billfish, tuna and other oceanic gamefish.

Manmade FADs recreate nature's FADs of drifting logs, weed lines and upwellings. A FAD

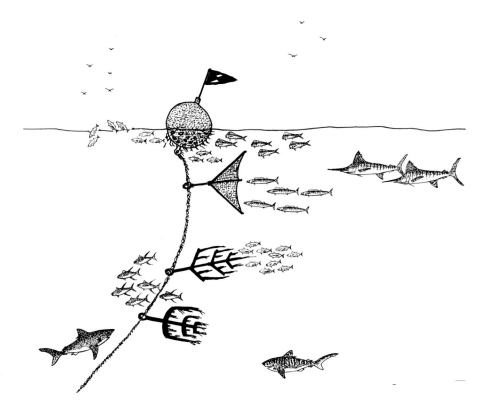

▲ FADs concentrate and hold passing fish and bait.

has the effect of a floating reef placed within range and visible to fishermen.

There is considerable debate wherever thinking fishermen, managers and scientists get together. They realize that manmade FADs help commercial and recreational fishermen by showing them where the fish should be. Those who argue against the installation of FADs are aware that they do not increase the gamefish population; they simply make them more accessible to fishermen around the FADs instead of the grounds, ledges, peaks and natural upwellings that concentrate the food for the predators. They feel that these natural food congregators are known and found only by knowledgeable and experienced fishermen who have learned to decipher the riddles of finding offshore fish. Those against the installation of FADs are concerned that the ease of finding the gamefish and the concentration may place too great a pressure on

existing stocks, as they only aggregate the population; they don't increase the gamefish population.

Despite the discussions and opinions of the pros and cons of manmade FADs, there is no doubt that they can make it possible for recreational fishermen to catch more fish and for more fishermen to find fish although the boat traffic will be heavy. McIntosh Marine of Fort Lauderdale, Florida manufacture and market FADs that are easily assembled and moored.

Apart from the proven benefit for those seeking the peak predator species, FADs provide an ideal environment for catching suitable bait species to be fished near where they were caught or kept alive ready for a fast run to some nearby likely hot spot.

FADs give potential for all anglers to fish their favorite boat-fishing methods. The areas around FADs can be trolled with baits, with lures of proven successful speeds, slow trolling with live or dead baits, drifting with live bait, dead baits and strips and casting with spinning or bait-casting tackle. Judicious use of chum and chunking will also add to activity around FADs even though sharks are logically included in the smorgasbord of big species attracted by the complete food chain activity in the area.

The FAD is an obstacle that will cause cutoff or breakoff so thought and care must be exercised in boat positioning and maneuvering. Depending on the position of boat and fish it is sound practice to restrain the impulse to lock up and fight hard until away from the buoy and its attendant underwater appendages.

NATURE'S FISH FINDERS

OCEAN CURRENTS

Ocean currents are nature's highways and food chain providers of the high seas. The warm water Gulf Stream, sometimes 800 kilometers (500 miles) wide and about 650 meters (360 fathoms) deep, is perhaps the best known 'River in the Sea'. This current, which runs at 4–5 knots through the Florida Straits, moderates the temperature of the land masses on its course as well as carrying the complete marine food chain, including gamefish.

In many places fishing is hot when the current is hot. In offshore fishing blue water is often considered an indicator of a warm current and big fish, but not all gamefish come from blue water. At times, action may come in green and brown water. Whatever the color, the dominating effect of the currents is known to successful fishermen. The current temperature and flow over the sea bed, coastal configurations, continental shelf and deeper canyons and dropoffs trigger the concentrations of microscopic plant and animal life that start the food chain.

Currents trigger upwellings of the deep ocean water, bringing nutrient-rich decaying and dead organisms to the surface. This concentration of minerals and salts stimulates the growth of plant plankton, which is the start of the food chain.

Plankton nurtures the microscopic animals that are the base of predatory life in the ocean. The current edges are most productive.

Cold water in the polar regions sinks and travels towards the tropics. The Humboldt Current of South America moves north along South America and is then deflected by the earth's rotation and the shape of the South American west coast to warm in the tropics. Similarly, the shape of Africa's west coast and the warm Guinea Current deflects the cool Benguela Current to the west. The west coast of Australia is unique in that it has a warm current instead of the cool currents that are generally present on west coasts of major land masses.

The currents and counter currents become ocean drifts as they weaken or are driven by the wind. Their direction is guided by that of the prevailing winds, the rotation of the earth and the shape of the coastline. Northern hemisphere currents circle clockwise; southern hemisphere currents circle anti-clockwise. Similarly, it is this 'coriolis' effect that causes the commonly observed phenomenon of water flowing down plugholes in opposite directions in the northern and southern hemispheres. Even though currents often appear to be streams running along the coast, in reality they meander in pools and eddies, surrounded by the circling edge of the current.

These pools and eddies are important to offshore recreational and commercial fishermen, who look for current and temperature edges. The edges are a guide to where to fish and are clearly shown on photographs from cameras and remote sensing equipment on orbiting satellites. This information is of primary importance to weather forecasters who pinpoint and predict the El Nino and counter La Nina effects that affect fishing as well as climate.

Ocean current waters run from areas of high pressure to low pressure with movements caused by melting ice, heavy rainfall and evaporation by the sun. Low temperatures make the ocean heavy and dense (high pressure), while high temperatures make it lighter and less dense (low pressure).

The currents are the hunting ground as well as the home of the gamefish, many of which wander within the currents rather than adhering to the defined migrations of other fish. Recording of tagged gamefish has shown that many species pass or congregate in the same area at approximately the same time and conditions each year.

The currents vary in temperature, velocity and direction from season to season and sometimes even from month to month. At some seasons, fingers of differing water temperature will push into the water along the coast. These fingers have the benefit of providing temperature edges but can have the disadvantage of pushing cool water in close to the coast and moving warm water further offshore out of range of sport fishermen.

Because the transoceanic currents pass between a number of continents, their names can be confusing. The current that has been named Gulf Stream off the east coast of the USA and Canada becomes the Gulf Stream Drift and the North Atlantic Drift, then the Portuguese Current, the North Equatorial Current and the Antilles Current

before again becoming the Gulf Stream. All stages of this North Atlantic current system are warm except the Portuguese Current.

The North Atlantic, South Atlantic, North Pacific, South Pacific and Indian Oceans have similar current systems where around three-quarters of the major transoceanic current is warm and the rest is cool. The winds that have most influence on these currents are the north-east trade winds in the northern hemisphere and the south-east trades in the southern hemisphere.

Not all billfish are long-range ocean wanderers. Some move only short distances and are subject even more to the effects of fishing pressures. Some species are associated with continental shelf habitat, while others are usually associated with the currents and drifts.

SEABIRDS — THE FISHERMEN'S EYES IN THE SKY

Since man first hunted fish, birds have been one of the most important natural indicators of where

▲ Trevally feeding on surface plankton in Bay of Islands, New Zealand while the kahawai work deeper.
Photo: Peter Goadby

▲ All pelicans have the same massive bill, graceful flight and ungainly landing whether in Australia or the Caribbean. *Photo: Peter Goadby*

fish and action should be. The world's great fishing grounds are naturally home to the birds whose fragile existence is dependent on the life of the sea. The best and most successful primitive fishermen were those who could read the pages of the ecological book revealed by the seabirds.

This has continued to modern times, despite the multitude of electronic devices that give today's fishermen even more visible indicators of fish and bait. The seabirds are more than natural guides. They have a unique beauty as well as purpose.

In some areas visiting and local people go to sea to watch and band seabirds. Man not only recognizes and respects these birds that survive the ruthless conditions of the water world, but realizes there is much to learn. Fishermen have a unique opportunity to watch and learn.

Seabirds link and bring together the marine world. The tropic birds with their graceful long twin tail feathers and powerful head and big eyes ride high over the big fish, indicating the presence of marlin (and tuna and mahi mahi).

Fishing at Walker's Cay in the Bahamas is a reminder of the link between tropic birds, man and fish. This is also so at low-lying Christmas Island, Kiribati, which has its own subspecies of tropic bird, a variation of the widespread white tails. The white-tailed tropic bird occurs in all tropical oceans, while the striking red-tailed tropic bird is an Indo-Pacific species not found in the Atlantic. All are valuable fish finders.

◄ Albatross of several species are a source of interest to anglers in temperate waters in the southern hemisphere.
Photo: Peter Goadby.

In Baja California visiting fishermen are often amazed by the large number of flocks of frigate birds; in other tropical waters they tend to fly alone or in groups of two or three. Along with gannets and pelicans, they are the dive-bombers of the offshore world. They ride over bait schools or big fish waiting for surface or bird action, poised to pick up small fish right on the surface or to harass other feeding birds into disgorging the food they have already taken. Frigate birds lack the natural oil on their feathers that enables other seabirds to set and live comfortably on the surface of the sea. Their marauding, harassing, aerial dogfight tactics force the other birds to disgorge the small fish, squid or crustacea they have swallowed, and the frigate birds pick it up before it hits and sinks below the surface. The piratical activities of these birds also extend to robbing chicks from the nests of other birds. The male frigate bird is very striking with its bright red balloon throat patel and glossy green–black feathers.

The eight pelican species of the world are perhaps the easiest of all birds to recognize; their massive bill and expandable pouch are like no other bird's. All the pelicans, except the Chilean pelican of the Humboldt Current, range from inland to coast and provide interest for the fishermen of bays and estuaries in particular. The Chilean pelican is the only known offshore species. Pelicans are graceful in flight and are most efficient hunters. While travelling in flight they carry their neck tucked into the shoulder, then while fishing they fly with the bill pointed down. When they sight their prey they suddenly stop as if shot, folding their wings as they drop to the surface with a resounding splash. At other times they paddle and hunt under the surface, picking up food from the muddy surface water and even from the shallow sea bed. If any efficient fish-hunting bird deserves the description 'cute', this is it.

In the southern hemisphere, offshore fishermen regularly have the opportunity to watch albatross and petrel species soaring and gliding on the thermals. The dive-bombing activity of gannets, known as boobies in many fishing areas, also indicates bait schools in the water.

The days with the greatest number of birds and most bird activity are, for those fishermen who know and recognize the messages they are giving, often the most successful and interesting fishing days.

◀ Great Barrier Reef trollings baits for black marlin. Those with a hook out of the throat are rigged to swim.
Photo: Peter Goadby.

ESTIMATING WEIGHT WITHOUT SCALES

IGFA rules provide that record claims must be weighed on scales on land and not at sea. The travelling fisherman can still gain a fairly accurate assessment of the weight of his capture if it is too big for any available scales. A time-proven formula that fits most species of gamefish and sharks will give a weight that is remarkably close to correct, though of course calculated weights are not eligible for record claims. First, measure the girth of the fish at its greatest part in inches, or convert your measurement to inches, e.g. 3 ft 4 in = 40 in. Measure the length of the body from the tip of the lower jaw to the middle of the crotch of the tail in inches, or convert to inches, e.g. 8 ft 4 in = 100 in. Square the girth, e.g. 40 × 40 = 1600. Multiply this by the length, e.g. 1600 × 100 = 16,000. Once you have made this calculation divide the result by 800.

The result is the fish's approximate weight in pounds, e.g. 16,000 ÷ 800 = 200 lb.

Please note that blue marlin may be 10 per cent above the calculated weight.

Charter captains in the Great Barrier Reef black marlin fishery have ascertained that a circumference of 50 cm (20 inches) at the butt of the tail on a black marlin is a positive guide to whether it will exceed the magic 450 kg (1000 lb) mark.

All tackle used must be submitted at the time of weighing. IGFA rules now say that at least 15.24 m (50 ft) of line plus the double, if one was used, in one piece and leader must be submitted with the completed record claim and photographs. Each year the IGFA issue their fishing rules with the current world record chart. The IGFA address is 3000 E Las Olas Boulevard, Fort Lauderdale, Florida 33316, USA. Membership of IGFA is open to clubs and individual anglers who receive a news sheet and patches direct from the world body.

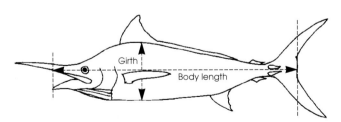

▲ Weight calculated by measurment for billfish.

INDEX